A World of Gangs

A World of
Gangs

Armed Young Men and Gangsta Culture

JOHN M. HAGEDORN

FOREWORD BY MIKE DAVIS

UNIVERSITY OF MINNESOTA PRESS

MINNEAPOLIS • LONDON

Globalization and Community Series, Volume 14
Dennis R. Judd, Series Editor

Additional information about the author and his work can be found at
http://gangresearch.net.

"The Rose That Grew from Concrete" reprinted with permission of
International Creative Management, Inc. Copyright 1999 by Tupac Shakur.

Photograph of favela at the opening to Part I by João Roberto Ripper
courtesy of Imagens do Povo Image Bank, a project run by Observatorio de Favelas
do Rio de Janeiro. Photograph at the opening to Part II, *One Way*,
courtesy of the photographer, James F. Short Jr.

Maps in the book were created by Patti Isaacs, Parrot Graphics.

Published by the University of Minnesota Press
111 Third Avenue South, Suite 290
Minneapolis, MN 55401-2520
http://www.upress.umn.edu

Printed in the United States of America on acid-free paper

Library of Congress Cataloging-in-Publication Data

Hagedorn, John, 1947-
A world of gangs : armed young men and gangsta culture /
John M. Hagedorn ; foreword by Mike Davis.
p. cm. — (Globalization and community series ; v. 14)
Includes bibliographical references and index.
ISBN 978-0-8166-5066-8 (hc : alk. paper) — ISBN 978-0-8166-5067-5 (pb : alk. paper)
1. Gangs. I. Title.
HV6437.H34 2008
364.106'6—dc22
2008000082

The University of Minnesota is an equal-opportunity educator and employer.

15 14 13 12 11 10 09 08   10 9 8 7 6 5 4 3 2 1

This book is dedicated to Bobby Gore
and the brave men and women
of Lawndale's 1960s Conservative Vice Lords

History has the cruel reality of a nightmare, and the grandeur of man consists in his making beautiful and lasting works out of the real substance of that nightmare.

—OCTAVIO PAZ, *The Labyrinth of Solitude*

CONTENTS

Reading John Hagedorn

MIKE DAVIS

Symptomatic of a more profound fallacy, the Library of Congress biblio-graphic system makes the subject "street gangs" a subset of "social pathology," when the accurate classification should be "urban history, street politics." Gangs, in the most straightforward sense, mint power for the otherwise powerless from their control of small urban spaces: street corners, slums, playgrounds, parks, schools, prison dormitories, even garbage dumps. For poor youth lacking other resources, these informal spatial monopolies, if successfully defended and consolidated, provide some measure of entre-preneurial opportunity as well as local prestige and warrior glamour. Gangs also frequently act as neighborhood militias to police public space, enforce (or resist) ethnic and racial borders, and, thereby, control access to jobs and housing. Although most gangs are ephemeral alliances, a few endure as charismatic icons of local identity; membership then becomes an inter-generational rite of passage, resonant with patriotic pride ("military service for the 'hood, same as my daddy," an LA OG once told me). If some gangs are vampire-like parasites on their own neighbors, others play Robin Hood or employer of the last resort; most combine elements of both predation and welfare.

The genealogy of gangs, broadly construed, is almost coeval with the history of the big city; despite the current identification of street gangs as the sinister seeds of organized crime and terrorism, they have also been the building blocks of urban machine politics from Republican Rome to Prohibition-era Chicago. The great gangs of the Roman hills, who controlled the city's grain supply, were a plebeian power to which even Caesar had to defer. In the city-states of Renaissance Italy, artisan gangs, the custodians of popular rights, were always ready to rollick, riot, and, if necessary, revolt. The famous fighting gangs of New York in the 1840s and 1850s (along with their doppelgängers, the volunteer fire companies) constituted the grass-roots of Jacksonian democracy in the city and provided street armies for both Tammany Hall and their "Know Nothing" opponents. Indeed, American gangs were often the proletarian equivalents to Skull and Bones and Beta Theta Pi—with some alumni ending up at city hall as well as on death row. The most powerful political boss in modern U.S. history, "hizzoner" Richard J. Daley, began his inexorable ascent in the Chicago Democratic machine as a gang chieftain and racist provocateur during the 1919 riots.

Gangs, in other words, are as ancient as the hills of Rome and as American as the spoils system (if not apple pie). If they share a generic logic—the informal ownership of the street through a local monopoly of force—their actual histories and raison d'être across time and space are incredibly diverse and unpredictable. Yet it has been the smug mission of modern American criminology and allied social science subfields to reduce complex realities and largely unexplored histories to simplistic pathologies. Despite all the pseudoscientific mumbo-jumbo (survey questionnaires, regression equations, behavioralist models, and the like), gang research in the post-war era, with a few honorable exceptions, only embellished the stereotypes originally brought to the slum by the charity reform movement of the 1850s: a fundamentally moralistic critique of poor people's supposed predisposition to crime and disorder. If the 1950s burnished classic studies with new theories of teenage rebellion and the 1960s shifted that emphasis to deviant subcultures, the overall methodology of "gang studies" through the early 1980s remained rooted in Victorian values, obsolete social science, and self-reproducing paradigms that ignored dramatic structural changes in urban life.

Although this traditional criminological approach saw itself as scrupulous and empirical, it was hopelessly entangled in mythology and wishful thinking, especially in its fetishism of laws and norms in lieu of any realistic theory of urban politics and intergroup conflict. Research on gangs was largely driven by episodic, media-incited outbursts of public hysteria over sensational killings or outrages; consequently, research budgets and agendas were (and are) heavily shaped by the priorities and biases of law enforcement and youth services organizations. The a priori consensus was that most street gangs were the urbanized equivalent of primitive tribes, recruited from broken families and disturbed psyches, pursuing essentially nihilistic objectives.

Sociological generalization supplanted any investigation of gangdom's complicated evolution since the nineteenth century. By the late 1970s, library shelves were groaning under the weight of monographs purporting to reveal the mysteries of adolescent street culture and *la vida loca,* yet most of the research was entirely ahistorical and wildly ignorant of the integral roles previously played by gangs in big city politics and European-immigrant economic mobility. Although race was prominent in psychological explanations of delinquency ("damaged Negroes," "underprivileged Mexicans"), few studies paid any serious attention to institutional racism, the continuous warfare over neighborhood boundaries, or the oppressive function of the police in minority areas. With the exception of William Whyte's famous participant-observer study of a North Boston street corner in the 1940s, most researchers depended on interviews with cops and probation officers, newspaper stories, welfare and school surveys, and, occasionally, the testimony of "informants." In the latter case, the typically anonymous gang member was briefly quoted to substantiate one of the researcher's contentions or generalizations, but never allowed to expound an opinion or present a point of view at any length. As with other primitive peoples, inner-city youth were not deemed to possess a rational eloquence.

All the more striking, then, when in 1988 John Hagedorn published his revelatory study *People and Folks: Gangs, Crime, and the Underclass in a Rustbelt City* in coauthorship with Perry Macon, a founder and "top dog" of the Milwaukee Vice Lords. The book began with a blistering critique of the geriatric authority of academic "gang experts," some of whom had not done any real fieldwork in decades yet still claimed a privileged understanding of the culture of the streets. As Hagedorn put it, there was "too much theory, too few facts," and he implied that gang studies had become part of obscurantist law-enforcement discourse that impeded any objective analysis of the destructive social forces at work in American inner cities.

The immediate occasion of *People and Folks* was national hysteria about the supposedly epidemic spread of Los Angeles– and Chicago-based "super-gangs" into their respective western and midwestern hinterlands. According to *Time* magazine, ABC News, and the National Association of Chiefs of

Police, big-time gangsters were systematically colonizing African American and Latino neighborhoods in smaller cities as part of a rapacious quest to build national markets for crack cocaine and other narcotics. Authorities warned that the spores of these outside gangs tended to grow in hothouse fashion, quickly overwhelming local law-enforcement resources; Milwaukee was often cited as a prime example of a peaceful city "invaded" in the early 1980s by teenage imperialists from Chicago.

In fact, as Hagedorn and Macon convincingly demonstrated in their reconstruction of the genealogy of Milwaukee's gangs, the "outside agitator" or "export" theory of gang growth was mostly bogus. Although some former Chicago gang members did arrive in the Wisconsin metropolis during the early 1980s (usually because their families were desperately trying to move them out of harm's way), the real impetus for gang growth was indigenous: an unemployment rate of 28 percent for blacks, soaring poverty, broken families, failing schools, persistent racial discrimination, and a brutal, bigoted police department. The cross-town busing of black and Puerto Rican students (supposedly in the name of desegregation) also inadvertently fostered gang affiliation by casting kids adrift in hostile schools far from their old neighborhoods. If the early 1980s breakdancing cliques and school-based gangs dubbed themselves Vice Lords or the Cobras, it was not because they had been recruited as franchises of the Chicago supergangs but simply because they wanted to appropriate some of the latter's subcultural celebrity. The urban anthropologist Mercer Sullivan later corroborated a similar phenomenon in New York City: what the press and police hyped as a gang invasion by LA Bloods and Chicago Latin Kings was "primarily a re-labeling of existing local rivalries."

In the same iconoclastic spirit, Hagedorn and Macon reexamined the contrasting stereotypes of gangs as irrational cabals of damaged children or highly lucrative drug mafias. What they found in Milwaukee were the ruins of once cohesive blue-collar communities: a postindustrial misery of unemployment and frustrated ambition living in the shadow of yuppie greed and conspicuous consumption. In the wake of deindustrialization, it was increasingly difficult for inner-city youth to "graduate" from their teenage associations into traditional working-class bread-earner roles; gang membership, as a result, tended to become more like a permanent vocation than a social phase. Gangs, in turn, more intensively cultivated subsistence crime, especially drug hustling, but the neglected neighborhoods and housing projects of Milwaukee evinced little of the fabled narco-wealth celebrated in the boasts of Compton rappers or depicted in movies like *New Jack City.* "Drug sales for most gang members," observed Hagedorn, "are just another low-paying job—one that might guarantee 'survival,' but not much more." And unlike those classical foot soldiers of machine politics, the violent Irish gangs in turn-of-the-century Milwaukee or Chicago, pariah black and Puerto Rican gangs had no access to traditional spoils or patronage resources.

The gang renaissance of the 1980s, in other words, was less a vast criminal conspiracy or epidemic of antisocial values than a spontaneous but shrewd adaptation of ghetto survival strategies to the hard, cold realities of the Reagan era. Certainly the Chicago and Los Angeles supergangs provided post–Horatio Alger status symbols to an aspiring grassroots, but, as Hagedorn and Macon repeatedly emphasize, the key preconditions for the gang resurgence arose out of local histories of economic restructuring and community defeat. (Law enforcement and penology also rapidly adapted to the same bleak topographies, but with much more lucrative results; indeed, their vested interests in the overlapping wars on drugs, gangs, and terror have become almost as entrenched and unreformable as the military-industrial complex.)

Twenty years on (and in a revised edition in 1998 that takes account of the radical impact of soaring cocaine sales on Milwaukee gangs), *People and Folks* remains an essential guide to clear thinking about street culture and the wages of injustice. It founded what might be called "critical gang studies" and gave new hope to all of us who despaired at the lurid caricatures and urban myths passing for social science. Hagedorn and Macon also gave inspiration to that minority current of American documentarists and writers who have tried to represent inner-city people coping with life in our postindustrial cities as rational actors and disenfranchised citizens rather than demons from the 'hood or romanticized outlaws. Watching an episode of David Simon's series *The Wire* on HBO—the closest thing to Émile Zola on the tube—is often like rereading *People and Folks.*

While Macon spent most of the 1990s entombed in something mislabeled a correctional institution, Hagedorn was fighting for reform inside the Milwaukee County child welfare bureaucracy; his compelling account of his experiences, *Forsaking Our Children* (1995), countered a mountain of lies about welfare reform and Clinton-era "compassion." Likewise, his edited anthology with Meda Chesney-Lind, *Female Gangs in America* (1999), challenged hoary clichés about girl gangs through fascinating case studies of gender politics in different inner-city subcultures. More recently from his new base at the Chicago campus of the University of Illinois, Hagedorn has worked with Bobby Gore, the legendary leader of the Lawndale Vice Lords in the 1960s, to reconstruct the sinister story of how the Daley machine and ultimately the Nixon administration sabotaged every effort by radicalized Chicago gangs to transform themselves into legitimate community organizations.

These remarkable studies of the impact of economic restructuring and postliberal social policy on communities of color in the Midwest clearly deserve the same scholarly laurels as those awarded to such works as William Whyte's *Street Corner Society: The Social Structure of an Italian Slum* (1943), St. Clair Drake and Horace Cayton's *Black Metropolis: A Study of Negro Life in a Northern City* (1945), and William Kornblum's *Blue Collar Community* (1974), but many criminologists regard Hagedorn as too dangerous a figure to be allowed to sit at the high table of academic honor. Their recoil from his work, of course, is quite understandable, since he prefers to consort with street kids instead of cops, runs a famous grassroots Web site (gangresearch.net) that averages more than two million hits per month, and excavates social histories that refute law enforcement dogma. On the other hand, anyone interested in urban issues from a progressive perspective—especially activists and academics who are tired of post-this-and-that jargon and yearn for serious, well-researched "ground truth"—will find an intellectual feast in this cycle of work.

A World of Gangs: Armed Young Men and Gangsta Culture transcends any academic genre. This is a book, quite frankly, that everyone needs to read and discuss, especially those, like my thirteen-year-old son, who are inheriting a divided world that my generation failed to reform or make more just. Hagedorn provides us with the first synoptic view of the myriad warrior nations and street governments that have arisen in the concrete deserts of neoliberalism. The globalization of gang lifestyles to the ends of the earth—from the frozen housing projects of Nuuk, the capital of Greenland, to the mean streets of Ulan Bator and Vladivostok—is one of the most striking and misunderstood phenomena of our time. Since the first edition of *People and Folks* was published, the debate about the "gang problem" has migrated from the front page of the local newspaper to the

columns of *Foreign Affairs,* from the neighborhood police station to the
Pentagon. In the past year, gangs staged an extraordinary semi-insurrection
in São Paulo, Brazil; fiercely battled United Nations troops in Port-au-
Prince, Haiti; were massacred by the police in Nairobi and Buenaventura,
Colombia; and provided an excuse for the mayors of Los Angeles and New
Orleans to demand federal intervention. Similarly, the violent specters of
two huge LA-born but now transnational gangs, MS-13 and 18th Street,
haunt a dozen cities in both North and Central America.

Ha   g is part of the continuum of crime
and r   n of geopolitics in the twenty-first
centu   the abandoned and betrayed youth
in our ghettos and favelas, we are all living in "failed" states, and we should
not be surprised by the angry social combustion that accompanies the
economic polarization of the new gilded age. His careful case studies highlight numerous social fractures and historical inequalities that have con-
verged to create a world of gangs, but savage capitalism (i.e., the kind of
ruthless, untrammeled marketplace celebrated in both the *Wall Street Journal* and gangster rap) remains the decisive substratum. Street gangs mir-
ror the inhuman ambitions and greed of society's trendsetters and deities
even as they fight to the death over scraps from the table of the international drug trade. But Hagedorn, characteristically, also finds hope in the
contradictory values of outlaw youth—selflessness, solidarity, and love amid
cupidity and directionless rage—and he maintains hope that a culture of
resistance will ultimately prevail over the forces of juvenile self-destruction.
Whether one shares his optimism or not, he makes an eloquent case that
the future of the world will be determined on the streets of our cities.

ACKNOWLEDGMENTS

What makes a book? *A World of Gangs* is an expression of powerful and contradictory influences on my life over the past ten years. While I have spent many hours reading and thinking about social theory, many of my "deeper" insights come from the streets or from home, not from my books or the university.

The idea for this book began with my dissatisfaction with the way the social sciences, including my own earlier book, *People and Folks,* had framed gangs. In many ways, Mac Klein started me on this journey through his invitation for me to participate in the Euro-gang Workshop near Frankfurt in 1998. I was repelled by the blatant exportation of U.S. gang research into Europe and began looking at the much more varied gang experience in the third world. What I saw there looked to me a lot more like what I was seeing in Chicago. Luke Dowdney's invitation for me to take part in the ten-nation study *neither War nor Peace* was one of the most decisive events in my intellectual journey. The groups of armed young men I learned about firsthand from researchers in Africa, Asia, and Latin America taught me that a global framework would be quite different from the stale "official definitions" of U.S. criminological reality. The Social Science Research Council's workshop "Youth in Organized Violence" in Pretoria reinforced this notion.

Among those I have learned the most from internationally are Luke Dowdney in Rio de Janeiro; Francisco Gutiérrez from Medellín; Mohammed Ibrahim of Nigeria; Surren Pillay from Cape Town; Elana Zilberg and

Philippe Bourgois, with their U.S.–Central American comparative focus; Agnes Camacho from the Philippines; John Pitts from London; Cameron Hazlehurst of New Zealand; Siri Hettige from Sri Lanka; and my student Nixon Camillien from Haiti.

Back in Chicago, these global influences were fed through the prism of my local research. For reasons that will appear obvious to readers, funding for my research is not likely to ever come from the U.S. Department of Justice. I am therefore extremely grateful to Karen Colvard and the Harry F. Guggenheim Foundation for funding my study of variation in homicide in Chicago and New York City and for supporting me as I reconceptualized my understanding of gangs. David Perry, director of the Great Cities Institute, provided both space and support for many years. His notion of "contested cities" and the urban planning course we held simultaneously via videoconference in Chicago, Belfast, Jerusalem, and Berlin were enormously influential in helping me look at cities through fresh lenses. At Great Cities, Nacho Gonzalez and Paul Goldstein are among my most trusted comrades, and I cannot thank Christiana Kinder of the GCI staff and Mary Austin from Criminal Justice enough for their loving help and concrete assistance. Lance Williams, Xavier Perez, and David Stovall have been generous in helping me understand Chicago's twenty-first-century streets.

My break from criminology has been slowed down on more than one occasion by Jim Short, who was always ready to question my more "extreme" conclusions and force me to think about them some more. Diego Vigil and Carl Taylor have been inspirations from within the U.S. academic "gang squad"; Loïc Wacquant and Saskia Sassen from without. Paul Elitzik is still my best friend even though he is no longer my publisher; my critique of the left was sharpened through our discussions.

The two people who shaped my thinking most were Bobby Gore and Dennis Judd. Bobby Gore was the spokesman for the 1960s Conservative Vice Lords. From Bobby, I learned about the flexibility of the form of the gang and how its negativity can be turned positive. Bobby and Chuck Spruell, Mac Herron, Noonie, JP, and so many of the other guys from 16th and Lawndale showed me both the power and the pathos of their "shattered dream." Bobby Gore is without question one of the most decent human beings I have ever met. It is no exaggeration to say that his unjust incarceration at the end of the 1960s was a principal reason why Chicago's gangs were not able to stay on their prosocial path and eventually reverted to the streets.

Dennis Judd provided intellectual encouragement for me to write this book and cosponsored an international working conference at UIC in 2002 on rethinking traditional criminology. Once I completed a first draft of about half of this book, he engaged me in what was one of the most remarkable critique sessions I have ever experienced. He urged me to be true to "my voice" and allow the inductive process, first taught me by Joan Moore, to speak. This book would not have been possible without Dennis's critical guidance. Pieter Martin simply convinced me that the University of Minnesota Press really wanted this book and was the best place to publish it.

This book is not just about gangs: it is about unnecessary suffering. For me, like Richard Wright, "the meaning of living came only when one was struggling to wring a meaning out of meaningless suffering." While I wrote the entire book during a sabbatical and residence at UIC's Great Cities Institute, I began writing while evacuating my wife's parents from New Orleans in the wake of Hurricane Katrina. My preoccupation with nihilism may have had some immediate, personal origins. I especially want to thank my late father-in-law, Dr. John Devitt, for his comments and insights on my work during that long drive north.

Tupac Shakur's poetic raps and the world of hip-hop were as influential in shaping my thought as any academic text. Iris Rivera and my daughter Tracey gave me important insights on hip-hop and gender. My daughter Katie and her husband Pat and their two kids, Eli and Rio, my son Marty and his son, Oscar, and my still-at-home sons Zach and Jess all taught me about life through their struggles and comments on my thinking. They have never stopped reminding me that I too often put work before family. For that failing of mine, I am truly sorry.

Then there is my debt to what I have read. The citations in the book display my respect for the intellectual shoulders on which I stand. Derrick Bell, bell hooks, and Cornel West convinced me to refocus the study of gangs within a racial lens, and Manuel Castells and Alain Touraine grounded my work within an overarching, noncriminological framework. But even a book of nonfiction like this owes much to the world's great literary works. Many writers have compelled me to look deeper and deeper into the human soul—Gabriel García Márquez, Joseph Conrad, James Baldwin, Jean-Paul Sartre, Herman Melville, Susan Sontag, Fyodor Dostoyevsky, Mark Twain . . . I cannot list them all. I believe the insights of social science badly need to be complemented by the far richer exposition of life, love, and meaning in literature.

Finally, my deepest debt is to my partner, Mary Devitt. She has been my soulmate through this book's entire ten-year pregnancy. She has again and again offered me both the clarity of her thought and the caring of her support. She is the love of my life. I hope, despite the stolen hours of writing this book, I am still the love of hers.

Why Are Gangs Everywhere?

The brown current ran swiftly out of the heart of darkness, bearing us down toward the sea . . .

— JOSEPH CONRAD, *Heart of Darkness*

Vigário Geral, a poor neighborhood, or favela, in Rio de Janeiro, appeared calm and peaceful. A small boy, no more than four years old, ran up to me and grabbed my hand and would not let go as my colleagues and I walked around. Shouts from happy kids playing soccer filled the background. Wires ran from the shanties to nearby power lines, siphoning electricity. It was hard to imagine that just a week before, seven people had been gunned down in the very alley where I was standing. Terceiro Commando, the gang in the next favela, had been allowed to slip into Vigário Geral, probably by police, and had opened fire. When I looked carefully, I could still spot one or two patches of faded brown blood.

Violence by gangs and other groups of armed young men is a worldwide phenomenon. Gangs today play a significant role in all kinds of violence, from ethnic riots to drug market conflicts, even to working for local tyrants in enforcing "law and order." While there have always been gangs, today's urbanizing world is producing them faster than ever and in myriad forms and shapes. High levels of violence by "nonstate actors" like gangs or terrorists have been an unsettling aspect of globalization. The evidence I present in this book leads to the uncomfortable conclusion that gangs are not going away soon, no matter what we do.

Like my first book, *People and Folks,* this study is fundamentally inductive, listening critically to the voices of gang members themselves and trying to understand the world as they see it. Their voices demand respect and recognition and are often defiant in the face of racism and oppression. They can also be destructive and threatening, and many gangs are no longer bit players in the life of cities. Gangs are unmistakable signs that all is not well and that millions of people are being left out of the marvels of a globalized economy.

People and Folks began by asking, what do we know about gangs? This book comes after more than twenty years of studying gangs, a move of my research from Milwaukee to Chicago, and participation in several international comparative studies. While much of what follows builds on what has been handed down by criminology, I also had considerable "unlearning" to do. Much of what I thought I knew did not hold up when I looked at gangs outside the United States and Europe. Many of the classic sociological theories seemed to be just plain wrong or no longer applicable.

Rather than update orthodox criminology, I turned to Manuel Castells's work on the information age to inform my project. I chose to sequester myself these last few years from the entrenched thinking of many of my academic colleagues and to avoid most academic meetings as I reexamined my own thinking. The results surprised me and led to this book, which has three main points.

Gangs are not a unique form but one of many kinds of armed groups that occupy the uncontrolled spaces of a "world of slums." Institutionalized gangs and other groups of armed young men have become permanent fixtures in many ghettos, barrios, and favelas across the globe and are an ever-present option for marginalized youth. Globalization is not the cause of gangs; their unprecedented growth results from massive urbanization, immigration, poverty, and weakened states. As today's gangs proliferate, they often morph into ethnic militias, drug posses, vigilantes, mercenaries, political parties, or even religious police. Gangs and similar alienated and angry groups are a fundamental and long-term characteristic of the global era.

Gangs are shaped by racial and ethnic oppression, as well as poverty and slums, and are reactions of despair to persisting inequality. While gangs can be of any ethnicity, I have found that they cannot be fully understood without analyzing the history of racial or ethnic oppression and the resistance to it. In the past several decades, many marginalized people and ethnic groups have consciously or unconsciously lost their faith in "progress," as they are confronted by the cold permanence of racism and oppression. In response, millions of young people have turned away from secular, Western identities and toward nationalism, ethnicity, or militant religions. Many young people have also been attracted to the nihilistic power of the gangsta persona and the street ethic of survival "by any means necessary."

It is in this power of identity, including the more life-affirming currents within the hip-hop lifestyle, where we can nurture a cultural counterforce to youth's nihilism, misogyny, and self-destructiveness. Encouraging cultural "resistance identities" and linking them to social movements, like those in the United States opposing gentrification, police brutality, or deportations, may present the best opportunity to reach out to our alienated youth. Some gangs have shown the ability to overcome their violent tendencies and may be brought into broader movements for social justice, though this task is admittedly daunting.

Globalizing Gangs

My challenge to criminological gang research begins with its method. Rather than lead off with the local, this book looks first at gangs around the world and the uncertain conditions they live in. The proliferation of gangs in Africa and Latin America is clearly related to familiar economic and social changes now associated with globalization—urbanization, immigration, and social marginalization. In many ghettos, barrios, and favelas where the state is more an idea than a reality, gangs and other groups of armed young men have flourished. But cities of all sizes in the United States and Western Europe, where the state is unquestionably more than an idea, are also home to a growing number of gangs. Gangs are not new in Africa or Latin America, and many predate globalization. Chinese Triads and the Sicilian Mafia have been around for centuries. No simple explanation exists to understand such disparate phenomena.

The gangs of this book, unlike those of criminology textbooks, are not stable, clearly defined entities. Today's youth gang might become a drug posse tomorrow or, in some places, even transform into an ethnic militia or a vigilante group the next day.[1] The changing shapes of gangs pose problems, but, I argue, also present opportunities for reducing violence and drawing some gangs into social movements.

Gangs, in other words, are one of many kinds of groups that are socialized in the prisons and streets and not by conventional institutions. In these turbulent times, members of gangs are angry, potent actors, armed young men (and sometimes women) who exercise power over areas or ethnic groups. "The state," Castells points out, "still relies on violence and surveillance, but it does not hold their monopoly any longer."[2]

Gangs and other armed groups are often in control of one or several neighborhoods, and sometimes even larger localities in cities of all sizes. While such powerful gangs are mostly found in Africa and Latin America, some U.S. gangs—notably the long-lasting ones in Chicago and Los Angeles—are more similar in many respects to their third world cousins than they are to American gangs of yesteryear or "troublesome youth groups" in Europe.[3] U.S. ghettos, like their sister slums in Africa, South Asia, and Latin America, are all part of what Castells calls a "Fourth World" of extreme poverty, resentment, and brutal, day-to-day struggle for survival.

Gangs in Chicago and Los Angeles are important for another reason. These gangs have *institutionalized,* or persisted for generations, and show no signs of going away. The United States is not the only place such institutionalized gangs are found: Cape Town and Rio de Janeiro are among the cities that have produced such gangs, as I discuss in chapter 2. While not all cities have institutionalized gangs—New York City does not, for example—conditions in many cities worldwide are ripe to produce more.

THE POWER OF IDENTITY—RACISM, RAP, AND CULTURE

So if gangs exist in strong states and weak ones, in advanced countries and the third world, in cities large and small, and among nearly every oppressed group, how can we explain them? First we need to recognize that the global era is not just a time of increased economic exploitation and polarization of rich and poor. Ethnic and religious violence has flared up everywhere, particularly after the demise of the Soviet Union.[4] The rise of nationalism, Islamic fundamentalism, and other forms of religious, ethnic, tribal, and racial identity are a nearly universal response of the socially excluded to a hostile world. "When the world becomes too large to be controlled," Castells says, "social actors aim at shrinking it back to their size and reach."[5]

This means that ethnicity, race, religion, and culture matter, and that especially includes gangs.[6] Today the resentments, alienation, and anger of racial and religious discrimination can be found everywhere, as, for example, in the 2004 uprising of youth in the *banlieues* of Paris. The alienation in the world's ghettos is so deep that Cornel West correctly labels this outlook "nihilism."[7] Gangs are the paramount expression of this nihilism.

But gangs have not always been so intensely or permanently alienated.

In the U.S. industrial era, gangs were organizations of ethnic youth who were as violent as any gangs today. One example is Chicago's Outfit, a loose collection of mainly Italian and Sicilian street gangs that unleashed an era of violence during the 1920s that closely compares with the carnage of the 1990s drug wars. Today, the sons and daughters of the Outfit are respectable Chicago citizens who can play down their past (and for some, present) illicit means of gathering wealth and power.[8]

An even better comparison, however, can be found in the conventional success of Chicago's Hamburg Athletic Association (HAA), a gang whose most famous member was Mayor Richard J. Daley. The HAA was formed on the mean streets of Chicago's Bridgeport neighborhood more than a hundred years ago, and its members clawed their way to political power by combining street smarts, violence, and cronyism. Chapter 6 compares the Irish American HAA with a similar gang, Chicago's African American Conservative Vice Lords (CVL), to highlight how racism has led to unfathomable degrees of despair and alienation. I not only rely on historical documents but also present my own recent, unpublished research on the CVL and personal anecdotes of my interaction with the HAA, both of which are still active today.

To properly understand gangs, we need to grasp the depth of the alienation among those who are left out. The studies that compare "gang and nongang," or measure degrees of "group cohesion" or "social disorganization," capture only a small part of a basically cultural reality. Starting with the "truly disadvantaged" in neighborhoods where "work disappears,"[9] Alain Touraine argues that

> those no longer defined by the work they do, largely because they are unemployed, define themselves in terms of what they are, and for many of them this means their ethnic background. Those counter-cultures are embodied in gangs, and often in forms of music, with a high ethnic content.[10]

In other words, *it's the music, stupid.* Gangsta rap and the worldwide embrace of hip-hop culture have been almost completely ignored by scholarship on gangs. Rather than revive musty academic notions of "delinquent subcultures" or ethnically neutral "cultures of poverty," I look at hip-hop and gangsta rap as examples of "resistance identities" of youth. The gangsta persona is a textbook glorification of gang culture, the very definition of what West calls "nihilism." It is in essence the tendency of the excluded to "direct their brutality against themselves and their immediate community rather than against their structural oppressors."[11] Understanding the *culture* of gangs, first of all, means understanding their music.

Rap's lyrics are often ludicrously violent and hypermasculine, reflecting hyperbole, traditional bad guys, and ribald fun. But the hatred of women that permeates so many rap songs also exposes the insecurities of powerless black men, seeking to exercise their will in a misdirected theater of misogyny. The worship of "clothes, hos, and bankrolls" by such rappers as N.W.A., bell hooks says, represents "the same old song. Black men want to be 'in charge'—in charge of the war, in charge of the women, in charge of the world. . . . Gangsta culture is the essence of patriarchal masculinity."[12] Within gangsta rap, as within gangs, women either conform to traditional identities or rebel: "fighting female," as Mary Devitt and I argued.[13]

But hip-hop is more than gangsta rap, and it is in its broader meaning that its promise lies. The origins and heart of hip-hop are diametrically opposed to the misogyny, violence, and drugs found in what can be called "corporate hip hop," as West has been tirelessly pointing out.[14] The alternative rapper Guru says,

> Yo, hip hop is a way of life. It ain't a fad. It ain't a trend. Not for those of us who are true to it. . . . It's our way to release tension, to let out the frustration that young people face in the world today. Over the years hip hop has evolved to represent what is happening now—the reality of street life. Rap is the oral expression of this. The tool, the literature. . . . it will still remain for some of us the raw essence of life. Peace.[15]

Gangsta rap, as much maligned by the older generation as exploited by multinational media companies, must be recognized as the tortured, angry, often poetic rebellion of ghetto youth. Rap's deeply racialized, "black Atlantic" identity and message is so powerful that white youth, even in U.S. suburbs, cannot help but see it as the definition of their own rebellion. The MTV gangsta is nothing less than the "Wild One" of our generation, Ice Cube's gold chains replacing Brando's leather jacket.

Like the favela youth I met in Rio de Janeiro, black youth in the United States have a sober realization that poverty, racism, and oppression will not go away soon. Many black people suspect that there is a permanence to racism that civil rights laws have not touched. They fight back, and not always constructively. "The fact that the powerful often win does not mean that a war is not going on," says Tricia Rose in her insightful *Black Noise.*[16] The face at the bottom of the well, to recall Derrick Bell's powerful book, is that of a black youth. And he is angry. And rapping.[17]

Hip-hop and its gangsta rap variant are cultural answers to the permanence of racism and oppression, a "resistance identity" in Castells's schema. It is the existential cry that no matter how bad things are, in Jesse Jackson's well-known phrase, "I am somebody." And that somebody is defined not by schools, police, respectable citizens, or by you and me, but by young people themselves through hip-hop and all too often gangsta rap. The real hero of hip-hop is still Tupac Shakur, whose work straddles the tension between "thug passion" and "revolutionary ambition."[18] He calls out lyrically in the name of ghetto youth everywhere: "Why am I dying to live, when I'm just living to die?"

The culture of the streets has been called by Philippe Bourgois a "culture of terror" and Elijah Anderson the "code of the street."[19] In reality, today this culture is defined by hip-hop, and this book challenges the not-so-benign neglect by criminology of this central cultural characteristic of the street and its gangs. I cannot forget what a young gang member on death row tragically told me: "Hip-hop is my life." To begin to understand the searing anger that forms the cultural scaffolding of gangs, download some hardcore rap and carefully listen to it.

Return to the City

In this era of the "global city," an understanding of the redivision of urban space and political economy is essential. Gangs, I argue along with Saskia Sassen, have a ubiquitous "presence" in polarized and uncertain urban landscapes.[20] Today, in our majority urban world, there are more of these uncertain landscapes than ever. UN-Habitat chillingly reports that more than one billion people now live in slums. In sub-Saharan Africa, three-quarters of urban dwellers live in such deteriorated conditions. China alone has 166 cities of one million or more. Lagos has become a city teeming with more than ten million people. Medellín, until recently the city at the top of the homicide charts, now has nearly as many people as Chicago.

It was industrialization and urbanization that saw the flowering of immigrant gangs in 1920s Chicago and prompted the first U.S. gang studies.

A similar, but more extensive, migration and urbanization process is now sweeping the third world, as I show in the first section. While the new economy is producing "Gold Coasts" in city after city, it is also producing countless slums and their inevitable gangs.[21]

Gentrification and the redivision of space are accompanying this urbanization worldwide. While the rhetoric on gentrification calls attention to falling rates of crime and increased "security," replacing poor dark people by rich white ones is seen on the street as a domestic form of ethnic cleansing, a "secret war," in my parlance. The racialized spaces of the ghetto, barrio, and favela are being redefined as places of confinement for the socially excluded and dangerous "other." Prison, as Loïc Wacquant argues, has become spatially and conceptually linked to the ghetto in a continuum of domination.[22] For gangs today, prison is part of the neighborhood and vice versa.

Gangs are a normal feature of today's contested cities, physically and symbolically divided by race, religion, ethnicity, gender, and income. As long as the new globalized economy and polity produce inequality and prolong suffering, gangs will be one of a panoply of angry, and often armed, responses.

The War on Terror, Social Movements, and Gangs

The most common public policy response to gangs is, of course, repression. The U.S. Department of Justice is *not* like Western criminologists—it does think about gangs globally.[23] The U.S. government has basically grafted the war on gangs and drugs onto the war on terror, the twenty-first-century version of our 1950s anticommunist crusade. A media-driven tsunami of implausible tales of "dirty bombs" and improbable alliances between Mara Salvatrucha and al-Qaeda has panicked Congress into supporting ill-conceived, draconian policies,[24] much like in the McCarthy era.[25]

Branding gangs a "national security threat" or "new urban insurgency" is consistent with a bipartisan Washington attitude that divides the world into good and evil.[26] These scare tactics divert us from understanding real-life gangs and the human beings in them and the reasons for their alienation. Such one-dimensional thinking is diametrically opposed to the logic and method of social science. This means research like *A World of Gangs* is likely to get short shrift in Washington, since it contradicts "official definitions of reality" and many policymakers' deeply held beliefs.[27]

This book seeks to remind the reader that gang members are real people, "social actors," reacting, sometimes destructively, to conditions of poverty, racism, and oppression. We should not romanticize gangs *or* underestimate the creativity of young people in forming organizations of the street. While most gangs remain unsupervised peer groups, others can be highly organized or deadly violent.

Can we deal with such people and groups rationally? Can we recognize ourselves in the "other"? Israelis and Palestinians had thought it inconceivable to sit down with each other, and the British government had sworn never to meet with the "terrorist" Irish Republican Army. Why can't we listen to the tortured voices coming from the ghetto and seek to find common ground? The popularity of gangsta rap is unmistakable evidence that the alienation of our youth is at a dangerous level.

This alienation cannot be overcome by government antigang programs, a few jobs, better schools, or "zero tolerance" police tactics. Some of these policies produce good effects, some bad, but most are irrelevant to solving the real problems of the underclass. As Diego Vigil says, "Basically, the street gang is an outcome of marginalization, that is, the relegation of certain persons or groups to the fringes of society, where social and economic conditions result in powerlessness."[28] Vigil has it just right. And given the entrenched nature of inequality worldwide, I repeat, *today's gangs are not going away soon, no matter what we do.*

The response I favor lies in bringing gangs and those on society's margins into broader social movements, while demanding they take steps to shed their violent, antisocial skin. This is a difficult task and, for most gangs, may prove impossible, as well as raise the eyebrows of many of my readers. However, one historical lesson of this book is that the gang is not a frozen form, unchangeably violent or terminally hostile. We either bring gangs and the underclass into the polity or run the risk of living in a permanent fortress society. The lessons of the 1960s, as I show throughout this book, suggest that the failure to include the underclass in social movements forecloses any possibility of significantly reducing inequalities and human suffering.

Those gangs that in the past have successfully transformed themselves into prosocial organizations, like Chicago's 1960s Conservative Vice Lords or New York City's 1990s Almighty Latin King and Queen Nation, have left a lasting impression on their communities. Their memories must be kept alive. However, criminology as a whole, with notable exceptions, does not even theorize the possibility of gangs as participants in social movements.[29]

The discipline of criminology today mainly produces research and evaluation for the state that are little more than studies in safe logic that leave untouched the racism and alienation that reproduces gangs.[30]

Research, Not Stereotypes

A World of Gangs is based on my research in Chicago and other U.S. cities as well as around the world. It is derived from my experience teaching and doing research in Chicago this past decade; from comparative research I have done through the Great Cities Institute at the University of Illinois–Chicago and discussion among the fellows and scholars;[31] from my research on the history of gangs in Chicago;[32] from an international working conference I hosted that produced the volume *Gangs in the Global City*;[33] from my participation in the early stages of the Eurogang research;[34] from research in Chicago as part of *neither War nor Peace,* a ten-nation study of children in organized armed violence;[35] from membership in the Social Science Research Council's workshop on youth in armed conflict;[36] from my research for a New York City–Chicago comparative study of violence for the Harry Frank Guggenheim Foundation;[37] from many fruitful hours of collegial discussion with scholars from Brazil, Colombia, Haiti, South Africa, the United Kingdom, Nigeria, Sri Lanka, the Philippines, and Germany, among other countries, as well as with my students; and finally from my own experience as an activist. I am also continuously learning through research for my Web site, http://gangresearch.net. *A World of Gangs* is both a product of my research contradicting previously trusted theories and a search for how to better reach our endangered youth.

Nearly one hundred years ago, Robert Park, a journalist turned sociologist, looked out at Chicago's "gangland" and led social scientists in a sustained effort to humanize the hobos, juvenile delinquents, and other "socially excluded" residents of the slums. The "Chicago school" studies were aimed to humanize, but they also explained why crime and violence occurred in specific areas of the city. Park argued that while the people who lived in "slum" areas were "marginal" to the city's workings, it was absolutely necessary for the city to include them as a part of society. This book, following in Park's footsteps, if not walking in his shoes, aims to understand gangs in the global city as *social actors* whom we ignore or attempt to eradicate only at our risk.

1

GLOBALIZING GANGS

Ghetto, Favela, and Township: The Worlds Gangs Live In

The township was desperately overcrowded; every square foot was occupied either by a ramshackle house or a tin-roofed shack. . . . Life was cheap. Gangsters—known as Tsotsis— . . . were plentiful and prominent; in those days they emulated American movie stars.

—NELSON MANDELA, *Long Walk to Freedom*

I begin with a seldom-asked question: why do gangs in some cities come and go, as in New York, London, or Buenos Aires, while in other cities, such as Chicago, Cape Town, or Rio de Janeiro, they become permanent fixtures of the landscape? There have always been gangs or groups of armed young men who have persisted over decades—even centuries, like the Triads or Mafia. But in this era of globalization such institutionalized gangs may become more a norm than an anomaly.

While others, such as Mike Davis, have called attention to the disturbing consequences of a "planet of slums,"[1] less understood is the related emergence, in these slums, of groups of armed young men. In many ways the next few chapters can be read as a companion to Davis's article and subsequent book *Planet of Slums,* emphasizing the ubiquitous reaction and resistance of alienated, angry, and well-armed young men.

A main source for the present volume is the study *neither War nor Peace,* in which my colleagues and I discuss gangs in ten different countries.[2] One of our most important findings was that in each country the presence of armed groups was an open invitation to successive cohorts of neighborhood youth to find in their local "gangs" a family, job, or identity, as well as thrills and excitement. The present chapter explores the concept of institutionalization, describing how gangs begin and grow and why they endure despite determined efforts of authorities to exterminate them.[3] However, my starting point for understanding persisting gangs is not a review of different kinds of U.S. gangs.[4] Rather, this brief chapter explores how urban conditions produce a deep alienation that, in certain circumstances, leads to institutionalized gangs.

GLOBAL URBANIZATION AND GANGS

In the 1920s sociologists in Chicago initiated research into gangs as part of a study of urbanization and industrialization. The rich empirical work of Robert Park and his colleagues described how the immigration of rural peoples into the urban maze created a "profound revolution in the psychology of the peasant."[5] This "revolution" was seen as the result of social disorganization, as traditional institutions lost power and the peasant became resocialized into an industrial order. It also seduced some of the children of those immigrants, as Frederic Thrasher documented, into street corner gangs.[6]

I revisit the Chicago school periodically throughout this book, but today urbanization has accelerated beyond the imagination of the scholars of Hyde Park. For the first time the population of the world is a majority urban, and this process is radically changing the face of Africa, Latin America, and Asia.

Urbanization, along with the miseries of poverty, has created classic conditions in poor communities for the growth of what Thrasher in 1920s Chicago called "gangland." In the world today, according to the influential *Challenge of the Slums* report, nearly one billion people live in what the UN defines as "slums."[7] Three-quarters of Latin America's half billion people now live in cities, and nearly one-third of them live in slum neighborhoods. Of the three hundred million urban dwellers in sub-Saharan Africa, more than 70 percent live in shantytowns or other dilapidated urban areas. In Asia, more than a half billion people live in desperate urban conditions. The West is not left out either. In the United States alone, twelve million people live in what the UN defines as "slums." People in the third world are flocking to cities as rural opportunities disappear, only to find equally bleak prospects. By the year 2020, the UN estimates, half of the world's urban population will live in poverty.[8] "Urbanization," says Davis grimly, "has been radically decoupled from industrialization, even from development *per se*."[9] Many urban areas are transforming into "megacities" of more than twenty million people. By 2025 Asia alone could have ten or eleven such cities. Mumbai, India, is projected in the next twenty years to have a clearly unsustainable population of thirty-three million.[10]

While the world's urban population is growing, so is its youth population, with 42.2 percent of Africa's population under the age of fifteen, twice the percentage in North America. Almost sixty million Nigerians are under twenty-five years of age.[11] In both Asia and Latin America, nearly one-third of the populace is under fifteen.[12] There are now one billion youth between the ages of fifteen and twenty-four.[13] What age constitutes "youth" is problematic, but, as Charles Green says of the black diaspora in the United States, Caribbean, and East Africa,

> The various age groups are linked by a common appreciation of "hip-hop" clothing and their wavering maturity level. They hang out together, belong to the same gangs, are without marketable skills, and are very likely to have fathered or mothered one child or more outside of marriage.[14]

Urbanization has had as far-reaching effects on youth in the third world as it did on second-generation Polish youth in 1920s Chicago. Gangs have appeared in all major Latin American cities, South Asia, and Oceania.[15] Youth gangs, as a subset of Africa's thirty-two million street children, have

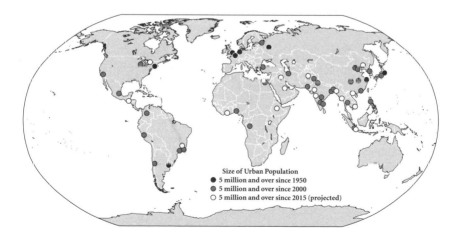

Cities and megacities since 1950. Source: United Nations, *World Urbanization Prospects* (revised edition, 1999).

also become a major issue in the world's fastest urbanizing continent.[16] Migration + cities + poverty + slums + discrimination + youth = gangs. Then and now.

POLARIZATION, SOCIAL EXCLUSION, AND THE RETREAT OF THE STATE

In the United States, criminology has used the term *social disorganization* to describe the conditions for the growth of youth gangs. In the global world of today, however, the parallel concept is *retreat of the state*.[17] The notion of social disorganization has some intuitive charm. The concept is that gangs form out of unsupervised peer groups, which are unsupervised because the formal institutions of society—schools, church, family—break down. When large-scale immigration from the countryside to cities takes place, the immigrants' traditional institutions are shattered, and the new urban institutions are not yet strong enough to replace them, especially for the acculturating children. Thus the Chicago school described gangs as the temporary product of the second generation, its members on their way up the ladder of ethnic succession.[18]

But such industrial-era concepts, intertwined with a belief in the inevitability of progress, fail to capture both the varied conditions today in the third world as well as the stubborn, dismal conditions in African American ghettos of the United States. The term *social disorganization* always had trouble explaining the myriad organizational forms within "slums," and the sociological concept is clearly inadequate to describe, for example, the "warlord politics" of failed states in Africa.[19] Rather than a temporary phenomenon during a period of "modernization," poverty and slums in much of the world have become an intractable reality, spawning despair and angry young men.

Manuel Castells presents a devastating picture of the polarization and social exclusion of the "Fourth World" in today's society.[20] Castells points out that industry has collapsed in much of Africa since the 1970s, and continentwide imports actually declined from 1980 to 1995. Since 1980, income inequality increased throughout most of the world, including the United States, Brazil, Russia, and Mexico, as well as most of sub-Saharan Africa. Inequality is highest in Latin America, while in South Asia it has decreased to some degree.[21]

Indeed, as Zygmunt Bauman chillingly points out, the 358 richest billionaires in the world have the combined income of 45 percent of the world's population. If these 358 Midases decided to keep $5 million each as pocket change and gave the rest away, they could double the annual income of half of the world's people. And, in that unlikely scenario, Bauman wryly adds, "pigs would fly."[22]

Castells ties the spread of "social exclusion" and "income polarization" to the neoliberal, free market policies of globalization and the "retreat of the state." This term is widely debated, since, for example, in sub-Saharan Africa there has never been much of a modern state to retreat from. But in essence, the concept includes both the process of economic adjustment by states in the third world and policies aimed at dismantling the welfare state in the United States and the West.

In other words, in today's world, as the market gains influence, the state "retreats" from providing social welfare. It cuts back the safety net for the urban poor, and alternative policies of "austerity, privatization, and militarization take hold," often mandated by the World Bank or the International Monetary Fund.[23] The state, particularly in the third world, cannot provide adequate employment, services, or security for vastly expanding poor urban neighborhoods; it exists mainly to "enable" the market.[24] Castells provides the transition I am going to explore in the pages ahead: "When and where there is no regulation and control by legitimate forces of the state, there will be ruthless control by the illegitimate forces of violent, private groups. Unfettered markets are tantamount to wild societies."[25] In some cities, gangs have exercised "ruthless control" of areas of cities for decades. I call that persistence "institutionalization," borrowing from theories of organization.

INSTITUTIONALIZATION AND GANGS

Major gangs in Chicago, Cape Town, and Rio de Janeiro have been around for more than forty years. These gangs have all spread outside their original neighborhoods and have a history and an identity that go far beyond wild peer groups. In other words, such gangs have institutionalized.[26]

The concept of institutionalization in organizations derives from American sociology and the work of Philip Selznick. He examined how the Tennessee Valley Authority adapted to changing political conditions and continued to flourish well after its New Deal origins.[27] Departing from classic organizational theory, Selznick found that an institution's main goal was not just to rationally accomplish a specific task, but also to find the means for survival.[28]

In elevating survival, or "unplanned adaptive change," over the task at hand, Selznick argues, institutions acquire an identity that is shaped by the need to adapt to changing conditions. These include rivalry with other organizations as well as power struggles by group leaders. As organizations institutionalize, they develop rituals and ceremonies that distinguish them from other similar organizations, and come up with an apocryphal organizational history. An organization produces a formal or informal structure with rules and role expectations, its members identify with the organization, and it gathers support from at least some elements of the broader community.

For example, the well-respected Lutheran churches in the United States distinguish themselves not only from Methodists and Catholics but also from one another, and have variations in liturgy, requirements for ordination, dogma, and sect-specific rituals. When I was growing up, it was considered morally questionable by my relatives for my family to forsake the Wisconsin Evangelical Lutheran Synod for the upstart American Lutheran Church.

That same religious fervor applies to joining a Chicago gang. A college student described his initiation as a teenager being blessed into the Black Gangster Disciples, making clear the power of ritual:

> After a long string of questions, including my concerns about the initiation process, I agreed. It felt right, like magic. . . . The first meeting I attended was held during the evening hours in the park across from our high school. . . . A circle was formed and all brothers crossed their arms right over left. I was instructed to follow. We opened up the meeting with a GD prayer and creed, which struck me as being amazingly poetic. I was informed that no disrespecting was to occur during the meeting. Profanity was not tolerated and "mouth shots" were to be allotted to the rule breakers. I was instructed to stand in the center of the circle as Darren approached me. He was the brother with the most rank at the time. I was ready for anything and kept my guard up just in case any unwanted gestures were made. Darren asked me to uncross my arms and grumbled prayers with a straight face as significant emblems were drawn across my chest with his index and middle finger, as would a priest. Afterward he shook my hand and smiled and said "You're Folks." These were my brothers now and I shook their hands lovingly.[29]

Institutions, Selznick found, are not in essence bricks and mortar, but systems of belief that "provide the individual with an ordered approach to his day-to-day problems, a way of responding to the world consistently yet involuntarily."[30] Selznick here is drawing on an earlier tradition derived from Émile Durkheim's and Max Weber's studies of symbolic systems of authority.[31] What is important for the present study is that institutions create "rationalized myths" about their structure and activities that have less to do with accomplishing set goals than with maintaining and preserving the organization.[32] Gangs "protect the hood" in the same way as "schools educate"—typically more myth than reality. "Myth-making," Jack Katz and Curtis Jackson-Jacobs argue, "is one of the central activities of males involved with gangs."[33]

Applying the concept of institutionalization to gangs, we can begin to understand why some gangs persist for decades despite changes in leadership and police repression. Institutionalized gangs are not merely an "expendable tool . . . of dynamic leaders" or sustained only by profits from drug sales. These gangs are "living organisms" instilling in their members, as well as the community, a belief in the organization itself.[34] This belief persists despite organizational performance,[35] since it is essentially cultural, not rational, and handed down as tradition through generations.

This is why police are unable to destroy institutionalized gangs, such as Chicago's Black Gangster Disciples, despite jailing the entire leadership of the gang, "cutting off its head," then naively expecting the body to die.[36]

> Q. If you cut off the head of the gang, will the body die?
> A. There's more than one head in everything. There ain't no drug spot that I know of that's only one person and that's the main person. You need more than one person. Just because of a situation like that. What if he gets caught, goes to jail, you can't do that. No, you need at least—two is good, but three is better. . . . They take the man down. It's still going on. The man, he just drops, he says okay, we're going to miss him, but we still must go on. The show must go on. It's like the circus. The show must go on.[37]

Institutionalization means that the gang's show goes on despite changes in leadership (killed, incarcerated, or "matured out"); it has organization complex enough to sustain multiple roles of its members (including roles for women and children); it can adapt to changing environments (police repression or civil war); it fulfills some needs of its community (economics, security, services); and it organizes a distinct outlook of its members (symbols, rituals, traditions, sometimes called a subculture).[38]

In ghettos, barrios, and favelas around the world, gangs are thriving. While most are wild adolescent peer groups that incessantly come and go, in some circumstances they do not go away but institutionalize and become major players in the life of their community and city. These gangs are nearly invulnerable to repression. To more thoroughly understand this concept and in what kinds of conditions such gang organisms best grow, the next chapter compares the history of long-lasting gangs in Chicago, Cape Town, and Rio de Janeiro.

chapter 2

Street Institutions:
Why Some Gangs Won't Go Away

> "This is madness, Aurelito," he exclaimed.
> "Not madness," Aurelliano said. "War."
>
> —GABRIEL GARCÍA MÁRQUEZ, *One Hundred Years of Solitude*

Gangs in Chicago, Cape Town, and Rio de Janeiro have been operating for decades. This chapter seeks to understand how and why such gangs persist.

The history of institutionalized gangs in these three cities, like that of any organization, is highly mythologized. In Chicago, gang members memorize the literature, laws, and prayers of their gang, and learn about past warriors and leaders, often with titles such as "kings" or "lords."[1] Such histories are memorized by gang members in prison and handed down from veteran Original Gangsters ("OGs") to eager young recruits. The Black Gangster Disciples have even put their history into book form.[2] In Rio de Janeiro, children learn to idolize drug faction leaders as heroes who have defied the state.[3] "Once they are members of the gang," Andre Standing reports about the "Americans" gang in Cape Town, "youngsters are taught the gang's history and rules, are encouraged to have the gang's tattoos and adopt clothing styles unique to the gang."[4]

Myths aside, the origins of gangs in all three cities can be found in the social movements of the 1960s, a time that plays an important role in my overall narrative. In both Chicago and Rio de Janeiro, the crushing of social movements by the state resulted in the incarceration of political leaders and gang members alike. But while the 1960s revolutionary movements were smashed in Chicago and Rio, the gangs in both cities got stronger.

During the same time in Cape Town, the anti-apartheid movement alarmed the South African government, which initiated a major displacement of the African and coloured population for "security" reasons. In the displaced communities of Cape Town, coloured gangs, like Rashied and Rashaad Staggie's Hard Living Kids, would arise in the 1960s and not go away, unlike more transient black African youth gangs in Johannesburg and elsewhere.

INSTITUTIONALIZED GANGS IN CHICAGO, CAPE TOWN, AND RIO DE JANEIRO

Prison

While Chicago school theory stresses the centrality of neighborhood to the growth of gangs, in today's world the prison also plays a crucial role in both the origins and continuing activities of gangs. The spaces of the prison and the ghetto coincide, as Loïc Wacquant argues.[5] In eight of the ten cities in the *neither War nor Peace* study, street gangs had strong links to prison gangs.[6]

In Chicago, Mayor Richard J. Daley declared "war on gangs" in 1969 and followed a policy of suppressing both gangs and revolutionary groups like the Black Panther Party. The major Chicago "supergangs," the Black Gangster Disciples and Black Disciples, the Blackstone Rangers, the Conservative Vice Lords, the Latin Kings and Maniac Latin Disciples, among others, grew stronger in prison and saw themselves as "political prisoners," while the more political Black Panthers and Young Lords fell apart.[7]

Many of Chicago's supergangs had also formed behind bars, not in neighborhoods. For example, the Conservative Vice Lords formed first in the St. Charles Illinois Youth Center, not Lawndale.[8] At its origins, the Blackstone Rangers, according to its adviser, John Fry, "more resembled a prisoners' organization than it did a gang or a community organization," and the Stones too began in St. Charles.[9] Gang leaders in Chicago today are nearly all incarcerated, but most still maintain control of key gang functions.[10] For example, one leader of the Latin Counts told me that for him to begin a new section in Bridgeport, he had to go to a federal prison to obtain permission from their incarcerated chief. Rather than prison being a place to send gang members in an attempt to break up the gang, gangs have adapted and have used prison to advance their interests.[11]

In Rio de Janeiro, the military dictatorship deliberately locked up the gangs and revolutionaries together to discredit the political activists, but found the same results as in Chicago. Bank robbers, like Rogério Lengru-ber ("Bagulhão"), learned methods of organization from the incarcerated urban guerrillas and adopted an organizational name—Comando Vermelho ("Red Command")—that suggests revolutionary influence.[12] On the streets, the CV is often called "the movement," as if it were a leftist group.

By the late 1970s, the new Rio prison-based gangs had transformed older marijuana networks into cocaine operations with local hierarchical con-trols and access to ample firearms. "Replicated almost identically in dif-ferent favela territories, local organization was based on military needs for defense and invasion and simple division of labour for the bagging and sales of drugs."[13]

Luke Dowdney goes on: "The Comando Vermelho's most powerful *donos* (leaders) are currently in prison from where they continue to control their territories via cellular phones and visiting colleagues." In 2002, on the orders of gang leaders in prison, all of Rio de Janeiro's commercial and manufac-turing concerns, schools, and buses were shut down for the day in a show of gang power.[14]

Irvin Kinnes finds that in Cape Town in the 1970s "prison gangs that tra-ditionally operated inside prisons started to recruit outside members, espe-cially those who belonged to street gangs." In turn, the wealth of the drug economy allowed some street gang members to buy their way into the more prominent, and feared, prison "numbers" gangs.[15] Street gangs and prison gangs became completely intertwined in Cape Town.

In all three countries, the incarceration of gang leaders after the repres-sion of social movements coincided with a spectacular increase in the num-ber and sophistication of gangs.[16]

Cocaine and Defensible Spaces

A major reason why gangs in all three cities have adapted and grown was an unintended consequence of the emergence of the drug trade, particularly cocaine.[17] In Chicago, like elsewhere in the United States, cocaine trans-formed gangs into economic enterprises, fixated on real and hoped-for profits. Chicago was a distribution center for the U.S. Midwest, and the gangs divided up the large Chicago market. In the 1960s the new black and Latino street gangs had replaced the Outfit as the main distributors of drugs for their communities and were well positioned for a central role in drug distribution.[18]

Both Cape Town and Rio de Janeiro had large domestic markets, controlled by the gangs, but both were also important transit points for drugs headed outside their respective continents.[19] Jackie Lonte, leader of the Americans gang, was credited with introducing crack to Cape Town after a 1970s trip to Brazil.[20] Fernandinho Beira-Mar ("Seaside Freddy"), a Rio drug lord, was captured hiding in the Colombian jungles with the left-wing guerilla group Fuerzas Armadas Revolucionarias de Colombia in what police called a "guns for drugs" pipeline.[21]

The importance of Rio de Janeiro as the major transit point of Colombian cocaine, rather than Buenos Aires, played a key role in providing Rio's gangs with the wealth necessary to maintain their organizations, safely protected in the defensible spaces of the favelas. By comparison, gangs in Buenos Aires have not persisted for generations or reached the organizational level of their Rio counterparts 1,200 miles to the north. As a port, Cape Town, not Johannesburg, is the natural transit point for drugs from South Africa, as well as from Latin America, and became the home for South Africa's institutionalized gangs.

Another reason why gangs in Chicago, Cape Town, and Rio de Janeiro institutionalized, and gangs in other cities did not, was their ability to sell drugs safely within defensible spaces.[22] This concept was initially devised to discuss ways to prevent crime, but a close reading of Oscar Newman's work can show its relevance for criminal organization.

When I first flew into Rio de Janeiro as part of the *neither War nor Peace* study, I took a cab from the airport, and my first glance at the favelas filling the mountainside hit me with déjà vu. Out loud to my befuddled Portuguese-speaking cabdriver, I said, "My God. It's Robert Taylor Homes writ large." Housing projects and favelas both provided defensible spaces for gangs to institutionalize, safe from enemies and police.

Rio's favelas, many of them built on the side of the mountains surrounding the city's exotic beaches and areas where the rich live, provide a true defensible space from police and rival factions. Rapid urbanization in the 1980s led to overcrowding and a vast expansion and criminalization of the informal economy.[23] The drug factions, Dowdney says, use the "favelas as defensible and strategic sales points within the city."[24] Police find it nearly impossible to locate "suspects" in Rio's dense living quarters, with narrow alleys and hostile population, just as gang members easily hid from police in Chicago's public housing towers. The favelas are different in this way from the spread-out *villas miserias* in suburban Buenos Aires.[25]

During an afternoon while I was in a Rio favela, a police invasion occurred, but the residents did not appear to be unduly concerned. Child lookouts shot off firecrackers to warn residents of the impending invasion. Gunshots indicated where the police were entering, and by the time the police arrived anyone they were searching for was long gone or safely hidden. Perhaps because this time the police were not serious in their excursion, they did not come in with armored cars and helicopters, guns blazing, as they often do.[26] Life in the favela went routinely on, before, during, and after the police invaded. "The power of drug trafficking," said one non-affiliated favela youth, "is greater than the government's power."[27]

Sudhir Alladi Venkatesh points out that within Chicago's black ghetto, drug dealing in housing projects like Robert Taylor Homes "was more private and not usually subject to police action."[28] The gangs saw the projects as an easily milked cash cow. As one Black Gangster Disciple told me in military terminology, "Basically you control the area. If you controlled the perimeter, you controlled the projects."[29] Venkatesh's history of Robert Taylor Homes provides an unforgettable ethnographic description of the defensible nature of housing projects that were built to contain Chicago's poor black population, rather than allow spatial mobility.[30] This had the unexpected result of creating public housing where, as the housing scholar Susan Popkin says, "the gangs had more power than the police."[31] Dense and crowded conditions, not only in public housing but within Chicago's poor black neighborhoods, have been a defining characteristic of that city's ghetto for nearly a century.[32]

In Cape Town, the Area Removals Act in the 1960s relocated tens of thousands of coloured and African peoples into neighborhoods segregated from white areas by law, highways, and violence, much like the history of segregation in Chicago.[33] White control was relaxed after the 1960s relocation and again in 1994 when the African National Congress (ANC) took power and security services became disorganized. Cape Town's gangs, not the police, according to Ted Leggett, "have been controlling the same turf for generations."[34] Defensible spaces appear to be important conditions for the institutionalization of gangs.[35]

Racism and Ethnic Identity

In all three cities racism and ethnic identity join economic rationality, a history rooted in social movements and prison, and defensible spaces as crucial factors in why gangs institutionalized in these cities and not others. In Chicago, the black and Latino gangs formed during the 1960s social movements adopted nationalist attitudes and were involved, in one way or another, with social movement politics.[36] The laws and prayers of all the major African American gangs are filled with nationalist rhetoric and Muslim references. Chicago's "People and Folks" alliances, now largely abandoned, were adaptations that lasted decades and aimed at stabilizing dangerous intra-ethnic rivalries.

Gangs in New York were just as prominent as Chicago's in the 1960s, but faded in the 1970s, unlike Chicago's resurgent supergangs. New York's mayor in the "urban crisis era," John Lindsay, adopted a policy of outreach to the gangs and even went out on the streets during the 1968 riots. At the same time that gangs like the Black Spades were dying out, hip-hop was deliberately introduced by former gang members into New York neighborhoods to combat gang violence. By contrast, in Chicago, the gangs stayed as the dominant neighborhood forces.

Mayor Lindsay's policies contrasted sharply with Chicago mayor Daley's "shoot to kill" orders after Dr. Martin Luther King Jr.'s assassination, and Daley's subsequent "war on gangs." Rather than fade away, like their New York cousins, Chicago's gangs all got stronger. By the 1980s the introduction of cocaine allowed now well-established Chicago gangs to reorganize as "ethnic enterprises,"[37] transforming turf into markets. However, in New York City, since the old gangs were defunct, new drug crews, not long-standing gangs, dominated the crack market. These gangs, with superficial ties to neighborhoods, were easily dismantled by intense police repression, while Chicago gangs could not be crushed.[38]

In Rio de Janeiro, the favelas are made up overwhelmingly of Afro-Brazilian and "Pardo," or mixed-race people, unlike the *villas miserias* in more ethnically homogenous Buenos Aires.[39] While Brazil is a supposedly "non-racial" society,[40] dark-skinned Brazilians have fewer opportunities, are politically underrepresented,[41] are disproportionately victims of violence,[42] and, according to the International Labor Organization, are heavily concentrated in the informal and illegal labor markets. Afro-Brazilian identity has a strong cultural presence within the favelas that have produced some of Brazil's most vibrant music.[43]

CAPE TOWN GANGS' RACIAL IDENTITY CRISIS

Cape Town's history of gangs, drugs, and ethnic identity provides a clear example of how these combined factors have contributed to gang institutionalization. In South Africa, it is mainly coloured, not black African gangs, that have institutionalized.[44] In Cape Town, the Hard Livings, Americans, Sexboy, and other gangs were founded after the relocation of the coloured and African communities in the 1960s into the Cape Flats. The newly formed gangs were the descendants of earlier *skollies,* or street corner gangs. These newer gangs took advantage of the introduction of cocaine as a profitable commodity in the early 1970s and added this new, lucrative product to *dagga* (marijuana) and Mandrax sales.[45] The gangs coexisted with the country's militant anti-apartheid movement, often giving support but also maintaining a suspicious distance.

During the apartheid state, coloured people and members of Cape Town gangs were both discriminated against and favored over black Africans, and both hopeful and fearful of the black-led movement. As the liberation struggle grew in intensity, the Americans gang, it was revealed in the Truth and Reconciliation Commission (TRC) hearings, collaborated with South African intelligence services and even assassinated anti-apartheid activists.[46] Black gangs in Soweto, argued Clive Glaser, declined as the "comrades" and other militant groups of black African youth gained in prominence.[47]

During the 1994 elections that ended the "ancien régime," the gangs physically attacked ANC candidates, including Nelson Mandela.[48] After the ANC victory, conditions changed again. Gang violence persisted as the economy in the Western Cape deteriorated. The vigilante group People against Gangsterism and Drugs (PAGAD) executed thirty gang leaders in 1998 alone,[49] including the Hard Livings leader Rashaad Staggie, who was pulled from his home, shot, and "set alight."[50] The gangs, which had already united in a cartel called the Firm aimed at regulating drug trafficking, responded by building a coalition of gangs and community groups, the Community Outreach Forum ("Core"). They called on the ANC to "repay" them for what they claimed was their earlier political and financial support. The ANC, however, in response banned gangs in the Prevention of Organized Crime Act (POCA), a law based on California's antigang Street

Terrorism Enforcement and Protection Act (STEP). No surprise—the gangs did not go away.

The coloured community has long experienced unease with its racial heritage. "If you want to know why we coloured have gangs," a local observer told Standing, "the problem is we coloured wish we were white. . . . we don't know who we are or where we came from."[51] Or wished they were black, given the strong, racialized influence of rap music in Cape Town.[52]

The disorientation under apartheid continued under new conditions in the ANC-led South Africa. Feelings ran high in coloured communities that conditions were better under apartheid. "De bruinmense," or the coloured, Bill Dixon and Lisa-Marie Johns conclude, are a "race apart" and deeply disturbed about their role in the new South Africa.[53] The Western Cape is still South Africa's most violent area, with rates of homicide highest for coloured communities.

What is significant in the Cape Town experience, as well as in the equally complex histories of Chicago and Rio de Janeiro gangs, is that changing conditions have not resulted in the demise of the gangs. Racism, inequality, the drug economy, defensible spaces, and prison are all factors that combined to form an ethnic identity that helped young men create a gang organization that could adapt to a changing environment and last for decades despite repression and loss of leaders.

ARE INSTITUTIONALIZED GANGS ORGANIZED CRIME?

American law enforcement today often labels gangs "organized crime," contrasting minority gangs to earlier (white ethnic) youth groups, in the belief that today's gangs have a tightly organized, hierarchical structure.[54] Gangs in Chicago and Los Angeles, including the much-demonized Mara Salvatrucha, are sometimes seen in conspiratorial terms as centrally organized and linked in a broad chain of drug distribution and terror.

What lies behind this paranoia is the belief that gangs, particularly the institutionalized ones I have been describing, are organized into pyramid-like bureaucracies, with "lieutenants" and "foot soldiers" carrying out the orders of a diabolical "chief, " as if gangs were a distorted reflection of a police department. While it may be human nature to see in the other a negative reflection of what is familiar, such simple-minded ideas are contradicted by much research as well as the last fifty years of organizational theory.

Are institutionalized gangs "organized crime"? If by this it is meant "do persisting gangs support and enrich themselves by the underground economy," the answer is yes, almost by definition. However, if what is meant is that gangs like the Latin Kings, Comando Vermelho, or Hard Livings are godfather-run, centralized, efficient crime syndicates, then the answer is no—or at least almost never, and if they ever are, then not for long.

The *neither War nor Peace* study found that armed groups varied structurally from the "militarized command structure" of Rio's drug factions to a "corporate structure" in Chicago's gangs to the informal "flat structure" of Cape Town's Hard Livings.[55] But what does this mean?

Comando Vermelho, the most organized of the gangs, Dowdney reports, "can be seen as a network of affiliated independent actors rather than a strictly hierarchical organization with a single head figure," a style of organization aptly described by the Brazilian anthropologist Alba Zaluar as "horizontal reciprocity networks."[56] In fact, "from 1986 onwards, the Comando Vermelho began to fragment internally and disputes for territorial control between donas became commonplace and increasingly violent."[57] In Cape Town, rather than a General Motors–like corporation, a gang leader described the operation as "a big chain, you know, like 7-11 franchises."[58]

This gang member is more attuned to organizational realities than most law enforcement officials. Institutionalized gangs might best be described as "networks" or "loosely coupled systems," a term Karl Weick coined to describe how schools respond to central direction but also maintain local integrity.[59] Both concepts are consistent with the organization of many decentralized businesses today and are a better fit for drug-selling institutionalized gangs than the rigid hierarchies of industrial-era behemoths like General Motors.[60]

In fact, the notion of "gangs as networks" fits Chicago gangs well, with each citywide supergang in reality a loose alliance of neighborhood branches, or "franchises."[61] While leaders can indeed call "hits" from prison and are typically major figures in the drug game, their influence over the day-to-day activities of their branches is often minimal and almost always exaggerated.

While all Chicago gangs have a formal structure,[62] the absolute authority of the leader may be more of a useful myth. Such fairy tales sometimes come in handy for gang members presenting a fearsome image of the efficiency of their gang to outsiders, like police or researchers. For example, I was told that Chicago's "Milwaukee Kings" (a different gang than the Latin Kings) has an "established hierarchy and chain of command," age-graded sections, a set of laws formalized into a constitution written in 1980, a juridical board, finance board, and even a historian! Still, the gang has been led for several decades by members of the same family and has been forced from its home turf by gentrification. While the gang's structure appears bureaucratic, it is in essence "family-based," with decisions made informally among kin.[63] This gang closely resembles the "quasi-institutionalized" East Los Angeles gangs described by Joan Moore.[64]

In the last years, as in Rio de Janeiro, Chicago's gangs have fragmented, and "renegade" factions have split off from the main gangs.

> R. . . . We ain't . . . too together. . . . You know why that happens, though, because niggers, you know what I'm sayin', get their head pumps up. Nigga don't wanna honor no violations no more. Nigga don't wanna pay dues. They don't wanna hang out. So renegades come from that. Nigga wanna do what he wanna do. Outlaw (say) "fuck it. I don't gotta ride with y'all. I do what I wanna do. I'm out for myself. I ain't be goin' to no meetings no more, I ain't be payin' no dues."[65]

Law enforcement officials have periodically crowed about their success in breaking up gangs in Chicago, Cape Town, and Rio de Janeiro. However, the fracturing of gangs into more decentralized segments is not necessarily a sign that repression "works" or notice that the demise of the gangs is imminent.[66] In Cape Town, the intense pressure put on the gangs by PAGAD and then their banning by the ANC resulted in further gang decentralization, which was seen by some law enforcement observers not as a good thing but as "a necessary strategy" by the gangs to allow themselves to survive. While it could be that the fracturing of gangs in all three cities is a sign of decline, it also might be a sign of health, of still-influential institutions surviving another "unplanned adaptive change." Significantly, as I write in 2006, gangs in all three cities show no signs of going away.

The Importance of Institutionalized Gangs

So why is the institutionalization of gangs in a few cities important? The reader cannot forget that most gangs do not institutionalize but are wild groups of kids that come and go as the peer group ages. To understand why some gangs institutionalize, we need to return to the last chapter. Globalization is urbanizing the earth's population, polarizing rich and poor, and creating vast spaces of social exclusion or slums within cities. By 2020, the UN predicts that half of the world's urban population will live in poverty.

As inequality is increasing and some areas of cities, regions, and entire continents are marginalized, immigration increases, and ethnic conflicts have accelerated. Minority ethnic, racial, or religious groups are often the most-neglected populations by third world and Western states alike. Large areas within megacities have admittedly become unmanageable, and armed groups are stepping in to manage the unmanageable spaces.

The good news is that conditions for institutionalization do not presently exist in all cities, as I have shown. Local policies matter. On the other hand, in more and more of the world's urban areas, conditions are ripening for the institutionalization of gangs or other armed groups. Once founded, these groups will not easily go away, as organizational preservation becomes the top priority and cultural traditions take hold. An increasingly frustrated and demoralized population will reluctantly turn to armed non-state actors who can provide security of a sort, a sense of identity, perhaps the sole local supply of jobs, and rudimentary services that the state cannot or will not offer.[67]

Cheryl Maxson and Malcolm Klein, supporting the paradigmatic claims of the Los Angeles school of urban studies, argue that gangs in Los Angeles, not Chicago, are today's model for gangs elsewhere.[68] They address the wrong research question. What is most important are not the differences between LA and Chicago but more their *similarities*—in both of these U.S. cities, local conditions have uniquely produced institutionalized gangs.

In LA and Chicago gangs are admittedly quite different from the "play groups" of nineteenth- and twentieth-century U.S. slums, but gangs in both cities are uncannily similar to their cousins in Rio de Janeiro, Cape Town, Kingston, Medellín, Mumbai, and Karachi. U.S. criminologists need to get out of their Eurocentric world and look to Africa, Asia, and Latin America for more meaningful comparisons.[69] It is the desperate urban conditions in the fourth world, including U.S. cities, that are more likely to produce institutionalized gangs today. What is cause for alarm is that the processes of institutionalization that produced gangs in LA and Chicago have also been at work in many U.S. cities in the last few decades, as well as in Europe and the third world. Moreover, the gangs of Chicago, Cape Town, or Rio de Janeiro are also similar to other kinds of armed groups. In fact, gangs can often quickly morph into an ethnic militia, a fundamentalist paramilitary group, or a drug cartel.

chapter 3

The Problem with Definitions:
The Questionable Uniqueness of Gangs

We didn't call ourselves gangs. We called ourselves clubs or clicas.

—LUIS RODRIGUEZ, *Always Running*

How does one make sense of this description of gangs in Kano, Nigeria?

Ayan daba (are) urban gangs who, through hunting and warrior traditions, have historical links to anti-colonial Islamic religious politics. These youths, highly skilled in the uses of weaponry and magic, have ambiguous roles in Muslim communities, where they have been employed by religious leaders to strong-arm public opinion. Ayan daba are considered "revolutionaries" who have Muslim ideologies and traditions. . . . (they sometimes) dress lavishly in a Muslim-style riga (dress), smoking a joint reminiscent of Cheech ('n Chong) slap a alamajiri (Qur'anic student) to the ground for forgetting to say his prayers. . . . (They also) have adopted a style of dress they associate with "West Side niggers," or Los Angeles–based rappers. In their sun glasses, chains, and baggy jeans, ayan daba show a broad interest in youth cultures around the world. . . . ayan daba serve as the vanguard for local political and religious leaders, earning the major part of their income from politically motivated thuggery.[1]

How do we make sense of gang members like these who say their heroes include Saddam Hussein, Osama bin Laden, Tupac Shakur, Bob Marley, and Nelson Mandela? Conerly Casey's vivid description of Kano gangs points out a most important feature of the global era: the lines of distinction between different kinds of groups of armed young men are just not so clear anymore. In fact, it is the same set of conditions I detailed in the last chapter—social exclusion, racism, and a delegitimized, weakened state—that produces angry young men who feed the worldwide networks of gangs, drug cartels, and death squads; religious, ethnic, and political militias; and revolutionary guerrillas, as well as the ranks of police and the military. Then there are the terrorists.

"Al Queda," Jack Goldstone goes so far as to say in a National Research Council essay, "is like gangs in U.S. central cities or social protest movements throughout the world."[2] This is not an outlandish claim, nor does it echo hysterical government charges that "gangs = terrorists." Goldstone is aware that it is fourth world conditions that produce angry young men and their rebellious identities and organizations. The specific content of those historical conditions determine what kind of armed group is likely to form.

Most criminologists share Malcolm Klein's view that "street gangs are, by and large, qualitatively different from other youth groups."[3] Herbert Covey has adopted this approach in his survey *Street Gangs throughout the World* and attempts to isolate, reify, and universalize what he calls the "true street gang."[4] Scott Decker and Frank Weerman's *European Street Gangs* also explicitly applies a Klein-like definition.[5] For Klein and Covey, gangs can be defined and categorized as various kinds of "crime problems" or delinquent peer groups that have distinct and unique characteristics.

But the gangs in Kano may cause some readers to doubt conventional criminological wisdom. In fact, while the twenty-first-century process of gang formation may sometimes look the same as it might have on street corners eighty years ago, it can also look radically different. To make sense of this I briefly survey below the different kinds of conditions that spawn gangs around the world, particularly how gangs respond to social control measures—or the lack of them—by the state.

Globalization and the State

The first gangs studied by sociologists in 1920s Chicago were rebellious, youthful by-products of immigration, urbanization, and industrialization. Park and his colleagues were imbued by a progressive spirit that saw the potential of the state for ameliorating conditions of poverty and treating delinquency, as well as replacing the broken traditions of the old world with a cosmopolitan civility.[6] In the industrial era, Alain Touraine argues, the belief in progress and civilization was fed by the spirit of class struggle in the West and by the hopes of national liberation in the third world.[7] The strength and very existence of these social movements were characterized by the vision of a soon-to-come better day—whether that meant prosperity under the welfare state, socialism, or an end to racial, ethnic, or religious oppression. Such sentiments can be seen in this passage from Richard Wright's *Native Son,* which anticipates Frantz Fanon:

> "What I killed for must've been good!" Bigger's voice was full of frenzied anguish. "It must have been good! When a man kills, it's for something. . . . I didn't know I was really alive in the world until I felt things hard enough to kill for 'em. . . . I feel alright when I look at it that way."[8]

To understand how perspectives have changed, compare Bigger's tortured hope with the cold, quasi-existentialist lyrics of today's West Coast gangsta rap group Cypress Hill: "Here is something you can't understand— How I could just kill a man."[9] There is no passion or ideals. The hope of a better world has disappeared. All that is left is the sober, nihilistic reality of a violent ghetto with no exit.[10] As one older Chicago gang member sadly told me, "Gangs today are different than 'back in the day.' They don't mean anything anymore."

Holding a full cultural critique for a later chapter, I focus here on optimism as one consequence of the modern project, whether in its liberal, nationalist, or Marxist form. This included a positive and hopeful view of the capacity of political action for alleviating the misery of the masses.[11] Events over the past century, however, have provided evidence of the incapacity of both liberal and socialist programs to significantly reduce human suffering.

The loss of faith in the state can be understood by looking at Susan Strange's book *The Retreat of the State.* Her central point is that a variety of actors other than states now exercise authority and control outcomes that previously were the domain of the state. While states were once "the master of markets," she argues, "now it is the markets which . . . are the masters over the governments of states."[12] Her examples range from the power of telecommunication firms to control the substance of information to the "big six" accounting firms and their management of mergers and acquisitions that help transnational corporations operate outside national law. She also includes a chapter on the powerful influence of mafias and drug cartels who profit greatly by corruption in a global criminal economy wholly outside the laws of states. As Arundhati Roy explains:

> The thing to understand is that modern democracy is safely premised on an almost religious acceptance of the nation state. But corporate globalization is not. Liquid capital is not. So, even though capital needs the coercive powers of the nation state to put down revolts in the servants' quarters, this set up ensures that no individual nation can oppose corporate globalization on its own.[13]

By the end of the 1990s, the IMF was imposing its neoclassical structural adjustment formula of cutting social benefits in more than eighty countries. When states refused to toe the line, like Kenya or Peru in the late 1980s, they were punished and, as in both examples, collapsed economically while informal and underground economies expanded.[14] Half of all U.S. foreign aid for third world countries is now given through nongovernmental organizations (NGOs) rather than the state.[15]

The demise of the state may be premature, however. "The state does not disappear," Manuel Castells adds. "It is simply downsized in the Information era."[16] Further, the counterpressures on the state are not just global, since "below the state there are communities, tribes, localities, cults, and gangs."[17] Steve Reyna explains that globalization has created "monsters" in the form of autarkic armed groups fighting to destabilize African and other third world states.[18] As Mike Davis says,

> Even within a single city, slum populations can support a bewildering variety of responses to structural neglect and deprivation, ranging from charismatic churches and prophetic clubs to ethnic militias, street gangs, neoliberal NGOs, and revolutionary social movements.[19]

What we can learn from a quick glance at the four corners of the globe is that gangs and other kinds of armed nonstate actors are a *normal* presence. The loss of faith in the state has been replaced by faith in more local, tangible bodies and, as Castells demonstrates, by the "power of identity."

WARLORDS, DRUG LORDS, TRIADS, AND GANGS

In the United States, Europe, South Asia, Latin America, and Africa, the complex conditions we lump together under the term *globalization* give rise to or support the prevalence of a bewildering lineup of gangs and other similar armed groups.

Warlords

The "retreat of the state" can hardly be used to describe sub-Saharan Africa, since many states have never been strong to begin with. Colonialism carved boundaries for countries that paid little attention to what Harvey Zorbaugh, in a different context, would call "natural areas."[20] Independence produced states and rulers that were propped up by some combination of foreign investment, military aid, and corruption. The end of the cold war produced a sharp cutback in U.S. and Western aid that devastated the states that had depended on the free flow of anti-Soviet or anti-American aid.

Jean-François Bayart terms the situation in sub-Saharan Africa as the "criminalization of the state," or the segmentation of the state into networks that include illicit trade and corruption. The situation is so grave that Steve Sampson seriously suggests that we should "conceive of the state as filling gaps where the informal sector does not operate."[21]

William Reno calls this the "shadow state," dominated by warlords—a state that is not so much "weak" as it is a crazy quilt of armed groups. Bayart claims these warlords and their minions are "thoroughly rooted in the realities of African life,"[22] meaning the domination of political life by personal and tribal networks that survive through the sale of drugs, arms, and trafficking in people.[23] Basil Davidson calls this "a kind of Tammany Hall–style patronage, dependent on personal loyalty, family, and similar networks of local interest."[24] Politics, economics, and crime go together like, well . . . like vampires and blood:

> Significantly for a possible future warlord politics, these agents of political violence transmute into networks of criminal violence and agents of enterprising local strongmen. . . . in several instances gangs took over neighborhoods and businesses.[25]

Drug Lords

The African situation differs from Latin American countries. As in Africa, there are regions of cities and countries, such as the favelas of Rio de Janeiro or the cocaine-producing areas of Peru, that are outside the state's control. Latin American states, however, have a longer history, marked by periods of repression, military dictatorship, and civil war, as well as by a struggle of all political tendencies to adjust to U.S. neoliberal policies.[26] The end of the cold war did not mean a sharp cutback in military and economic aid, which instead increased to push Washington's "war on drugs."[27]

The central role of cocaine in the global criminal economy, with its prime growing areas in Bolivia, Peru, and Colombia, has transformed the politics of the entire region.[28] Left-wing guerrillas in Colombia and Peru, as well as right-wing militias, have struck up relationships with the Medellín and Cali cartels.[29] In Mexico, the drug cartels, which by the late 1990s dominated the cocaine trade, prospered mainly because of official corruption as well as their willingness to use violence.[30]

There is little faith in the ability of governments to produce change, and death squads of all sorts exercise a terrorizing power. There is "mounting anger" at the inability of the criminal justice system to solve the problem of violence. Paul Chevigny explains that this fear and anger provides an opportunity for states to mix together "an explosive brew of state power and vigilantism."[31]

Social change is more rhetoric than reality for those stuck in urban barrios and favelas. For example, I was in Rio de Janeiro in 2003 as part of the planning group for the *neither War nor Peace* study. We were meeting soon after the election of Luiz Ignácio Lula de Silva, the progressive Workers Party president. "Lula" was seen by many Brazilians as a savior and viewed at first by the United States and the World Bank with alarm. After three or four days in Rio and its favelas, and dozens of hours of conversations, I had not heard anyone even mention the name "Lula." I finally asked why, and the cold responses all were a variant of: "What Lula does in Brasília has little effect in our favelas. . . . After he gets done paying the foreign debt and buying off the military from a coup, there won't be anything for us. . . . Things are the same in the favela no matter who is in power." Lula's election meant no change for the operations of the drug factions.

Triads and Tigers

In South Asia, a region where overall inequality is *decreasing,* the "developmental state" is both strong and legitimate, but also has long coexisted with a variety of nonstate armed groups.[32] While thriving states like China and Japan have relatively homogenous populations, they also coexist with still-vibrant Triads and the Yakuza.[33] Other countries like India and Pakistan are deeply divided by religion and ethnicity, with each religious group having its own militias.[34]

The "Golden Triangle" has long been the world's leading source of heroin and has played a similar role in Southeast Asia as cocaine later did in Latin America. The story of the exporting of heroin is filled with both the violence of armed groups and the connivance of the French and American military and the Kuomintang of "nationalist" China.[35] The lessons of the economic miracles in South Asia are that dynamic economies do not mean the disappearance of gangs. The illicit trade in drugs, sex, and other goods has been functional for states, which have profitably and corruptly coexisted over long periods with armed groups.

Gangs and the Loss of Legitimacy

Finally, to bring it all back home, in the world's only superpower, the United States has seen its legitimacy and reach sharply criticized by conservatives. The calls to reduce taxes and cut back on the welfare state are part and parcel of the Ronald Reagan Republican raison d'être that "government *is* the problem." Conservative ideology supports a strong military and law enforcement while advocating the rollback of public services and a reverent reliance on the market. While the UK has enthusiastically embraced the "neo-liberal agenda,"[36] other European states have taken a different tack.

At the same time, in U.S. ghettos and in many immigrant suburbs of European cities, the state governs as much by force as by a declining legitimacy.[37] Gangs and youth in the United States, France, the UK,[38] and elsewhere see the police as the enemy and resist any formal controls. For example, Elijah Anderson describes the Philadelphia ghetto:

> In some of the most economically distressed and drug and crime-ridden pockets of the city, the rules of civil law have been severely weakened, and in their stead a "code of the street" often holds sway. . . . The code of the street emerges where the influence of the police ends and personal responsibility for one's safety is felt to begin, resulting in a kind of "people's law" based on street justice.[39]

The importance of gangs in contemporary U.S. cities is spelled out by Castells: "The making of a sizeable proportion of the underclass's young men into a dangerous class could well be the most striking expression of the new American dilemma in the information age."[40]

DEFINITIONS AND FLEXIBILITY

Recalling the Kano gangs at the beginning of this chapter, I find it difficult to see gangs worldwide as sharply delineated from other armed youth groups. Gangs, in my studies, do not appear to be just a local "crime problem" but can be conceptualized as one of many angry responses to widely varied conditions in a globalized world.[41]

It is this cultural response and its power of identity that I explore in the remaining chapters. As Henry Giroux points out: "Within this postmodern youth culture, identities merge and shift rather than become more uniform and static."[42] Edward Said adds, "No one today is purely *one* thing."[43] Craig Calhoun reinforces Giroux's and Said's take on the current era:

> It is not just that collective identities and ways of life are created, but that they are internally contested, that their boundaries are porous and overlapping, and that people live in more than one at the same time.[44]

If gang members' identities are internally contested and constantly switching, how can a hard and fast definition describe such a changing reality? The search for a more precise gang definition by criminology is, on the one hand, an old-fashioned positivist venture, trying to tack down and quantify gangs as a static, clearly delineated form. Liberal criminologists also have a desire to portray Western gangs as basically disorganized peer groups, worlds apart from what seem to be more-organized groups of armed youth, particularly in the third world. Defining a "true street gang" is also useful to the U.S. and Western criminal justice officials who are seeking to "enhance" already severe penalties with longer sentences for a crime being "gang-related."[45]

Certainly young people themselves do not get hung up over the term *gang,* and most members of institutionalized gangs insist they are "organizations." Others call their gangs "crews," "sets," or other terms. Former Chicago white ethnic gang members told me they belonged to Irish or Italian "clubs" and that "gangs" were a black and Latino thing.

To limit gangs to wild peer groups—as do James Short and Joan Moore[46]—slights the variety of institutionalized gangs, the history of political activity by gangs, and the transformations gangs often make from juvenile delinquents to organized criminals, pawns of political parties, religious or ethnic militias, or even revolutionaries. The best definition of gangs, as I have argued, is an amorphous one: they are simply alienated groups socialized by the streets or prisons, not conventional institutions.

Young people, particularly armed young men, are everywhere filling the void left by weak, repressive, racist, or illegitimate states. They fill that void in a number of ways—as supervised youth groups, as entrepreneurs who want only to be left alone to make their money, as political actors fighting for reform or power, or even as armed pawns of the state.[47] If there is any constant in today's gangs around the world, it is their *changing* forms, how they can be categorized at one point in one way, and then a few months or years later they can adapt or become something quite different.

chapter 4

From Chicago to Mumbai:
Touring the World of Gangs

Thus what had begun as a fight for social and economic justice has
degenerated into a caste conflict with a veneer of class struggle.

—PRAKASH SINGH, *The Naxalite Movement in India*

What marks the form of the gang today worldwide is its flexibility, its ability to shift gears, to grow up from a wild peer group into an illicit business,
working for political spoils or acting as thugs for ruling powers. As Michel
Wieviorka observes in central Africa: "In Brazzaville the downwardly socially
mobile youths form groups that, depending on the period, may be part of
the political militia or again may be armed gangs."[1] Thus gangs do not
represent "stages" in some natural process of evolution, with unsupervised
peer groups inevitably growing into "third generation" political gangs.[2] For
example, in Kosovo,

part of the Kosovo Liberation Army has become an official police force under
the tutelage of the international community, another part a political party
seeking state power, and still other sections operate as independent bandit
groups intimidating or corrupting local officials, and robbing aid missions
with military precision.

Steve Sampson concludes: "Liberation armies, political projects, local protection, and banditry come together."[3] It is this perplexing, diffuse, and
often incoherent phenomenon that this chapter addresses.

Much, but not all, of the data presented here comes from *neither War nor*

Peace. This study is remarkable for its comparison of various groups of what it calls "COAV"—children in organized armed violence. What strikes the reader is that the voices of youth in such diverse settings as Mindanao, Cape Town, San Salvador, and Chicago sound so much the same. Some of these armed groups are gangs, others ethnic militias, still others private security forces of the state, but their reasons for joining the armed group, their participation in violence, or their ties to family all sound similar. Without the specifics, it would be difficult to tell from which country the quote came or whether it was a youth in a gang, militia, or death squad.

U.S. criminologists have created typologies that categorize gangs by neighborhood opportunity structure,[4] by the nature of ethnic organization,[5] and by size, age range, territoriality, internal differentiation, longevity, and criminal versatility.[6] Rather than follow these traditional, Eurocentric types, I have chosen to categorize gangs as mainly (1) unsupervised peer groups similar to traditional notions of the "true street gang"; (2) street organizations, mainly in poor neighborhoods, that desire minimal state interference in their economic, social, or cultural activities; (3) politicized oppositional groups, like ethnic, religious, or territorial militias, that advocate reform, overthrow, or takeover of the state; or (4) vigilante bands or violent tools of those holding state power. But no matter where they are located, "gangs" often change from one form to another, as they are influenced by other armed groups and the boundaries between them so often fade away.

Alienated, Unsupervised Peer Groups

The typical youth gang goes from play group to gang in a "group process" just as Frederic Thrasher described a century ago. Thrasher, more so than many of his successors, also identified a range of possibilities of what might happen to the gang as its members age. But the old master did not imagine situations like Freetown or Medellín.

In Freetown, Sierra Leone, gangs called *rarri* boys formed in colonial times in crowded and poor neighborhoods and developed their own way of life, centering on fighting over territory and engaging in petty crime. But after independence in 1961, politicians recruited the *rarri* boys to provide muscle in elections, like early U.S. voting gangs, although *rarri* boy culture and music even then was interested only in the "good life." The civil war in the 1990s, however, transformed *rarri* boys from thugs into child soldiers, focused on what Ibrahim Abdullah creatively calls "revo (loot) shon";

to keep them obedient, the *rarri* boys were fed with drugs.[7] The end of the civil war has produced roving bands of unemployed youth with an abundance of small arms, bitterness, and a need to survive. From gangs to child soldiers and back to gangs is the Freetown story.[8]

In Medellín, in the early 1980s, guerrilla organizations like M-19 and FARC began "peace camps" that recruited youth into what would become powerful urban militias. These militias were formed to counter the influence of more than four hundred criminal youth gangs, which at the time had more than ten thousand members. The militias engaged in a sort of nonethnic "cleansing," or antigang vigilantism, that by now is a familiar scene around the world.[9] The drug cartels naturally formed ties to the local gangs as agents for drug distribution. But the success of the left-wing militias and the strength of popular antigang sentiment in Medellín led cartel czar Pablo Escobar to both mouth revolutionary rhetoric and call for "law and order," turning on his local gang allies.

The militias and gangs were also adapting and changing roles. The gangs learned from the militias and began to repair their relations with the community, doing "social work by day and violence at night." Unlike most other armed groups, these are not made up of only armed men: "All of Colombia's irregular armed groups recruit women and girls to serve as combatants."[10] The 1980s were a time of many murders by children hired as hit men, called *sicarios*.[11]

In the 1990s the left-wing militias began to recruit youth based more on fighting ability than on politics and linked with Escobar and the cartels. Lines between gangs and militias were blurred. After the death of Escobar, the cartel decentralized, and many of the groups that had worked for Escobar returned to Medellín's slums. The highest rates of violence in Medellín were the product of a five-way war between the gangs, the militias, the right-wing paramilitaries, the cartels, and the state. Later, to confuse matters more, the gangs, the right-wing paramilitaries, and the cartels formed a new alliance.[12]

What is important in these stories of Freetown and Medellín is that civil war and institutionalized armed groups forced youth gangs to alter their forms and behavior. Gangs developed in Medellín and Freetown like youth gangs everywhere, but the civil wars in both cities—and the vast wealth of the drug traffickers in Medellín—have made it difficult to distinguish the gangs from other armed groups.

Gangs in More Stable Conditions

In other places, unsupervised peer groups do not grow up around institu-tionalized armed groups or suffer through the turbulence of civil war. In China, delinquency is apparently leading to gang life for an increasing num-ber of "underprivileged youth." Sun Dongdong, a forensic psychiatrist at Beijing University who studies youth crime, said, echoing Western crimi-nologists, "They form gangs to fight the emptiness."[13]

Similarly, in Sydney and Melbourne, Australia, research has found that gangs are engaged mainly in "petty theft, graffiti, and vandalism," with no apparent links to professional criminals or institutionalized gangs. Gangs in Australia, though, Rob White finds, are highly "racialized," and many are drawn from minority ethnic groups, where the gang was a way to show "social presence" in the face of marginalization.[14] This differs from the experience of Maori youth in New Zealand, who grew up in the shadow of Black Power and other ethnic gangs that have institutionalized over the past forty years and provide not only a "social presence" but also illicit eco-nomic opportunities for Maori youth.[15]

The European and U.S. gangs described in Malcolm Klein's Eurogang book are mainly of the unsupervised peer group type, although the skin-head gangs that Joachim Kersten describes from Germany appear out of place, and such gangs have a wide range of level of organization and ori-entation.[16] The bickering between Klein, Jerzy Sarnecki, and others over whether to call Europe's unsupervised youth groups "gangs" reflects the problems in looking at gangs using only the United States and Europe as models. Klein's "Eurogang paradox" means that while European gangs are not like the stereotypes of U.S. gangs, neither are U.S. gangs. While this is insightful, Klein is actually proposing that Europeans adopt a narrow, U.S. crime-based, "group process" definition of gangs. He is saddling Euro-pean scholars with a "comparative perspective" derived only from gangs in Western countries.[17]

The problem can be understood if we look at Kenya and what seems at first a straightforward description of a "true street gang." Gangs in Kenya began as gangs do everywhere: youth are "enticed into criminal activities because there is no one to monitor or supervise them."[18] Even during the Mau Mau uprising, "crime merged imperceptibly with rebellion" as gangs like the Forty Group joined in the violence.[19]

After independence, this process accelerated as Nairobi's population ballooned to nearly three million. The gangs in Nairobi, focused on survival, targeted foreigners and tourists for kidnapping and carjacking as well as participating in more standard activities in the underground economy. Civil wars in Somalia and other nearby states have made small arms easily available, and rates of violence shot up in the 1990s. The end of the cold war meant a reduction in foreign aid, and the Moi government used its corrupt police force to step up political violence while neglecting security from street crime. A strong vigilante movement then arose and targeted the gangs with "necklacing" and lynching.

Recent reports find that Kenyan gangs have now actively joined a political process that emphasizes tribal and ethnic divisions. All this has led Herbert Covey, a follower of Klein's definition, to despair: "In countries similar to Kenya, it is difficult to separate street gangs from civil war or law-violating groups."[20] *That* is precisely my point.

While unsupervised youth groups, male and female, continue to arise spontaneously in urban centers, the existence of institutionalized gangs, like the Colombian cartels and paramilitaries or the Chinese Triads,[21] bends the form of area youth gangs to the needs of the older armed group. Civil wars, ethnic and religious hostility, the drug trade, and deep-seated feelings of insecurity in the face of street violence have all worked to make the form of the unsupervised youth gang susceptible to radical alteration of its shape. This erodes the distinctions between gangs and other armed groups and has led me to reject traditional criminological categories.

Laissez-Faire

Some armed groups are not unsupervised youth who can be taken and shaped by more powerful forces. Some of these groups are the *shapers*, institutionalized gangs or other nonstate armed actors with powerful self-interests. One set of these armed groups is less interested in politics and more often simply wants the space to run its businesses and activities with minimal state interference. Like U.S. conservatives, these gangs believe in laissez-faire.

The need to stay out of politics can be seen in the different strategies of the Medellín and Cali drug cartels in the 1990s. While Escobar and his Medellín network declared war on the Colombian state after failed attempts to enter the political process, the Cali cartel refused to get drawn into the war. It relied on corruption and collaborated with state security forces to debilitate Escobar's cartel in order to allow business in Cali to proceed unhindered.[22]

The Marashea gangs in cities near the gold mines in South Africa have persisted for more than fifty years by making money off miners through providing *dagga* and women. Gary Kynoch points out that "the Marashea established, protected, and expanded spheres of influence independent of larger political and ideological concerns."[23] The Marashea both fought against and collaborated with the apartheid state and the ANC in order to organizationally survive.

In Chicago, one lesson gangs have drawn from their attempts to enter the political process is that it may be better to mind your own business. The following lament comes from the official history of the Black Gangster Disciples (BGD): "Our trouble as an organization began when we started dealing in big city politics. Before that, we were largely overlooked."[24]

For many BGD leaders, as well as the Conservative Vice Lords and other institutionalized Chicago gangs, involvement with politics meant targeting by police and the political machine. If one wanted to do business without hassle, one should avoid politics, as this young Vice Lord told me in 2004: "I think . . . it's peaceful if you mind your own business, stay out of other people's business, nothing happens."

Institutionalized gangs in Chicago, as elsewhere, reoriented themselves to the drug trade, and the need to do business unencumbered became paramount, as this BGD member explained:

> From my observations the higher-ranking Gangster Disciples were placed in that position because of their drug connections rather than their leadership abilities. The more money one had within the gang, the more influence and power that coincidentally followed. The regents and mayors were known to be no nonsense type individuals. They usually planned the amount of a drug that a particular dealer was to receive. They acted as the American Stock exchange by buying low and selling high. . . . Drugs became synonymous with the Gangster Disciples within the neighborhood. They controlled the community, not in a political manner, but rather by coercion, money, and drugs.[25]

In East Los Angeles, Joan Moore has documented an almost century-long tradition of institutionalized gangs reinforced by waves of new immigration.

Gangs like White Fence are a "specialized structure of the barrio" that can be seen as a "symbolic challenge to the world." East LA gangs began as part of a Chicano "self-help" movement, not as a politicized revolutionary organization.[26]

Similarly, the drug factions in Rio de Janeiro are explicitly apolitical. They avoid involvement in city and national politics and concentrate on making money. The "traditional absence of the state" in the favelas makes the drug factions a kind of "state within a state."[27] However, the drug factions control the economics and security of the favelas while having no pretenses to confronting the power of the state citywide or being burdened with responsibility for all essential services.

Other gangs described in *neither War nor Peace* also are characterized by a laissez-faire attitude toward the state. After the civil war in El Salvador, *pandillas* or *maras,* territorial youth gangs, exercised a higher profile.[28] The ideologically driven conflict of the eighties gave way to a more survival-focused nineties leading into the new century.

Most of the *maras* in El Salvador are united in two major gang constellations, the Mara Salvatrucha 13 and Calle 18, both gangs with origins in Los Angeles. At the end of the civil war, many young people whose parents had fled the conflict and illegally entered the United States either returned or were deported to El Salvador. While in the United States, they had joined gangs and were literally "bringing the neighborhoods back to my country," as one gang member told Elana Zilberg.[29] In 1997 alone, more than 1,500 youth suffered a "forced repatriation" that has confused identities and created a new kind of transnational gang. The civil war of the 1980s was replaced by a war of terror against the *maras,* of both a government crackdown and death squad executions by "la Sombra Negra" and other vigilantes with ties to the old right-wing regimes.[30]

While the El Salvador gangs have ties to drug cartels, the civil war has given them and many others a bad taste for politics. As the journalist Silla Bocanero said, "Until recently, a rebellious youth from Central America would go into the mountains and join the guerillas. Today, he leaves the countryside for the city and joins one of the street gangs engaged in common crime without political objectives."[31] While many El Salvador gangs are unsupervised youth out only for *vacil,* or thrills, the form of the gang in El Salvador, Ecuador, Guatemala, and other post–civil war countries is a rejection of politics and focus on survival,[32] what is sometimes called the "privatization of violence."[33]

From another angle, it can be asked what happens to "child soldiers" when wars are over. This question has haunted Asia, Latin America, and Africa and is compounded by economies that often cannot provide jobs even for educated youth. Donal B. Cruise O'Brien calls this the "lost generation" that may be of "continental proportions" in struggling Africa. During the Liberian civil war, the "Small Boys Unit" of Charles Taylor was kept armed and "under control" as a potent fighting force. As the fighting ended, these young people were desperate for an identity in a hopeless future: "Some young people see a solution in the life of the warband, others turn to God, the identities of soldier, or religious believer."[34]

Similarly in the Congo the groups of armed young men left over after the civil war created a "nightmare" for residents of Brazzaville. "The intensified struggle for power among politicians suddenly created a demand for young men as militia men. . . . After the war of 1983–1994, life never returned to normal. Armed young men have been a serious problem ever since."[35]

Depoliticization and demoralization affects the Arab world and other regions as well. In Palestine, the political environment overshadows, but does not eliminate, criminal gangs. In cities like Cairo, however, the policies of repression of the Sadat and Mubarek governments have foreclosed collective action and channeled much economic activity into the illegal arena of gangs with "elaborate internal organization."[36] In South Asia, gangs have sprung up in the wake of the end of U.S. intervention and now control "flesh markets" for tourists and for export.[37] Massive urbanization has created squatter communities and a survival economy that stays depoliticized in the face of a strong, repressive, developmental state.

Demoralization and depoliticization also characterize the chaotic transition of Eastern European socialist countries to capitalism. Gangs and "mafiyas" have emerged, as state institutions have weakened and unemployment skyrocketed. These new criminal organizations eschew politics for business.[38] For example, in Albania, a World Bank report states, "The loss of adult authority leaves young people free to rebel and unite in gangs bent on violence for the sake of self-assertion as much as for easy earnings." The criminal economy includes up to 25 percent of the young men aged 18–25 and has become a "structural feature in Albanian life."[39]

In situations of demoralization and lack of trust in the state, young people often latch on to an identity, sometimes of gang member, that wants cultural or individual expression with little concern, or desire, for a project of broader societal change. Thus the retreat of the state has a cultural effect, as Manuel Castells notes, of reinforcing communal, ethnic, religious, or local identities. One character in a popular film about Nigeria's vigilantes sums up this anticosmopolitan attitude by wearing a T-shirt that says: "f—— the world, save yourself."[40]

But sometimes these identities are not depoliticized but actively seek to reform, overthrow, or take over the state.

GANGS AND POLITICS

In the United States, Irish and other "voting gangs" were long involved in electoral politics. In contemporary Mumbai (Bombay), Bal Thackeray, stealing a page from the political book of Chicago's first mayor Daley, bases his political power on the "direct action" of gangs of youth. Thackeray has in effect cloned Daley's Democratic Party, Irish Catholic, neighborhood precinct organizations with his Hindu Shiv Sena Party and its Shakas (precincts). Shiv Sena is ubiquitously flanked by its *mandels* or clubs, where youth, *goondas* (gangsters), and other militants both work the elections and participate in violence much like Chicago's earlier ganglike social athletic clubs strong-armed electoral foes.[41] In Mumbai today, politics and the underworld are as intertwined as Chicago ever was under Capone or the Daley regimes.[42] Arjun Appadurai describes a Mumbai political machine that works hand in glove with organized crime and real estate interests in precisely the same manner as their Chicago counterparts.[43]

By the 1960s in the United States, gangs were inspired by the civil rights, nationalist, and revolutionary movements and were drawn into political activity. Similarly, in South Africa, the black Totsis and youth gangs participated in mass protests organized by the ANC and the more militant Pan African Congress during the Soweto uprising. Nelson Mandela advocated efforts to win the gangs over to the cause of liberation, though the rise of the "comrades," a militant ganglike youth group, took center stage as the gangs withdrew.[44]

African American gangs in Los Angeles were heavily influenced by the 1965 Watts riots, called by some "the last great rumble."[45] LA gangs, like those in Chicago, were impressed with the Black Panther Party and were shocked by the police killing of BPP leaders in 1969 (Bunchy Carter and

John Huggins in LA, Fred Hampton and Mark Clark in Chicago). In the wake of the destruction of the BPP, LA's black youth who were "searching for a new identity mobilized as street gangs."[46] After the 1992 riots following the acquittal of the police who beat Rodney King, the Crips and Bloods put up a common program for reconstructing Los Angeles—"Give Us the Hammers and Nails and We'll Rebuild the City"—that was perhaps the most comprehensive proposal offered to resurrect and redeem Los Angeles. Officials refused to take the gangs' offer seriously.[47]

In New York City, the Almighty Latin King and Queen Nation transformed themselves, David Brotherton and Luis Barrios argue, into a social movement in the 1990s. While this transformation was short-lived because of intense police repression, it has major significance for the study of gangs. The involvement of the ALKQN with politics is far from unique.[48]

In the last decades in Chicago, gang politics has become more mundane, as gangs attempt to worm their way into the machine through electoral politics and familiar Chicago-style corruption. Larry Hoover complained that he was considered dangerous because he advocated involvement of the streets into politics. He told the Geto Boys in a recording on their *Resurrection (Screwed and Chopped)* album that Daley was "afraid" of him because of his political potential. One BGD member agrees and told me: "Hoover was talking politics, that's why they were scared. You can't let no man like that get out." And another said of the BGD CEO: "He's a great man, he almost did something."[49]

In Chicago, gangs are also deeply involved with Latino politics, as this Latin King leader explained to one of my classes:

> So while these guys were trying to build something, Billy Ocasio and Luis Gutiérrez [major Latino politicians] noticed that. And mind you the reason they don't like us is because one of them used to be a Latin Disciple and the other one used to be a Gent. So they used to be Folks and they still have animosity against Latin Kings. . . . But when they need to get elected who do they come to? They come to the Latin Kings. . . . We help 'em out in exchange for jobs. And those are the back street politics that are played in this city. Everywhere. Right now . . . there's some politician or commissioner somewhere making a deal that if everybody found out about it, it'd be over. It'd be the end of their career.

The new Daley machine is actively soliciting the quickly expanding Latino community in building a majority (antiblack) political coalition and has hired gang members as part of its "outreach," leading to several scandals. Other gang members explained that they regularly made payoffs to aldermen and police, an old Chicago tradition. Some police officers and prison guards are also gang members and "help out" their own gang and go hard on their rivals.

Politics is no stranger to gangs in Jamaica either. Jamaican gangs had their origins in the 1940s and were organized by "yards," or certain sectors of the city where rival political groups concentrated. The *neither War nor Peace* study distinguishes between *area gangs,* which control entire communities with a Don who has a patronage relationship to the local political party, and *corner gangs,* which may or may not be tied to politicians.[50] All accounts of Jamaican history tie the violent persistence of gangs and local gunmen to their direct ties to the Jamaican Labor Party (JLP) of Edward Seaga and its rival People's National Party (PNP) of Michael Manley. The gangs have become part of the politics of patronage in Jamaican cities and dense ghettos, such as Craig Town or Tivoli Gardens. In 1975 twenty-five thousand people turned out for the Kingston funeral of the political gunman "Burrey Boy."

The intensity of the political violence grew to such an extent that the gangs and other public figures attempted to stem the tide. Bob Marley, in the famous "One Love" concert on April 22, 1978, coaxed Manley and Seaga to join him onstage to shake hands. The impetus for the peacemaking, according to Laurie Gunst, was the gangs themselves, whose imprisoned members talked to each other and cried out, "No more war."[51] But, Gunst continues, peace in the ghetto threatened the interests of the two parties, and a wave of police repression fractured the truce.

By the early 1980s, the lure of cocaine had internationalized the Jamaican gangs, or "posses," and this addictive substance had become the scourge of Kingston ghettos. The U.S. market beckoned, and the big money of cocaine smuggling loosened dependence on the political parties. Dons still control entire areas of Kingston, whose gangs, thanks to the politicians, are a classic example of gang institutionalization.[52] While the gangs have drifted away from politics, and fewer corner gangs have proliferated, the neighborhoods are still divided both by gang and by political loyalties, maintaining the deadly mix. By 2004 gang violence had reached extremely high levels, in part the result of thirteen thousand deportations of gangsters from the United States back to Jamaica.[53]

While the mix of politics and crime has persisted in Jamaica, demoralization and political opportunities in Northern Ireland, Colombia, and Peru have led political organizations to function as criminal gangs. In Northern Ireland, the Protestant militias, once fiercely anti-Catholic, have turned on themselves in a quarrel over drug markets. One resident in the Protestant stronghold of Shankhill told me that "Johnny Adair and his brood," referring to the Ulster Defence Association's top dog, are "nothing now but a bunch of gangsters."[54]

The much ballyhooed dismantling of Colombia's armed militias has prompted their commanders to turn to politics, winning local elections by an improbable Chicago-style 95 percent of the vote. The *Caracas Journal* reports,

> As some 23,000 paramilitary fighters have disarmed here over the last two years, their top commanders have declared their intentions to play a role in politics. But signs are emerging that the role is a dark one, as commanders use bribery and intimidation to control local lawmakers and even blocs of representatives in the Congress while they reshape their militias into criminal networks that traffic in cocaine, extort businesses and loot local governments.[55]

From the left, in Peru, the Sendero Luminoso (Shining Path) Maoist guerrillas have also turned their military defeats into opportunity by allying with local cocaine growers, like the infamous Tito Lopez, in Peru's Huallaga Valley. Peru, in fact, grows the majority of the world's cocaine, which is purchased from growers by Colombian cartels, which process it for delivery to world markets. The guerrillas have profited from providing protection to the growers, and their "communist" program for Peru has been fatally corrupted.[56]

In the opposite process, in Algeria, after the 1991 elections were nullified, the government banned the FIS (Front Islamique du Salut) and suppressed its Muslim supporters. This radicalized the alienated *hittistes,* youth "living in and from the street." Street youth saw Islam and the mosques as sources of inspiration and rebellion against a government that appeared atheistic and communist and resorted to terrorist tactics.

The repressive atmosphere became more complicated as delinquent gangs, operating under the protection of Algerian security forces, began stealing and demanding protection money from shopkeepers. In response, Muslim youth in the Armed Islamic Group (GIS) attacked the gangs. However, as in Medellín, no sooner had the GIS swept the gangs out than it, and look-alike Islamic gangs, took the delinquent gangs' place, demanding protection money and controlling the underground economy. Violence raged in Algiers in the 1990s in a war between the government security forces, the GIS, the Islamic gangs, and the delinquent gangs. By the end of the decade, the government's power had manifested itself in disillusionment with politics and a reversion to criminality.[57] Similarly, in Haiti, prior to Rene Preval's election, the Aristide "popular organizations" "had been reverting to more traditional forms of extortion, such as carjacking, kidnapping, and armed robbery."[58]

The uprising of Muslim gangs and youth in France in the fall of 2005 was a warning that fourth world conditions exist in European cities too. What seems clear from press reports is that gangs have joined youth in a political protest, similar to the 1960s social movements and gangs described here. Whether the gangs in Europe's immigrant ghettos and slums will maintain a political outlook or revert to "laissez-faire" is unclear.[59]

A final political example of gangs is the Muhajir Quami Movement (MQM), a party representing Pakistani migrants from India after the 1948 partition. By the 1980s Karachi had become a major port for the shipment of heroin from Afghanistan to the West and guns from the West to Afghanistan. The fall of the military regime led to democracy in 1988, and the MQM grew as the voice of what it called a new ethnic group. Its success, in no small part, Oskar Verkaaik argues, was due to small groups of friends who partook in violence and "fun" and recruited other youth to the MQM banner. The MQM won the local elections in Hyderabad, but the military takeover of Pakistan's government led to the party's fracturing. Accused of abusing power during its heyday, in the aftermath of General Muhammad Zia-ul-Haq's police state, "the MQM fell apart into locally organized groups resorting to anti-state militancy and crime."[60]

These disparate examples of gangs in politics also show the volatile and transient nature of gangs and similar armed groups and their potential to become political actors. Some gangs have dipped in and out of politics; some political groups have become gangs and vice versa. The skeptical claim that the political activities of gangs are more "rhetoric" than action is simply ahistorical and wrong.[61]

Gangs as Vigilantes or Death Squads

Sometimes gangs oppose the state, but sometimes they work for the powerful. Some are secular, and others are religious fundamentalists. Consider Islamic Taliban gangs in Afghanistan a few years ago: gangs of youth filled with religious fervor called "bands of hope" were, in effect, a moral police used to intimidate sinners. Anyone who strayed from strict fundamentalist doctrine was threatened, and the young toughs "tore from the bodies of women what they judged to be indecent dress." Priceless art was destroyed and literature burned.

Oh, did I say Afghanistan? I meant to say Florence, Italy, at the end of the fifteenth century. The "bands of hope" were young Catholic thugs organized by the Roman-appointed dictator, Girolamo Savonarola, to force wayward citizens to return to Church doctrine and a strict morality. The burning of art and literature was the infamous "bonfire of vanities" that destroyed some of the most precious artworks of the Renaissance. The roots of religious intolerance and the use of angry young men by state and church alike go back a long time.[62]

Contrary to the sensationalism of the mass media, today it is not only Muslim youth who burn art and a few of the ungodly. For example, human rights groups reported in overwhelmingly Christian Rwanda that mass murder and rape were carried out by the army and also by informal paramilitaries like the Hutu *Interahamwe* ("Those who stand together") who were attached to the ruling party. These

> gangs of the displaced use the camps as bases from which to launch raids to rove and kill local people. Some of this banditry may be purely criminal, but other instances are politically motivated efforts to destabilize local government control.[63]

The fratricidal savageness in these "civilized times" is carried out by groups outside the official channels, as with "Arkan's Tigers," who ethnically cleansed Serbia in the name of both their Eastern Orthodox God and Slobodan Milošević.[64] These groups are often thinly disguised military or police forces, acting under cover so that "plausible deniability" by their political leaders can be maintained.[65]

While most of what we define as "death squads" are state military or police officials killing extrajudicially, some groups performing these functions do not originate within the state but are indigenous armed groups, often acting as vigilantes to restore "law and order."[66] Bruce Campbell recognizes that "death squads may be privately constituted, almost always involve the support and participation of elements outside the government and develop considerable independence from their backers."[67] In this section, I describe those armed young men who were *not* officially organized by the state and have mainly originated in group processes largely *outside* official religious or state structures.

For example, in Nigeria armed ethnic militias and "self help" security forces, particularly the Egbesu Boys, Bakassi Boys, and Oodua Peoples Congress (OPC), have arisen as a "result of growing crime and violence over the last ten years and the inability of law enforcement agencies to provide adequate protection."[68]

While Human Rights Watch and others have linked the vigilante actions to traditions within Nigerian society,[69] others point out that it is the weakness of the current state that is the proximate cause of vigilantism:

> Nigerian governments have virtually told Nigerians to fend for their own protection. My hometown of Okpara with its environs has a population that is more than 20,000 people in Delta State. It has no police station. Indeed, there is no presence of government in the daily lives of its people. That is, the Nigerian state and its governmental agencies are *absent* from their daily lives.[70]

The three groups discussed in Mohammed's chapter on Nigeria in *neither War nor Peace* have different ethnic origins and unique histories, but they all arose from groups of unsupervised youth, as these who formed the OPC who

> were recruited as school dropouts that had joined area boy gangs (gangs of street children involved in petty crime) or other delinquent groups. A 20 year-old member who had joined the OPC at 16 told researchers he had done so as ". . . another way of identifying with my ethnic group, Oodua."[71]

All three groups recruited youth both to defend their ethnic group and, like People Against Gangsterism and Drugs in South Africa, to stop crime in the absence of effective public safety services by the state. "Bakassi Boys interviewed for this study expressed the belief that the primary objectives of the group are the protection of ethnic interests and the fighting of crime in their communities."[72] The Egbesu Boys were pulled together from existing groups of youth not only to maintain order in oil-rich Ijawland but also to defend their ethnic group against central Nigerian government forces and to demand a more equitable division of the oil profits.

While all three groups have ties to some units of government, the Bakassi Boys, made up primarily of Igbo tribal members, have been the most prominent, actually being incorporated in August 2000 "by the Anamra state government under the name Anambra State Vigilante Services."[73] The Bakassi Boys are known for horrific acts of violence and brutality, executing hundreds extrajudicially, and have become a parallel force to the admittedly corrupt police in several states. While the Bakassi Boys have received direct payments from the local state, they also have extorted money from shopkeepers to pay for protection.

Nigeria is not the only example of gangs being put to use by governments as a violent tool against ethnic opponents. In Indonesia, for example, an IMF-induced crisis set off anti-Chinese rioting. Ethnic Chinese hold dominant positions in Indonesia's economy, and "gangs of knife-wielding youth . . . pillaged Chinese-owned stores."[74] As in Central America, Indonesian death squads have also targeted street children, criminals, and other minority groups.

A different kind of state-sponsored gang is the Civilian Volunteer Organizations (CVO) of the Philippines. These groups sprang up under the Marcos regime as self-defense organizations, supplementary to the army, during the war against communist and Muslim guerrillas. After the fall of Marcos, the Constitution of 1987 mandated the dissolution of armed groups, but the COV became tied to the political interests of the mayors of towns, and what is called *datu* and their *pagali* (strongmen and their clans). The CVOs became private armies that protected the *datu* and his family and worked at the behest of the mayor.[75]

These youth were organized as political tools, often hired assassins, similar to the *sicarios* of Colombia. Like other politically involved gangs elsewhere, these state-sponsored groups mixed politics, violence, and the underground economy, what Agnes Zenaida V. Camacho calls "dark business ventures."[76] The CVOs "double as dealers'" of *shabu,* or amphetamines, and other drugs. As in Kenya and other countries, kidnapping for ransom is particularly attractive.

Finally, Haiti offers a politically incorrect example of the significance of armed gangs who do the state's dirty work no matter who is in power.[77] During the Aristide regime, the Cannibal Army, led by "strongman" Amiot

(Cuban) Métayer, was a gang that ruled the Raboteau slum in Gonaives, the city where Haitian independence had been proclaimed two hundred years ago. The Cannibal Army was one of many "popular organizations" that used force and intimidation on behalf of the beleaguered Aristide.

Métayer was sprung from prison by his gang, but then murdered, his brother and followers believed, on orders from Aristide. The Cannibal Army abruptly turned on the president and united with forces with ties to the old Duvalier regime. They seized and held Gonaives, killed police whom they called "drug dealers,"[78] then marched on Port-au-Prince, forcing Aristide's removal.

Since then, gangs loyal to Aristide and those opposed have battled in the Soleil, Bel Air, and other slums called cités in Port-au-Prince. The UN peacekeeping force MINUSTAH has also intervened and joined the fighting, typically against pro-Aristide gangs.

> The interim government's failure to restore stability left a power vacuum allowing armed groups to flourish. Former soldiers, armed Aristide supporters and criminal gangs are contending for control of different parts of the country. The level of violence has skyrocketed . . . , challenging MINUSTAH's ability to control the situation.[79]

The various kinds of gangs, of course, also have a long history of recruiting youth into the underground economy, which at times is the only means of support in Port-au-Prince cités.[80] The Preval government, breaking with U.S. policy, came to power pledging to negotiate with gangs of all persuasions.

CONCLUSION: THE POWER OF IDENTITY

Globalization has created impossible conditions in many cities and countries. Such desperate situations produce all sorts of "monsters" and armed groups trying to survive and make sense out of their situation. While most gangs are still unsupervised peer groups, the form of the gang can no longer be confined to delinquent gangs of Chicago school fame. The existence of institutionalized gangs and other armed groups alters the shape and prospects of the "true street gang." While the underground economy may become a solution to the gang members' problem of survival, religious, ethnic, or communal identity becomes the solution to the problem of meaning.

11

RACE, SPACE, AND THE
POWER OF IDENTITY

chapter 5

No Way Out: Demoralization, Racism, and Resistance Identity

Knowing there was no escape, no way out, the slaves nonetheless continued to engage themselves. To carve out a humanity. To defy the murder of selfhood. Their lives were brutally shackled, certainly—*but not without meaning despite being imprisoned.*

—DERRICK BELL, *Faces at the Bottom of the Well*

It should be no surprise that desperate conditions in ghettos, barrios, and favelas produce angry and alienated groups of armed young men and women. But the last section's review of "the world of gangs" also emphasized the salience of ethnicity, race, and religion to gangs. Responses from the streets to marginalization are often deeply racialized or colored by ethnic or religious interpretations.

Admittedly, not all gangs are from minority groups. The Nigerian Bakassi Boys, for example, defend the regional ruling Igbo group by terror and violence. Death squads are often composed of men from dominant groups that are threatened by minority rights and use extralegal means to suppress the other; the Ku Klux Klan has been a famous form in the United States.[1] The early skinhead gangs were, as one member put it, "identity groups."[2]

Neighborhood-based white gangs also have a strong sense of racial identity. In Chicago, for example, these gangs become what whites see as "the last of the Mohicans" holding "down the fort," since "their neighborhood is under siege" as Latinos and blacks move in.[3] A white Gaylord sadly comments: "It was apparent that the entire neighborhood was going through an ethnic and cultural change, and the reasons for the Gaylords to stay no longer existed."[4] The Gaylords were being displaced by Puerto Ricans whose gangs sometimes recruited some of the remaining whites.

> I've often felt sympathy when I see a White guy in a non-White gang. It's like his identity had been lost or stolen. I guess his family couldn't afford to escape the incoming culture, and he got taken up in it.[5]

The Latin Kings were one of the gangs that displaced the Gaylords and were seen as "part of the violent immigration pushing in to many neighborhoods in Chicago." Michael Scott, the insightful Gaylord author of *Lords of Lawndale,* adds, "To this enemy, the Gaylords probably appear as oppressive racist roadblocks preventing his progress."[6] Racial identity is crucial in understanding the motivations of gangs of all ethnic groups.

But such gangs as the Gaylords are often cited to support the thesis that U.S. gangs aren't just black and Hispanic—they can be of any race. Most gang researchers follow Walter Miller's view of gangs as basically a "lower class" phenomenon or, like Irving Spergel, subsume ethnicity in ecological concepts.[7] While there are several researchers like Diego Vigil, Joan Moore, Felix Padilla, and Carl Taylor who highlight the historical structures of racial oppression,[8] most contemporary gang researchers give little, if any space, to the analysis of the impact of racism.[9]

Among the few to confront the subject, Spergel examines what he calls "controvertible" evidence to support the impact of racial discrimination. He argues that racism is insufficient to explain why some youth and not others join gangs or why many gangs have a multiethnic composition. He asserts that racism has declined over the years, while gang problems have increased.[10]

The laudable intention of progressive scholars like Spergel is to debunk the racist canard that violence, gangs, and crime are "essentially" characteristics of any racial group. But this perspective also typically assumes that racial oppression is not as important as class, neighborhood, or level of social organization. If we only "control" for labor market participation, broken families, and level of education, for example, the racial effect "disappears" or fades away.[11] Minority gangs therefore can be understood basically as the latest version of the white ethnic gangs of yesteryear. To paraphrase Malcolm Klein's views, gang similarities far exceed their racial or ethnic differences.

But this notion, to chance a phrase, throws away the sheet but saves the Klansman. To control for joblessness, poor education, or other characteristics of the black and minority experience is to strip away some of what makes racism racism and shapes identity. The deracializing of gangs is one of the most egregious errors of Western criminology, a "pernicious premise," to use Loïc Wacquant's pungent phrase.[12] In this section I argue, with Moore, Vigil, Taylor, and Padilla, that today's gangs and other groups of armed young men cannot be understood without an analysis of the history of racial, ethnic, or religious oppression and resistance.

This short, more theoretical chapter explores how racism shapes the identities of alienated, impoverished youth, particularly African American gang members. It ties together three ideas that have not previously been linked. "Demoralization" was cited by the father of gang research, Frederic Thrasher, as a seminal characteristic of gangs. I show how this concept has changed since the industrial era and link it to Manuel Castells's fundamental idea of "resistance identity." Finally, I connect these terms to Derrick Bell's notion of the permanence of racism, linking all three concepts to explain the crucial significance of race in understanding gangs.[13] These three concepts together provide an explanation of how oppressed people organize meaning in a more uncertain, unequal, globalized world.

DEMORALIZATION

In the industrial era, demoralization had a very different meaning. For Thrasher, who devoted a chapter of *The Gang* to the concept, demoralization in the 1920s meant the adherence of gang members to deviant values and actions. In his view, the gang's

> demoralizing influence on its members arises through the dissemination of criminal technique, and the propagation through mutual excitation, of interests and attitudes which make crime easier (less inhibited) and more attractive.[14]

Further, Thrasher argued that "the boy usually acquires in the gang an attitude of fatalism, a willingness to take a chance—a philosophy of life which fits him well for a career of crime."[15]

Thrasher derived his ideas from the far richer and deeper analysis of Robert Park, who in turn was building on the theories of his mentor, Georg

Simmel.[16] Park and Simmel were exploring the impact of the city on migrants and immigrants who left their plows for the factories in the late nineteenth and early twentieth centuries. Classic sociology was largely concerned with understanding how the weakening hold of religion and old world traditions "de-moralized" the modern, urban newcomers. Émile Durkheim's notion of "anomy" was the first attempt to label these feelings of "normlessness" that the radical disruption of urbanization had on the simple, god-fearing mind-set of European rural folk.[17]

As the industrial era progressed into its "Golden Age,"[18] Robert Merton would revise Durkheim's views by theorizing that U.S. and Western culture had placed an overriding emphasis on "success." The consequent inability of people to attain their deeply ingrained success-goals would result in "anomie," and they would adapt to their condition in different ways.[19] Many adult gang members roughly corresponded to what Merton called "innovators," who accepted U.S. cultural goals of success but were alienated from manual labor and found alternative, illicit, means to make money. Merton also argued that there were "rebels" (like himself) who both rejected the goals of success and conventional means to attain them, as well as conformists and demoralized "retreatists" (like drug addicts) who saw no hope of success whatsoever.

Demoralization, as used by these scholars, was fundamentally related to the industrial era, or modernity. It described feelings about the loss of the old world, its gods and traditions, and the challenge of a new, urban, more scientific time. In such a more "enlightened" world, race and ethnicity were assumed to be "declining in significance." Demoralization, it was thought, was an unfortunate by-product of humanity's inevitable climb to the higher rungs of a secular "civilization."

The views of Merton, and more so the work of Richard Cloward and Lloyd Ohlin, became a theoretical rationale for "progressive" social change. Indeed, Cloward and Ohlin's *Delinquency and Opportunity* was adopted as a model for Lyndon Johnson's war on poverty, and Cloward would go on to become a key adviser to several sixties' activist organizations.[20] But those same social movements would prove to be the beginning of the end of the industrial era, what Alain Touraine calls "mid-modernity."[21] It is in the lessons of the worldwide 1960s social movements, and particularly their lack of success in changing conditions for the third world and the racial minorities at the bottom of the social structure, that the concept of demoralization would undergo a profound revision, underscore the significance of race, and define the parameters of the power of identity.

The Defeat of the 1960s Social Movements

The 1960s, for a brief time, recaptured in the United States, and across the globe, a rebirth of optimism. Youth, inspired by such diverse figures as Vladimir Lenin, John Lennon, John F. Kennedy, and Bob Marley, surged to the barricades to demand that capitalism live up to its promises or relinquish power. Frantz Fanon called on the "wretched of the earth" to rise up, make violent revolution, and create a better life. Huey Newton's Black Panther Party called on U.S. black youth to "seize the time" and hailed the "lumpen proletariat" (and its gangs) as a potential revolutionary force. In France, Daniel Cohn-Bendit led students to unite with militant workers and demand sweeping change.

The powerful social movements of the 1960s, however, would not fulfill the dreams of the "truly disadvantaged." Repression drowned many rebellions across the globe in blood, as happened in Indonesia, Argentina, Chile, and the Congo. In the United States, the state clamped down on black, Latino, Native American, and youth rebellion, replacing the war on poverty with a war on crime, as its police gunned down and jailed Black Panthers and other radicals and rebels. By the end of the 1960s, some in the black movement were advocating "revolutionary suicide," an eerie foreboding of suicide bombers today.[22]

For Cornel West, the hope of the 1960s was shattered by the failure of the U.S. government to live up to the promises of the war on poverty for black people, abetted by a subsequent void in African American leadership. The killings of Malcolm X, Martin Luther King Jr., Medgar Evers, Fred Hampton, and others were a chilling reminder to black people of the fury and power of racism. As bell hooks put it, "After the slaughter of radical black men, the emotional devastation of soul murder and actual murder, many black people became cynical about freedom."[23] As chapter 2 showed, the decline of social movements also had the unforeseen consequence in some large cities of strengthening gangs.[24]

West argues that "nihilism" among African Americans spread after the 1960s, though the concept is fundamentally rooted in the "psychological scars" of slavery and centuries of racism.

Nihilism is to be understood here not as a philosophic doctrine that there are no rational grounds for legitimate standards or authority. It is, far more, the lived experience of coping with a life of horrifying meaninglessness, hopelessness, and (most important) lovelessness.[25]

Since the 1960s, West goes on, racism has intensified, and U.S. black people have developed a "passionate pessimism" about "America's will to justice."[26] By the mid-1970s, the main lesson for the black "underclass" was that while a black middle class had demonstrably benefited from the 1960s upsurge, no lasting relief from poverty or racism came either from the politics of the street or from the ballot box.[27] I wonder, Tupac Shakur raps, if even "heavens got a ghetto?"[28]

An even more imposing obstacle than repression, however, was the restructuring of the world economy that began in earnest in the 1970s, the beginnings of globalization. Deindustrialization ate away at the U.S. working class, particularly its African American workers, who were late gaining a foothold in heavy industry in such cities as Chicago and Milwaukee.[29] The moving of factories to the third world, as I showed in chapter 1, has not even significantly reduced poverty and polarization there, and in Africa and many other places has increased it.

David Harvey points out the consequences of globalization for solidarity of the oppressed:

Gangs and criminal cartels, narco-trafficking networks, mini-mafias and favela bosses, through community, grassroots and non-governmental organizations, to secular cults and religious sects . . . are the alternative social forms that fill the void left behind as state powers, political parties, and other institutional forms are actively dismantled or simply wither away as centres of collective endeavor or social bonding.[30]

The adoption of religious identities, particularly Islam, has swept the world and exercises a strong influence in the United States, even within gangs. Monster Kody, the legendary Crips leader, was attracted to Islam in prison, for example, because unlike Christianity, Islam was a religion that advocated resistance to oppression. "Islam," Kody said, "is a way of life, just like banging."[31]

Today's complex, uncertain world has made a lasting impact on the consciousness of people of all classes. While highly skilled "symbolic analysts" have some control over their lives, the bulk of the world's people are help-less in the face of decisions made in banks in New York, London, or Tokyo.[32] Even the wishes of governments may have little effect on the decision of, for example, where Intel puts a new chip factory. Unelected bankers and market forces often have more power in this global world than presidents or parliaments.[33] Those with technical jobs can always find work elsewhere. Those without information-related skills are left with nothing.

This means that those on the bottom of the social structure, like the African American urban poor, have become "demoralized" in a new way. A faith in democracy, elections, or local or national leaders is no longer enough to guarantee security or "progress" in the global economy. Elec-tions and formal democratic processes do not work so well, particularly for the dark ghetto. The hope that things will eventually get better has been exposed as a myth of modernity, useful only to those who want to keep the people under control: "The assertion that progress leads to affluence, free-dom and happiness, and that there is a close connection between these three objectives, is no more than an ideology to which history has constantly given the lie."[34]

Demoralization today means, for large segments of the U.S. black com-munity, as well as for many Latinos, other U.S. minorities, and much of the third world, that survival and identity are delinked from the political goals of the state and abstract notions of democracy or hopes of socialism. Demoralization means "both the process of losing touch with morality as it is stripped out of our lives, and the way our culture has lost its sense of purpose."[35] But the costs of demoralization do not just produce drug addicts, like Merton's "retreatists." In the global era, these intense feelings of demoralization become the occasion for the socially excluded to resist the myths of modernity and create new forms of identity among them-selves—and their gangs.

RESISTANCE IDENTITY

John Gray describes "modernity" as "the hope that human beings will shed their traditional allegiances and their local identities and unite in a univer-sal civilization grounded in generic humanity and a rational morality."[36] But this does not describe today's world. In the "network society," when states themselves have little control over economics, in whom do people put their faith? For the information workers or "symbolic analysts," their new god may be technology, and a cosmopolitan identity is in vogue. But for the masses, technology is a god that too often fails or flees. While postmodernism has been a fashionable response among the elite and educated, for the majority, and those seen as the "other," more certain sources of meaning are needed. As Zygmunt Bauman puts it,

> Where the state has failed, perhaps the community, the *local* community, the physically tangible, "material" community, a community embodied in a *territory* inhabited by its members (and no one else who "does not belong") will purvey the "being safe" feeling which the wider world evidently conspires to destroy.[37]

While in the industrial era, a faith existed that political action could bring lasting change and provide a secular "working class" or "civic" identity, the sober realism of people today demands an identity closer to home. Castells calls this "resistance identity" or, provocatively, the "exclusion of the excluders by the excluded."[38] He means that the "socially excluded" defensively create religious, ethnic, or racialized identities to protect their personality and community against the uncertainties and injustices of globalization. "Anyone who is no longer defined by their activity," Touraine says, "soon constructs or reconstructs an identity based upon their origins."[39]

Castells goes on to explain that this production of identity is what is behind the growth of fundamentalist religion, and also ethnic and racial identities in the African American ghetto and elsewhere. Like West, Castells also argues that the failure of the social movements of the 1960s provided the key element in this new sense of nihilist identity, or as he calls it, a "culture of urgency."[40] People were left "with no other choice but either to surrender or to react on the basis of the most immediate source of self recognition and autonomous organization: their locality."[41] Castells's territorial "resistance identity," exemplified, he says, by "gang based social organization" has, in fact, become deeply racialized. LA's Monster Kody models this in his dramatic soliloquy:

> Who is Monster Kody? . . . I am Monster Kody . . . a person, a young man, a black man. . . . Anything else? . . . No, not that I know of. . . . What is Monster Kody? A Crip, an Eight Tray, a Rollin' Sixty killer . . . a black man. . . . Black man, black man, BLACK MAN.[42]

In the same vein, an unknown Vice Lord told me,

> Just because you're in a gang doesn't mean you're a bad person. Everybody
> needs something to stand for. Everybody needs something to believe in. That's
> why people become Christians. Got to believe in something.[43]

To more fully understand how demoralization and resistance identity apply
to U.S. gangs, we must explore "the permanence of racism" in the United
States and the Western world.

THE PERMANENCE OF RACISM

Why do I say that racism is "permanent"? Is this just a rhetorical flourish
or a bow to trendy theorizing? No. In the language of social science, to say
that racism is permanent is to say that it is not a *dependent* variable or a
factor to be explained or dissected into its components. Racism is an *independent* variable, like education, family structure, or religion, that has varying levels and must be included in all analyses. I do not agree with those who
say that racism is necessarily less important than economics or that if we just
add more jobs, racism will fade away.[44] I am sympathetic to Albert Memmi,
who, in asking if economics was the "motive force" behind colonialism and,
by implication, racism, said, "The answer is maybe—not certainly."[45]

There has been a shift among scholars in interpreting the influence of
racism, with a renewed appreciation for W. E. B. DuBois and a grappling
with Michael Omi and Howard Winant's "racial formation" thesis. Among
feminists, hooks represents the best of this tradition, integrating race, class,
and gender in ways that make much contemporary social science uncomfortable.[46] Robin D. G. Kelley's popular book, *Yo' Mama's Disfunktional!* was
consciously written as a "defense of black people's humanity and a con-
demnation of scholars and policymakers for their inability to see complexity."[47] Kelley is among many African American intellectuals who have raised
sharp disagreements with white social science's interpretations of black people's lives.

Bell, one of the country's foremost legal scholars, has taken to fiction and
storytelling to explicate his drive "for new directions in our struggle for
racial justice; a struggle we must continue even if—as I contend here—
racism is an integral, permanent, and indestructible component of this society."[48] But rather than accept that the permanence of racism must lead to

nihilism, Bell existentially asserts, *"We must acknowledge it, not as a sign of submission, but as an act of ultimate defiance."*[49] Tupac, as usual, has a rap that expresses this view succinctly in his song "Keep Ya Head Up":

> Say there ain't no hope for the youth and the truth is
> it ain't no hope for tha future . . .
> And even though you're fed up
> Huh, ya got to keep your head up.[50]

I find Bell's brave comments, Tupac's rap, DuBois's framework, and Winant's historical analysis convincing.[51] This perspective, and Bell's recommendations for struggle, forms the basis for my later exploration of hip-hop as a "black Atlantic" culture of resistance.

Black People as America's Other

Racism has been a stable pillar of the politics and culture of all Western and European societies, dating back at least to the shameful justification for the slave trade. The notion of the permanence of racism contradicts Gunnar Myrdal's modernist idea that racism is mainly an atavistic behavior of a feudal past.[52] Rather, the dehumanization of slaves, Edward Said explains, is but one example of the European creation of the other, the "Orientals" who ought to be granted Western "benevolence" so they can become "civilized."[53] This persisting fear of the other haunts Europe today, from neo-Nazi skinheads in Berlin,[54] to racial violence in London,[55] to anti-immigrant politics in France, the Netherlands, and elsewhere, to widespread anti-Islamic hatred, racism, and bigotry.

In the third world, Basil Davidson reminds us, ethnic, racial, or tribal violence is a disturbing legacy of the arbitrarily drawn state boundaries and policies of colonialism.[56] One horrific example is the genocide in Rwanda, whose unique ethnicities of Tutsi and Hutu were created by Europeans from occupational differences.[57] The collapse of the "apparent state" in Africa,[58] and its substitution by gangs of warring armed young men, can be directly attributed to the legacy of colonialism and the cold war politics of the superpowers, not historic, "essentialist" tribal antagonisms.

September 11 has not only exposed widespread global hostility to the United States, but the resulting U.S. war on terrorism has unveiled the American people's latent fear of the other and a violence just below a "civilized" veneer. Said sadly asked "whether there is any way of avoiding the hostility expressed by the division of, say, men into 'us' (Westerners) and 'they' (Orientals)."[59] This division has long applied to black people, who, as Ralph Ellison said, either were "invisible" to white America or were feared and demonized.[60] As Elijah Anderson eloquently describes:

> The master status assigned to black males undermines their ability to be taken for granted as law-abiding and civil participants in public places; young black males, particularly those who don the urban uniform (sneakers, athletic suits, gold chains, "gangster caps," sunglasses, and large portable radios or "boom boxes"), may be taken as the embodiment of the predator.[61]

In Western society, the scapegoat has been irrevocably racialized, and his "dark skin has a special meaning," which white people "have come to associate with crime."[62] Even gangsters from areas and republics south of Russia like Georgia are called the "n-word" by Muscovites.[63] Richard Sennett's historical description of the "fear of touching" is startlingly applicable to white Americans' reaction to African Americans.[64] Bell, echoing DuBois, defines the "permanence of racism" with the cold statement: "Black people will never gain full equality in this country."[65]

DuBois himself plunged to the depths of despair in an emotional chapter in *The Souls of Black Folks* on the death of his firstborn. He writes of his "gladness" of his son's death, that "my soul whispers to me, saying, 'Not dead, not dead, but escaped; not bond but free.'" He concludes with unrestrained desolation: "Well sped, my boy, before the world had dubbed your ambition insolence, had held your ideals unattainable, and taught you to cringe and bow. Better far this nameless void that stops my life than a sea of sorrow for you."[66] Sethe's killing of her daughter in Toni Morrison's *Beloved* follows tragically in this tradition.

This perception of the intransigence of racism offends a liberal faith in progress implicitly held by many of those who research gangs. It also clashes with the optimistic worldview of modernity and the hopes of a rising minority middle class.[67] While Jennifer Hochschild has pointed out that it is precisely the African American *middle* class that is most disillusioned by black "progress,"[68] the real victims of the failure of the modernist civil rights movement are William Julius Wilson's "truly disadvantaged," or what he earlier called the black underclass.[69]

Wilson's analysis of the impact of deindustrialization on Chicago became the paradigm for my understanding of gangs in Milwaukee. My first book, *People and Folks,* quintessentially argued that the loss of industrial jobs transformed black and Hispanic gangs from unsupervised peer groups into "post-industrial gangs," focused more on economics than delinquency.[70] After a decade of research in Chicago, however, my views have evolved, and I now define "demoralization" as not only the hopelessness of economic mobility but also the hopelessness of social mobility, and the sober recognition of the intractability of racism. A consideration of the historical structures of racism in Chicago, and how it has impacted gangs, led me to make a theoretical break with the Chicago school and look for more robust frameworks, which I found in Castells, Touraine, West, Bell, and others.

chapter 6

A Tale of Two Gangs: The Hamburgs and the Conservative Vice Lords

"Anyone ever tell you this is a white man's beach?" Morris asked Alford.
"You know we don't want n   o here!" Buddy said.

—JAMES T. FARRELL, "For White Men Only"

This meaning is not without interest to you, Gentle Reader;
For the problem of the Twentieth Century is the problem of the color-line.

—W. E. B. DUBOIS, *The Souls of Black Folk*

Once upon a time there were two gangs. One was a good, civic gang. The other was a bad, violent gang. One gang has lasted for many decades, and its leaders became leading citizens of the city. The other gang has also been around for decades, but its leaders have been killed or sent to prison. One gang is predominately male, proud of its ethnic traditions and neighborhood, and its members are very prosperous. The other gang is also predominately male, proud of its ethnic traditions and neighborhood, but most of its members are poor and out of work. One gang is Irish from Bridgeport. The other, from about four miles away in North Lawndale, is African American.

First and foremost, this story is more about race than space.[1] It explains how demoralization and Cornel West's concept of nihilism have an objective basis in the historical structures of Chicago's racism.[2] It points out vast differences between the industrial era and the information era, and the effects of the economic and social changes on both gangs. Heuristically, the comparison is a map to the step-by-step process I went through in shedding my allegiance to the Chicago school on my climb to more explanatory frameworks.

The Gangs of New York . . . and Chicago

The story begins not in Chicago but in New York, and may be familiar to those who saw Martin Scorsese's cinematic adaptation of Herbert Asbury's book *The Gangs of New York*.[3] Eric Monkkonen coined the term "voting gangs" to describe the Irish and Yankee gangs in New York City that used their physical skills to aid politicians of their ethnic group. The gangs of early New York City were more than teenage delinquents: they were "toughs intimidating voters (or sometimes other voting gangs)." Electoral violence in New York City in the nineteenth century was "a utilitarian tool, a part of northern politics, yet also the tool of criminals."[4]

First among the ethnic groups who expertly practiced the art of political violence were the Irish, who dominated the big-city machines in the nineteenth and early twentieth centuries.[5] The Irish in Chicago learned from their New York cousins and called their voting gangs "Social Athletic Clubs" (SACs). Frederic Thrasher found that 243 of his 1,313 gangs in Chicago were SACs, and another 192 were adult or "mixed" adult and youth.[6]

What were these clubs? One of the most famous, the Hamburg Athletic Association (HAA), was founded in 1904 in Bridgeport, an area of Chicago described by Mayor Carter Henry Harrison II as "a semi-legendary, all-Irish segment of the south division, where men were men, and boys either hellions or early candidates for the last rites of the church."[7] Clubs like the HAA, and Ragen's Colts in the adjacent Back of the Yards, were sponsored by local politicians who fervently practiced the fine art of electoral thuggery.

One history of Chicago elections explains:

> Social clubs were organized at the ward level to boost the campaign of a favorite son, or slate of candidates. The pageantry of torch-light rallies, colorful parades, and bombastic oratory set in smoke-filled meeting halls scattered across the city, provided an important sense of neighborhood identity and ethnic pride—the hopes, fears, and prejudices vested in the candidate fortunate enough to descend from the same dominant nationality found within the ward.[8]

"The tendency of the gangs to become athletic clubs," Thrasher said, "has been greatly stimulated by the politicians of the city."[9] SACs like the HAA were made up of adolescent and young adults with "feeder" groups of even younger kids affiliated with their older brothers and neighbors. The sociologist Edward Sutherland described Chicago's SACs in 1924:

> At the present time a good many gangs are flourishing under the leadership and protection of the politicians. These are frequently called athletic clubs and are fostered even among young boys, evidently with the expectation that political support will be gained in the future. In return for present support and expected future support the politicians extend protection to the boys in their depredations.[10]

Politics in Chicago, like New York, was intimately tied up with the rackets, which, until Al Capone's consolidation of power in the Prohibition years, was controlled by the Irish and their "clubs." "Scratch a club man," Thrasher claimed, "and you will find a gangster."[11] Gangsters, according to Thrasher, were normally "younger boys who have probably been favored by the politician and who have gradually become criminals, in which roles they are probably even more useful to him."[12]

In this sense the HAA was not different from the Dead Rabbits or other classic voting gangs of New York. It grew in an interstitial area southwest of the Loop and thus was a perfect example of the Chicago school's definition of a gang. But Bridgeport was not only an interstitial zone, it also was located across Wentworth Avenue from the Black Belt or Bronzeville, the home of Chicago's black community.

The 1919 Race Riots

This accident of geography is more significant than all the concentric zones of Chicago school theory put together. The proof of this brash assertion lies in the long-term consequences of the horrific events of 1919.

Irish-black hostility has a long history in the United States. The New York City draft riots during the Civil War were spearheaded by Irish gangs assaulting and murdering African Americans.[13] In 1864 four hundred Chicago Irish dockworkers "went on a bloody rampage" against black workers whom they believed were after their jobs.[14] At the end of World War I, racial tensions were simmering in Chicago as in many other cities.

The key events underlying these tensions were the migrations to Chicago and other northern cities of tens of thousands of black workers to fill

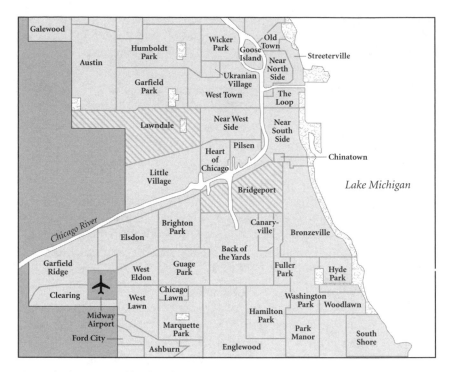

Central Chicago neighborhoods

jobs left by the Irish, Polish, and other white ethnics who went off to war.[15] When these soldiers returned, blacks held their jobs, and racial violence flared across the industrial Midwest. Significantly, the jobs in Chicago's stockyards filled by African Americans were geographically located in the Back of the Yards, just to the south of Bridgeport. African Americans often had to fight their way to work past a couple of miles filled with angry, racist Irish "clubs."

In the spring and summer of 1919 racial violence between black and white gangs exploded on the Wentworth Avenue divide, and, in those few months, twenty-four black homes in the "neutral zone" were bombed. On June 21, 1919, two black youths were brutally murdered by white gangs.[16] Tensions boiled over at the end of July, as a black youth was drowned after crossing an imaginary line in Lake Michigan separating black and white. But while other race riots flared and died down, the Chicago riots were kept burning by the SACs. The HAA was specifically named as one of the chief culprits.

What followed was carefully documented by the 1922 Race Relations Commission report.

> Gangs and their activities were an important factor throughout the riot. But for them it is doubtful if the riot would have gone beyond the first clash. Both organized gangs and those which sprang into existence because of the opportunity afforded seized upon the excuse of the first conflict to engage in lawless acts. . . .
>
> It was no new thing for youthful white and Negro groups to come to violence. For years, as the sections of this report dealing with antecedent clashes and with recreation show, there had been clashes over baseball grounds, swimming-pools in the parks, the right to walk on certain streets, etc. . . .
>
> Gangs whose activities figured so prominently in the riot were all white gangs, or "athletic clubs." Negro hoodlums do not appear to form organized gangs so readily. Judges of the municipal court said that there are no gang organization among Negroes to compare with those found among young whites.[17]

In fact, the drive-by shooting, popularly associated with Capone in the next decade, got its start in earlier East St. Louis and the Chicago race riots.[18] White club members would drive into the Black Belt and open fire, hightailing it out after discharging their firearms. But the invasion of the Black Belt was met by violent black resistance, as the World War I veteran Harry Haywood relates:

> It was rumored that Irishmen from the west of the Wentworth Avenue dividing line were planning to invade the ghetto that night, coming in across the tracks by way of Fifty-first Street. We planned a defensive action to meet them. . . . It was not surprising that defensive preparations were under way. There had been clashes before, often when white youths in "athletic clubs" invaded the Black community. These "clubs" were really racist gangs, organized by the city ward heelers and precinct captains.[19]

Still, black resistance would be inadequate against the white gangs, who, the Race Relations Commission suggested, intimidated witnesses and were often protected by police. For example, nine black families had moved into homes three blocks west of Wentworth Avenue, Chicago's Mason-Dixon line. During the riot, two hundred Ragen's Colts assaulted these homes, trying to burn them down and throwing bricks and rocks and opening fire. Police came and left, doing nothing while the Colts told white neighbors: "If you open your mouth against Ragen's we will not only burn your house down, we will 'do' you."[20]

The HAA was one of the active participants in the rioting, and its sponsor, Eleventh Ward alderman "Sonny" Joseph McDonough, was the city's most vociferous inciter of white violence and racial hatred. McDonough falsely said that he was shot on July 30, and he wildly claimed that the Negroes had enough ammunition to last for "years of guerrilla war." He told the local press that black people

> are armed and the white people are not. We must defend ourselves if the city authorities won't protect us. . . . I saw white men and women running through the streets dragging children by the hands and carrying babies in their arms. Frightened white men told me the police captains had just rushed through the district crying "For God's sake, arm. They are coming, we cannot hold them."[21]

The Race Relations Commission doubted that any of the events described by McDonough actually occurred. The commission also debunked the alderman's inflammatory claims of black terrorists planting bombs. The effect of McDonough's vitriol was to heat up the level of racism in the Irish community to fever pitch and must have had an effect on his star HAA protégé, Richard J. Daley. To his dying day, the first Mayor Daley refused to comment on his role in the violence as a seventeen-year-old HAA member. A few years after the riots, Daley would be elected president of the HAA and serve for fifteen years until promoted by McDonough, beginning Daley's step-by-step rise to the mayor's chair.[22]

For Thrasher the events of 1919 did not merit much analysis, taking up less than one page of the more than five hundred pages of his classic work, fewer pages than those describing two small Chinese American tongs. For Thrasher and the Chicago school, the events of 1919 were just another example of the pattern of cultural conflict in the city's interstitial zones.

> In the growth of Chicago it has repeatedly happened that one immigrant or racial group has invaded the territory of another, gradually driving out the

former, only to be itself displaced later by a still different cultural or racial group. This process of invasion and succession is both personal and impersonal and involves both competition and conflict.[23]

Harder to understand is Thrasher's assertion that after the race riots there existed two types of African American neighborhoods: "In one type the negroes and whites have become adjusted to each other and friction is either non-existent or negligible. In the other there is friction."[24]

He further writes of the "obliteration of race and nationality distinctions in the gang" and that racial divisions within the gangs were "superficial."[25] This perspective can only be described as delusional. To say that Chicago race relations in the 1920s exhibited "friction" is like saying there is "friction" between Israelis and Palestinians, or between Serbs and Bosnians. The 1920s began, in the concise words of Arnold Hirsch, an era of "hidden violence" that forcibly kept black people from leaving the south side ghetto. This violence, painstakingly documented by Hirsch, took the form of bombings and riots anytime black people sought to escape the confines of their assigned "place." "Friction" indeed.

We know from historical research that, after World War I, black people were the only ethnic group with concentrations of more than 90 percent in neighborhoods. Other ethnic groups had enclaves, but only black people lived in a ghetto.[26] By 1930, restrictive covenants, real estate contracts that forbade owners to sell to black people, would cover more than three-quarters of Chicago homes, keeping black people to a slim south side Black Belt. "If the restriction of the district can't keep them out," a white religious leader said in 1928, "the Irish will."[27] While other ethnics would invade slum areas, succeeding earlier groups, then moving on themselves, black people would be forced by law, tradition, and violence to stay caged in a segregated "black metropolis."

While it has been recognized that the lack of *mobility* of African Americans is contrary to some of the ecological concepts of the Chicago school,[28] the geographic *stability* of the Irish also contradicts aspects of the Chicago school's "ethnic succession" model. Many Irish did not move out of the city as they assimilated because their prosperity was tied to city politics and its patronage. Already by 1900, nearly half of all Chicago city employees were Irish.[29] By the late 1990s, Bridgeport's land values soared with gentrification, and those Irish who stayed became quite wealthy and determined to hold on to their property.

Nonracial ecological theory kept Thrasher and his Chicago school colleagues blind to the realities of racism in Chicago. Perhaps they were too close to events and did not understand what W. E. B. DuBois had been writing at the time about the fundamental nature of the color line.[30] They saw white racism as just another manifestation of ethnic conflict and ignored the persisting reality of racial violence. They also misunderstood the significance of Chicago's most prominent institutionalized gang, the Hamburg Athletic Association.

THE HAMBURG ATHLETIC ASSOCIATION AND THE MACHINE

The HAA is an unquestioned success story. It has lasted now for more than a century, and its clubhouse still stands at 37th and Emerald in the old neighborhood, two blocks from where its most famous member, Richard J. Daley, grew up and lived as mayor. The HAA is a good example of what happens when gang kids are provided with conventional opportunities through athletics, social activity, religion, and politics.

What has happened to the HAA? Today its clubhouse is still a center of activity for the neighborhood. It sponsors basketball games on its gym floor, which it bought from the Minneapolis Lakers when that team moved to Los Angeles in 1960. It has a weight room and a clubhouse area where every Friday night its members come to talk and "exchange ideas."

I was invited to the clubhouse by "James," a longtime HAA member, through connections with one of my students. James even made a videotape of a tour of the clubhouse for one of my classes and answered questions about its history. I later spent an evening with James and other HAA members discussing the nature of the club and how it was or was not a gang. "We're a gang of do-gooders," James told me many times, "a civic-minded gang." He derided any notion that the HAA was ever a gang like those today. "We're not the Gangster Disciples," said one club member, Matt Danaher, to a reporter in 1996.[31]

Indeed, the HAA membership today includes firemen, policemen, city managers, plumbers, and carpenters. In the mid-nineties, the *Chicago Sun-Times* estimated that 70 percent of HAA members were city employees, a percentage that would undoubtedly be elevated if city contractors were included. At the clubhouse and a nearby restaurant, I met high-ranking officials in the police department as well as several members who made a living by providing services to the city. Waste removal and other services have been contracted out to the mayor's political allies and have replaced civil service as Chicago's principal form of patronage.

HAA members today have the same last names as the members back in 1919, James said, and "only the first names have changed." The club is intergenerational, "handed down from father to son." "The men of the club personify family values," said HAA member Dannaher to the *Sun-Times*. Wives also play a supportive, auxiliary role but are not members. Was the HAA ever a gang? No, according to James; it was just a group of friends getting together to share a common, Irish life. He criticized William Tuttle's book *Race Riot* for believing that the HAA could be a social club and an athletic club and a street gang, saying it was difficult for it "to be all three at the same time."

What the HAA provided for street toughs from Bridgeport was an avenue out of the gang and into conventionalized politics. Its members were not choirboys but street kids who found in the HAA both comradeship and entrée into a similarly tough political life. For example, here is the HAA's Richard J. Daley as mayor, in 1961, responding to the pleas of an Italian housewife, Florence Scala, for the city to stop a plan to level the homes in her neighborhood to make room for the University of Illinois–Chicago: "Nobody gets tough with me. I know how to handle myself. I know how to protect myself. I come from the kind of neighborhood where we know how to protect ourselves."[32]

Maybe there is something to the adage that you can take the boy out of the gang, but you cannot take the gang out of the boy. A retired police commander whom I spoke with recalled his "club" days in Bridgeport as a youth. When I asked him what happened to all his wild friends, he thought for a moment, then answered, "I guess they all became police officers."

The HAA is an "institutionalized" gang in every sense of the term—it has persisted despite changes in leadership; has a younger generation waiting to join; has built an organization with multiple political and social roles; has adapted to changing conditions of being on the outside, to being consummate political insiders, to now being in a fierce fight within the machine with the rising Latino voting bloc; has provided jobs through patronage and social activities for the community; and has rituals and ceremonies like marching in the St. Patrick's Day parade under its colors and banner. It has institutionalized within Chicago's all-powerful Democratic machine.

James is right to be proud of his club. The HAA fulfilled its purpose and provided economic and political opportunities for Bridgeport's neighborhood kids and a way to make their lives meaningful. Club youth became well-to-do citizens and even mayor. The HAA still possesses influence on the second Mayor Daley, though the Latino community has recently cut into its patronage and now makes up more than half of Bridgeport's population.

While conventional political science may see in this the normal workings of "machine politics," the role of the HAA and other clubs in the 1919 race riots would set in concrete the racial principles on which Chicago was built. As Adam Cohen and Elizabeth Taylor put it, "Daley's modern Chicago was built . . . on an unstated foundation: commitment to racial segregation."[33] If, for the HAA, it has been the best of times, for the Vice Lords it would become the worst of times.

SHATTERED DREAMS

The story of the Conservative Vice Lords (CVL) begins not in Chicago but in the South, as black people migrated north in large numbers after World War II. Chicago's Bronzeville, on the south side, was overcrowded and could not contain a fast-growing black population despite the years of "hidden violence" and absolute political dominance of the Irish machine. Black gangs in Bronzeville, from the 1919 race riots into the 1950s, would be street corner kids, very much like Thrasher described. "Policy," or illegal, gambling was one road to mobility, but it was controlled by older African Americans with no room for the gangs.[34] The black metropolis was segregated and overflowing by the 1950s. *Someplace* had to be carved out of Chicago's hodge podge neighborhoods to house a youthful and growing black population.

That someplace was Lawndale, a predominately Jewish neighborhood on Chicago's west side. By 1930 half of the population of Lawndale were Russian Jews, and white dominance continued into the 1950s. At that time, politically, the area was run by Jake Arvey, a "kingmaker" in Chicago politics. The Twenty-fourth Ward was described by President Franklin Roosevelt as the "best Democratic ward in the country."[35] In 1960 it may have won Illinois and perhaps the presidential election for John F. Kennedy by returning a vote of 24,211 to 2,131 over Richard M. Nixon, an astounding total that few believe was on the level.[36]

The west side was also the home of gangsters and had been the site of numerous killings by the Outfit, the "west side bloc" of aldermen who controlled any and all anticrime legislation. One historical essay describes it: "The 24th Ward had a history of drug trafficking, numbers running, and prostitution. Mobsters were believed to be the guiding force in the district. It was a malodorous mix of crime and crooked politics, to say the least."[37]

During the 1950s Lawndale's white population dropped from 87,000 to less than 11,000, while that of African Americans grew from 380 in 1940 to 13,000 in 1950 and then to more than 113,000 in 1960. While white politicians and gangsters held power in Lawndale, by the end of the fifties it was clear to Arvey and his ally and protégé, new mayor Richard J. Daley, that a black face was needed for the machine. Benjamin Lewis was appointed committeeman in 1961 and lived the high life of graft in this crime-scarred district, like his white predecessors. Soon after Lewis was reelected by an overwhelming margin and had hinted at some independence from Daley's machine, he was gunned down February 28, 1963, the last in a long list of Outfit murders of politicians. No killer was ever found, and Lewis's many corrupt dealings gave the Chicago police "too many motives."[38]

But while the white machine lumbered on and white gangsters dominated the rackets, there was restless stirring on the streets of Lawndale. "We began as a social athletic club," says Bobby Gore, one of the top leaders of the Conservative Vice Lords. But Gore's wry comment reveals both the similarities and differences between the CVL and the HAA.

McDonough sponsored the HAA, but the CVL would have an unsympathetic white alderman as it formed and then, for a few years, machine-token Lewis. The gang grew by assimilating a variety of neighborhood gangs in Lawndale, including the well-known Clovers. The CVL was a group of street toughs, but its ranks also included talented individuals like Gore, who shone as a member of a popular singing group, the Clevertones.

The CVL would officially come together in St. Charles, Chicago's juvenile prison. Like the HAA, it started as a "group of friends" who called themselves "vice lords" because, as the "the white man . . . was said to be the lords of all vice so we just took their title. Instead of being known as the mafia . . . we just wanted to be vice lords," said Edwin Marion Perry, or "Pep," the CVL's original leader. The CVL united other clubs and gangs in Lawndale under its banner and grew to be the largest gang in Chicago.[39]

As the CVL, the Egyptian Cobras, and other west side gangs formed, they fought not only among themselves but with the white gangs trying to hang on to their neighborhood. One CVL leader, Bennie Lee, describes his upbringing:

> My family moved out of K-Town in 1967. We moved on Cicero and Jackson. This was a predominately white neighborhood. My family was one of the first black families to move in that area. You have to keep in mind this was in the sixties. Racism and Jim Crow laws were still in effect. During the summer, we would have to walk through the majority white neighborhood to get to the swimming pool. The whites would attack us. These would be adult whites as well as young white boys our age. The adults would urge them on to attack us. . . .
>
> There were two swimming pools on the west side for us. One was in the near K-Town area at Garfield Park (3600 west), and Columbus Park, which was 5500 west. We decided to go to Columbus, which was closer. The whites felt we were invading their neighborhood. So it was these conditions that caused racial tension. The word got around the neighborhood that my brothers and me had the courage to fight the whites, so other brothers would join us to go swimming. So in that time we became recognized as a gang. We were forced to band together for protection.[40]

The racial solidarity formed in the process of struggling for territory was similar to the experiences of "ethnic succession" described by the Chicago school, but would have a very different, and violently tragic, ending.

The best narrative of the life history of the CVL is David Dawley's *Nation of Lords,* which documents the CVL's transformation from a gang into a community organization. While the HAA's street toughs also transformed their gang into a conventional group of "do-gooders," there is no record of the HAA ever repudiating its violent role in 1919 or later, and in conversations with me, members of the HAA minimized their club's role.

On the contrary, Gore tells of the CVL leaders meeting in the mid-1960s and despairing of CVL gang violence and the negative influence they were having on young people. "The kids are the ones who are actually losing," Gore told the other CVL elders after a group of young kids approached them, asked for guns, and said they wanted to follow in the CVL's footsteps. In the midst of the civil rights movement, rising levels of black pride, and a growing political influence of black people in Chicago, the gang leaders decided to change course.

Why did they change? One founder, Noonie, told me, "A lot of it was Bobby [Gore]. *And* it was the right thing to do." They became CVL, Inc.

This remarkable story can be followed on the Web site gangresearch.net, in pictures and first-person interviews with Gore and other leaders of the gang, as well as in Dawley's book. The CVL started businesses and youth and cultural centers and ran a community cleanup program with the Blackstone Rangers called "grass not glass." They took part in parades and celebrated their heritage, just as the HAA had done in Bridgeport. They attracted to their side the pride of Lawndale, great athletes such as the Golden Gloves champion Chuck Spruell, the National Football League star Mack Herron, the artist Don McIlvaine, and the world-famous drummer Willie "The Touch" Hayes. They became a "gang of do-gooders," a "civic-minded gang,"[41] who wanted their piece of the pie. While Pep left to attend Dartmouth—with which the CVL sponsored scholarships for Lawndale youth—the new CVL leader Alfonso Alford summed up their new stance.

> Like society itself, we are in a time of change. Just as we used to fight each other on the street, we now stand together in a different fight for life—the life of a city, the life of a neighborhood and the life of a people who have been declared unemployable, uneducable, and unreached.[42]

At first, politicians began to court the CVL, especially since the Twenty-fourth Ward was a treasure trove of votes. Edward Hanrahan, running for state's attorney, would praise them in a visit to the House of Lords, and the CVL would sponsor an open house for the Chicago police. The CVL worked to stop gang violence citywide. "The things we are doing to each other, we can't have it no more. You see. Because our problem is not among ourselves," said Gore to a citywide meeting of gang leaders. The CVL even adopted a less confrontational slant toward Mayor Daley and the Chicago machine. They worked closely with new black alderman George Collins, a staunch member of the machine, until his elevation to Congress, and they also forged ties with the local police commanders and businessmen.

The CVL, Inc., received funding from the Rockefeller Foundation and Republican fund-raisers like W. Clement Stone. Their youth activities were funded by Sammy Davis Jr., and they were the toast of the town. Chicago's leading journalist, the *Sun-Times*'s Irv Kupcinet, wrote, "The CVL, once regarded as a hardened street gang, has made a complete about-face.

Its purpose now is to provide activities and motivation for the blacks in Lawndale."[43]

All their good works surely would prompt the machine to reach out to them, like it had to the HAA before. "We thought the mayor would grab us and kiss us," says Gore, with an ironic smile and an underlying tone of sadness. But it was not hugs and kisses that made up the machine's response. It was war.

The War on Gangs

In 1969 Daley had had enough. The riots after Dr. Martin Luther King Jr.'s death and the police riot at the 1968 Democratic Convention were the tip of the iceberg of political stirrings among the African American community, particularly those at the bottom of the social structure. The Black Panther Party (BPP) and its charismatic leader, Fred Hampton, had established a major following on Chicago's streets. Black street gangs in Woodlawn, Englewood, and Lawndale had united smaller gangs under their banners and had begun to get involved with politics.

The gangs formed a coalition, "LSD," or "Lords, Stones, and Disciples," to take on the city and the construction trades and to demand jobs for the black community. "We were going to take Chicago on a trip," laughs Gore, making a pun on LSD, the popular hallucinogenic drug. But this was deadly serious business. In a series of meetings, including some coordinated by Euseni Perkins of the Better Boys Club and the author of a history of Chicago's black gangs,[44] Hampton met with leaders of the gangs and urged their political involvement and the creation of a united front. Perkins gets it just right:

> Fred [Hampton] was trying to organize these gang members into a political entity. He challenged them to stop the killing, shooting, and so forth and to come together and develop a political perspective. This is what the Jewish gangs did, this is what the Italian gangs did, this is what the Irish . . . Definitely the Irish. . . .
>
> The Irish controlled Chicago at one time. You got the mayor, the police commissioner, the park commissioner, just about every commissioner, every high office in the 30's and 40's you have an Irish. And yet Irish only consisted of about 3 or 4% of the population, maybe 5% that's all. But they literally controlled Chicago. . . . But that was because of the formation of these

gangs that helped them to develop this power base and they came here as immigrants. . . .

Black gang members began to say well they did it, we can do it also. But there's always two standards toward black criminality and white criminality. There's always two standards. They did it, okay that was righteous. But we ain't gonna let you do it.[45]

Mike Royko, a white journalist, sets the proper context in his biting biography of the "Boss."

Daley had seen the same thing happen before. He recalled Ragen's Colts, the Irish thieves and street fighters who became the most potent political force in Canaryville, and his own neighborhood's Hamburgs, who got their start the same brawling way before turning to politics and eventually launching his career. There lay the danger of the black gangs.[46]

Just as the HAA had helped Irish politicians seize power in Chicago for the Democratic Party and dispense patronage to their own, in fine Chicago tradition the black gangs were following the same path. While the HAA and other "clubs" combined violence with the hard work of campaigning to get their start, once in power Daley could use the police powers of the state to crush his enemies. As Noonie said, Mayor Daley

didn't want to see us prosper. We were getting with politicians and things. . . . Just like they started the Hamburgs, (he thought) these black boys would follow that path. . . . Can you imagine 10,000 guys with mothers and fathers and sisters and brothers who are voters? . . . One day Bobby might be the mayor.[47]

What was in essence a familiar contest for political power became a violent campaign of terror against gangs and the BPP. On May 9, 1969, Mayor Daley and his handpicked State's Attorney Hanrahan officially declared "war on gangs." In a press statement they used the words of organized crime and terrorism to change the fundamental way gangs were viewed:

Gang claims that they are traditional boys' clubs or community organizations ignore the violence and destruction of social values in the neighborhoods they terrorize.[48]

These are almost the same words as those used in the 1922 Race Relations Commission report describing the HAA, Daley's own gang. But the mainly

Irish police force in 1919 had no interest in suppressing the Irish clubs—surely many were members. Fifty years later, the police were eager to smash the black gangs. The political interests of the gangs and all the good deeds of the CVL were ignored, and the very idea of gangs—now mainly black and Latino—was criminalized.[49]

The war was swift and effective. As Lord Slim, who was a teenager at the time, told me: "They started lockin' up Lords. They got them on drug charges, anything they could. No one was left." In the fall of 1969 Leonard Sengali, the Blackstone Rangers spokesman, and Alford were both indicted on trumped-up murder charges. Sengali's case was thrown out of court, and a jury quickly found Alford innocent. Two weeks before the notorious Hanrahan-led police killings of BPP leaders Hampton and Mark Clark, CVL spokesman Gore was also arrested on a phony murder charge. Denied the attorney of his choice, Gore was forced to go to trial quickly without adequate preparation or location of numerous eyewitnesses who could clear him. The trial was flooded by a media-driven antigang hysteria, and, with a police force arresting and threatening potential Lawndale witnesses, Gore was convicted.

Daley pressured foundations and corporations to cut off funding for the CVL and vetoed a major job-training grant approved by a federal agency for the CVL. Coupled with Gore's incarceration, the cutoff of funds demoralized CVL members and the Lawndale community. With private jobs scarce and access to public jobs through CVL programs gone, youth reverted to the streets. There would be no niche in the political establishment for Gore and buddies. Rather than ride his popularity to city hall, Gore would spend the next eleven years in Stateville Correctional Center.

"Once Bobby went down," Noonie said, "guys didn't have jobs and stuff and there was money to be made selling drugs." "A lot of us were mad," adds JB. "They figured that if they cut off the head, the body would die."[50] But the CVL did not die; it was reborn, no longer a pro–social community group based on foundation and government funds but an economic organization, living off drug dollars.

The Institutionalization of the CVL

While the HAA institutionalized within the Democratic machine and political system, CVL members and their youthful followers were cut off from jobs and other conventional means to escape the streets. The dope dealers became the main game in town and one of the only employers for the youth that were the CVL base. "They used the Vice Lords for protection as they built their drug empire," Noonie said, not without bitterness. Slim adds:

> I started seeing Cadillacs on the corner. All these guys with tailor made clothes and capes on 'em. Where this comin' from? . . . then the drugs hit the neighborhood. . . .
>
> Bobby and them tried to keep the drugs out of the neighborhood, to make it a positive thing. . . . But after all of them left, somebody brought the drugs into the neighborhood and that's what the chiefs relied on for money: drugs.[51]

But the impression made by the CVL on the minds and hearts of its long-time members would not allow the gang to go away. Slim adds, "Noonie was the one who kept it going. He said 'I ain't gonna let this die.'" When younger kids tried to put up graffiti for a newly invented "RIP Boy's," Noonie and his buddies took action.

> We aint been nothing but Vice Lords, I ain't gonna be any RIP or nothing else. I got about seven of my friends and we made them take it all off the walls. . . . We Vice Lords and that's what we are going to continue to be.[52]

The CVL did not die, but institutionalized on the streets, supported by drug profits. The incarceration of so many of its members did not break the gang but gave it another space to occupy and training to rebuild on a criminal basis. When other gangs tried to claim Lawndale drug-selling spots, the CVL taxed them and reorganized around individual drug entrepreneurs. It was not the CVL of old, but the spirit would not die. As Noonie explains,

> It was just in my heart, it was because of Pep and Bobby I was proud to be a Vice Lord. It meant something to me. I didn't want that to be forgotten. I just had to build it back up.[53]

Slim says:

> The name had to go on because of what we accomplished. We couldn't let that die. I want people 100 years from now to say the Conservative Vice Lords did something for the neighborhood.[54]

Spruell, the Golden Gloves champ and a close friend of Gore, sees what is happening as so different than the sixties. "We were trying to help people . . . but the kids today are out for themselves." Still, JB explains why the CVL will not go away, despite repressive police tactics. He says the CVL will live on

> because of their children. You can't kill something that is steady being born, you can't kill a spirit that is willing to fight, not against ourselves so much as against conditions.[55]

The Permanence of Racism

How can the story of the HAA and the Vice Lords be told without race being at the center of the discussion? The different paths of these two gangs were part of the racial wall that has divided Chicago and America into "two separate societies, one black, one white." While the HAA members found jobs and a future in their gang activities tied to the Democratic machine, the Vice Lords would find only demoralization and despair. West's notion of nihilism fits the outlook of a defeated, depressed, and powerless group. It was all the worse because the CVL had come so tantalizingly close to success.

While the CVL programs were being demolished, Lawndale and Chicago were beginning the process of deindustrialization, with factories leaving and the middle class fleeing. Lawndale was written off, and arson became a tool for landlords to rid themselves of property that could not get high rents and pave the way for today's gentrification. With the CVL defeated, the salt of the earth of Lawndale would have no voice.

Harold Washington's ascension to power gave the old Vice Lords and black people in Chicago a brief glimmer of hope. As Slim said,

> People got more relaxed especially with the mayor we had before who thought we were the scum of the earth. But Harold came to visit us, and he was a positive guy, he told us he needed everyone.[56]

But when Washington suddenly died, Slim relays how cynicism once again embraced the community.

> Everyone was bitter (after he died) they say: all that could help us would be the black man runnin' the city and now they get rid of him, just like they did to our dreams. People turned hard, it got rough in the neighborhood.[57]

Vote totals, which had dropped sharply after the repression of the 1960s and had risen to elect Washington, fell again.[58] By 2000 more than half of all adults (male and female) in Lawndale were in jail, in prison, or on probation or parole, and more than 70 percent of all males had a criminal record.[59] Lawndale had an official unemployment rate of 26 percent. While gentrification is seen as a solution to Lawndale's problems, it is not a solution for the current residents, who are being displaced to make room for an advancing middle class.

As I learned the story of the CVL firsthand and investigated the HAA as well, my more basic analysis in *People and Folks* of the role of deindustrialization and gangs became a bit more complicated. It was not primarily economic factors that transformed the CVL into a drug business. The devastation in Lawndale caused by deindustrialization followed a path to perdition paved by racism.[60] The CVL would follow a third world trajectory of social exclusion, not climb the ethnic succession ladder like the Irish HAA.

To understand why the CVL did not end up like the HAA, racism is an indispensable independent variable. Race, not class, DuBois said, was the fundamental dividing line of the industrial era. This tale supports Michael Omi and Howard Winant's assertion that "we should think of race as an element of social structure rather than as an irregularity within it; we should see race as a dimension of human representation rather than an illusion."[61]

Black and, in a slightly different way, Latino gangs were seen not as successors or rivals to their white Irish counterparts but as the other—something alien and dangerous, threatening white civilization with the heart of darkness. But while this chapter supports Derrick Bell's notion of the permanence of racism, the global era causes us to look at racism in a new light.

As I earlier pointed out, the insecurity and oppressiveness of globalization has meant a return to local, ethnic, and religious identities. These "resistance identities" seek to reclaim meaning, self-determination, and self-respect in an era of the dominance of global corporations and U.S. military hegemony. In ghettos, barrios, and favelas around the world, the dispossessed and their gangs forged cultural responses to the dominant white culture and society. Among those responses were hip-hop and gangsta rap.

chapter 7

Reconsidering Culture:
Race, Rap, and Resistance

You should be thinking about a culture when you say, "hip-hop."

—KRS-ONE

How can anyone understand the outlook of gang members today without exploring the meaning of gangsta rap? Rap is an immensely popular, worldwide cultural genre, its hardcore version sensationalizing the gangster lifestyle. But it has not been a topic considered particularly important by the field of criminology or the study of gangs. The lack of social science analysis of gangsta rap is a consequence of criminology's systemic deracializing of both gangs and culture. It is a good example of what Robin D. G. Kelley means in his blistering critique of the lack of "complexity" in white social science.[1]

This brief chapter argues that culture has assumed a much greater importance in the global era than in the classical sociology of modernity.[2] On the one hand, American mass culture operates as a ubiquitous homogenizing force, with rap becoming the music of choice for youth worldwide as media companies "merchandize the rhymes of violence."[3] On the other hand, rap and hip-hop have also become a contagious culture of rebellion, the precise definition of what Manuel Castells means by "resistance identity." Tricia Rose says:

> Like generations of white teenagers before them, white teenage rap fans are listening in on black culture, fascinated by its differences, drawn in by mainstream social constructions of a black culture as a forbidden narrative, as a symbol of rebellion.[4]

What we are witnessing in hip-hop is the creation of a powerful global identity based on street experiences that are filled with multiple meanings, contradictions, and intense cultural struggle. This "complexity" is not understood by mainstream social science. Those, like Cornel West, who have realized the importance of hip-hop are often cited in a politically correct manner that "race matters," but politely ignored when their philosophic attention turns to hip-hop.[5] Many who write about gangs today remain ignorant of basic facts, even the difference between hip-hop and gangsta rap, and are unaware of the crucial role of gangs in the history of hip-hop culture.

As I discuss in the next chapter, engaging in the ongoing, fierce struggle within hip-hop over the misogyny and "thug life" of gangsta rap may be the single most important contribution we can make to tap the energy of the streets and heal the breach between generations, races, gender, and classes.

Culture and Industrial Age Social Science

The Chicago school sociologists took cultural matters seriously but believed that "culture" mainly referred to the traditions of the old world, which the modern world threatened by the mechanical rhythms of the factory and the anonymity of urban life. The modern era meant the replacement of the chains of culture by the freedom of science,[6] and "American" culture was not at first a central concern. Later, in the major industrial-era studies of gangs, American culture and subcultures were seen as dependent on social structure, as "largely situational," in Ulf Hannerz's terms.[7] For Richard Cloward and Lloyd Ohlin, in their classic work *Delinquency and Opportunity,* "retreatist," "fighting," and "criminal" gang subcultures were "ecologically" derived from different kinds of neighborhood opportunity structures. The typical reader of this classic work might not realize that the violent subculture being described was in fact African American gangs in New York City housing projects and criminal subcultures based on the Mafia in Sicilian or Italian neighborhoods.

A studied deemphasis on race and ethnicity still dominates research on gangs today and gets its theoretical rationale from the social disorganization tradition, currently exemplified by William Julius Wilson and Rob Sampson. For Wilson, culture is basically "a response to social structural restraints and opportunities."[8] In an important article, Sampson and Wilson argue that the culture of the streets is antagonistic to community organization.

The basic thesis is that the macro-social patterns of residential inequality give rise to the social isolation and ecological concentration of the truly disadvantaged, which in turn leads to structural barriers and cultural adaptations that undermine social organization and hence the control of crime. . . . our argument is that *if cultural influences exist, they vary systematically with structural features of the urban environment.*[9]

Culture, in this view, is responsive to variations in social structure; therefore, the attention of policymakers, logically, should focus more on jobs and education, not the "culture" of the poor.[10] Wilson, Sampson, and other social disorganization theorists are arguing against the more conservative view of a "culture of poverty," which posits the existence of a debilitating "underclass" culture that is independent of structural forces. Wilson's work is a stern rebuke to those who argue that the culture of the lower class is self-perpetuating and therefore will not budge even with more opportunities for jobs or education. Wilson also consciously seeks to alter the discourse of social change from race to class, deflecting policymakers from finding the "hidden agenda" behind his "universal solutions."[11]

Within the gang literature, Walter Miller represents the conservative culture of poverty view, arguing that gangs have not changed over the decades, since their behavior is the result of a stable "lower class culture." Gang members' street-oriented outlook is made up of "focal concerns" of "trouble, toughness, smartness, excitement, fate, and autonomy."[12] While in my previous work I have criticized Miller's views by pointing out that the live-for-today cultural traits he ascribes to the lower class are also characteristic of the rich,[13] what should be noted here is that Miller's culture of poverty is deracialized and ethnically neutral. For an anthropologist, Miller's disregard of race and ethnicity is striking.

In Miller's work, as with that of Cloward and Ohlin, Albert Cohen, and other subculturists, ethnicity and race, as well as religion, are virtually absent in explaining how gang members make meaning in their lives. Their "delinquent subcultures" produce meaning through gang members' nonracial, antisocial, and criminal acts. This is, at best, extremely one-sided. Anyone who spends any time on the streets knows that for black, Hispanic, Asian, *and* white gang members, ethnicity and race are crucial aspects of their lives.[14]

Classical criminology of all strains defines the behavior of gang members in terms of their "deficiencies," their broken families or disorganized neighborhoods. While personal, familial, and community problems certainly are influential in understanding gangs, they lead us away from racial oppression and understanding the source of the alienation that is so fundamental to inner-city gangs and their culture.

Some researchers of black communities in the social disorganization tradition do emphasize race and culture. Notably, Elijah Anderson has examined how black street corner men construct a deeply racialized meaning of their lives in Chicago and Philadelphia. I have already highlighted Anderson's view of the "anonymous black male" as America's "other." But Anderson, true to his social disorganization roots, also argues that a "we/they" dichotomy is simplistic, that "the underlying issue is class."[15] Anderson's ethnography, I believe, is shackled by his Chicago school, nonracial, ecological training.

More significant for this chapter, however, are Anderson's views of the "code of the street," which he sees as a "cultural adaptation to a profound lack of faith in the police and judicial system."[16] The core of Anderson's book of the same name revolves around categories of "street and decent."[17] While decent families struggle for respectability, street youth

> sometimes model themselves after successful local drug dealers and rap artists like Tupac Shakur and Snoop Doggy Dogg. . . . Highly alienated and embittered, they exude generalized contempt for the wider scheme of things and for a system they are sure has nothing but contempt for them.[18]

Though Anderson mainly seeks to explain how cultural street codes lead to violence, his "lack of faith" is closely related to West's thoughts on nihilism within the black community. Anderson sensibly explains the code as being rooted in a history of masculinity that has a tragic echo in today's truly disadvantaged black neighborhoods.

> The code is not new. It is as old as the world, going back to Roman times or the world of the shogun warriors or the early American Old South. . . . But profound economic dislocations and the simultaneous emergence of the underground economy that thrives on the "law of the jungle" implicit in the code have exacerbated conditions in many communities.[19]

Anderson's powerful portraits stretch the limits of modernist social theory by simultaneously elevating a racialized outlook while also "explaining" it as mainly an adaptation to the new deindustrialized world. The "code of the streets," Anderson implies, will change as economic conditions improve. While this is hard to contest, the more important point is to understand how people react and make meaning when their life chances do *not* improve. This is one meaning of the permanence of racism.

The insight that street culture reproduces the social relations of society has been convincingly portrayed by Philippe Bourgois, Lisa Maher, and Kathleen Daly, as well as Jay MacLeod, who consciously follows in Paul Willis's footsteps.[20] But street culture, as these scholars are aware, is not just reproduction but also resistance, and it is those forms of resistance that merit more investigation.

The global era, I have sought to show, has resulted in economic and social polarization in much of the world. Along with the global reach of the mass media, neoliberal policies have spawned cultural opposition, with religious, racial, and ethnic identities becoming the main source of meaning for literally billions of people. To better understand the racialized culture of the street, and the centrality of hip-hop to it, I need to briefly revisit the theories of Manuel Castells and his mentor, Alain Touraine, before "droppin' science" on the stage of hip-hop culture.[21]

THE DISSOCIATION OF CULTURE AND SOCIAL STRUCTURE

The concept of the dissociation of culture and social structure is simple to understand but has explosive consequences for social theory. What Castells and Touraine mean is that the world today is fundamentally torn by the battle between unfettered markets and local, religious, ethnic, and racial identities. The class struggles of the industrial era, though still very real, no longer describe the most serious and important conflicts in the world, which revolve around religion, race, and ethnicity—in a word, identity. Touraine explains the fundamental contradiction of this new era:

> Whilst the law of the market is crushing societies, cultures, social movements, and the obsession with identity is trapping them into a political arbitrariness which is so complete that only repression and fanaticism can sustain it.[22]

That elites manipulate some of these conflicts does not make them less real or destructive.[23] Our "unitary" civilization is decaying, and what is being assaulted with even more vehemence in the era of globalization is the ability of social actors, other than the cosmopolitan global elite, to make society rational, that is, to produce actual social change for the less advantaged.[24] This depoliticizes the many and creates dangers for both the global elite and the poor.

> The poorest define themselves in terms of a religion; the richest by appealing to a reason, which is, they believe, exclusively theirs. . . . On the one hand, the liberal call for an open society easily becomes cultural imperialism. On the other, the appeal to identity produces dangerous moral majorities and still more dangerous national fronts.[25]

There is a profound and reasonable cynicism among the vast majority of the world's people about their inability to produce social change, whether through elections or revolution. "With no Winter Palace to be seized," Castells says, "outbursts of revolt may implode, transformed into everyday, senseless violence."[26] Among the most excluded, like the African American underclass, their resulting no-exit-in-sight nihilism becomes a "culture of urgency." Like Touraine, Castells fears the violence and bigotry implicit in the power of identity, which necessarily means defining one's self or group in opposition to an other. The potentially fearsome consequences of the fanaticism of identity parallels the self-destructiveness of street culture in Bourgois's work.[27]

Castells, however, goes beyond Touraine's dark analysis and social reproduction theory and argues that it is the very creation of resistance identity that can also replace outdated industrial-era socialist or liberal ideals with new hope, what he calls a "project identity.[28] Arjun Appadurai, in the same vein, defines culture as "the mobilization of group identities."[29] Similarly, bell hooks suggests,

> It's exciting to think, write, talk about, and create art that reflects passionate engagement with popular culture, because this may very well be "the" central future location of resistance struggle, a meeting place where new and radical happenings can occur.[30]

While the industrial era was marked by the ability of humanity, with its machines and its culture, to subdue nature, the information age creates the possibilities of a culture that can have the power to transform humanity, by asserting the self-worth and dignity of people and social movements in the face of, and in spite of, an all-powerful technology. Touraine explains, "Industrial society had transformed the means of production; postindustrial society transforms the ends of production, that is, culture."[31]

The shift to an information society is more than the replacement of one set of elites by another. "In the richest countries," Touraine explains, "youth culture, the messages of the media, and the attractions of mass consumption mean that social demands are now expressed in nonpolitical ways."[32] Those with power are those who define the cultural models that are propagated worldwide through the ubiquitous mass media. Castells's "resistance identities" are the desire for nonsocial relations in an overflowing sea of information, whether in the form of propaganda, advertising, or Web sites in the millions. The construction of these identities is a life preserver to save people from drowning in a flood of information. The danger is that the power of identity can retreat, as Touraine, Castells, and hooks fear, into a bigoted world of racism, essentialist nationalism, and misogyny, or else lead to a surrender to consumerism that only reproduces existing relations of power. These are the precise contradictions that divide and define hip-hop culture.

chapter 8

Street Wars: Hip-Hop and the Rise of Gangsta Culture

When we made Hip Hop, we made it hoping it would be about peace, love, unity and having fun so that people could get away from the negativity that was plaguing our streets (gang violence, drug abuse, self hate, violence among those of African and Latino descent).

—AFRIKA BAMBAATAA, http://www.zulunation.com/hip_hop_history_2.htm

Hip-hop today is torn by a searing "culture war" between two different resistance identities: a defiant but life-affirming "black Atlantic hip-hop" and the consumer-oriented "corporate hip-hop" that now controls gangsta rap. This chapter seeks to understand the contradictions within hip-hop and how they shape, and are shaped by, the multiple conflicting identities of gang members.[1]

Rather than locate a "gang subculture" in different kinds of neighborhood "opportunity structures," or as an epiphenomenon of larger, more "fundamental" structural forces, this chapter argues that hip-hop is a central way for gang members and other young people (and some not so young) to make meaning out of their lives. Consistent with my argument in the last chapter, I see culture as reflecting and reproducing structural conditions, but also rising above them as a powerful, independent force in its own right. In other words, culture is responsive, but also transformative. It is reproductive, but also productive.

In the face of desperate ghetto conditions and the permanence of racism, some claim that "hip hop has become the primary vehicle for transmitting culture and values to this generation, relegating black families, community centers, churches, and schools to the back burner."[2] While this may be an overstatement, in many ways the key to understanding gangs is to "get" their music: where it came from, what it represents, why they like it, and what potential it can tap.[3]

GANGS AND HIP-HOP: A BRIEF HISTORY

Hip-hop is a worldwide street culture and consists of four elements: MCing (or rapping), DJing (spinning and scratching records), breakdancing, and graffiti art.[4] Some say that "Rappers Delight," a 1979 song by the Sugar Hill Gang, is the source of the term *hip-hop:* the song begins with the lyrics "da hip da hop, da hippity da hip hip hop and you don't stop." Others say Lovebug Starski coined the term much earlier.[5] Gangsta rap is a subgenre of hip-hop, and while it is a hyperbolic representation of street culture, it is also a big moneymaker for media conglomerates like Time Warner.

Hip-hop had its immediate origins in the music, dance, and art of African American and Latino youth in the South Bronx in the early 1970s. As a musical form, it is notable that it came from the streets, not the studios. Like the "devil's music" of the blues,[6] it is not based in middle-class experience but in an expression of the dispossessed's misery and defiance of racism and poverty.[7] The South Bronx of the seventies was the perfect environment for the rise of hip-hop. Some 170,000 black and Latino peoples had been dislocated because of Robert Moses's Cross-Bronx Expressway and other "urban development" projects.[8] Communities were shattered and left leaderless. Arson cleared out whole areas, making the South Bronx look like it had been bombed. The area became the symbol of the desolation and poverty of blacks and Puerto Ricans in the United States.

In Chicago and Los Angeles, similar situations of turmoil produced powerful gangs that became entrenched in their communities. New York City too had well-known gangs, and many more of them at the time than Chicago or Los Angeles. If ever an opportunity existed that would allow gangs to persist and become major forces in their communities, it would have been the South Bronx in the 1970s. Yet, unlike Chicago and LA, older gangs in the Bronx faded, with the inevitable new, younger ones taking their place. Why?

In chapter 1 I alluded to the reasons: New York City under John Lindsay did not declare war on gangs, as did Richard J. Daley in Chicago and Samuel Yorty in LA, but attempted to reach out to the ghettos. The importance of Lindsay's modest social opportunities policy may not have been what it did but what it did *not* do—try to suppress gangs by large-scale incarceration. Rather than prison aiding the institutionalization of gangs and assisting them to become the center of youthful rebellion, the streets hosted a new musical form.

The key figure is not Lindsay, however, but Afrika Bambaataa, the "godfather of hip-hop." As one of the first MCs, his vision for hip-hop has remained one pole of an intense cultural struggle among youth today. Bambaataa, whose given name is Kevin Donovan, was a "warlord" in the Bronx River Project division of the Black Spades, one of that area's largest, most-feared street gangs. Unlike Bobby Gore, a Chicago singer (the Clevertones) and leader of the Vice Lords, Bambaataa was not targeted for arrest and prison. Instead he left the gang and turned his talents to use music to lure kids from the violent life of the streets.

Bambaataa was enthralled with all types of musical styles and seized on and popularized the rapping of street youth, the scratching of records, and roles of DJ and MC at street parties. His music joined with other innovators, like Kool Herc, a transplanted Jamaican who introduced the Trenchtown system of setting up large speakers on street corners, turning South Bronx neighborhoods into raucous block parties.

Bambaataa early on saw that music and the not-yet-named hip-hop had the potential to pull kids from the self-hatred and destructive behavior that is an all-too-common response to poverty and racism. "At some point he started to believe," S. Craig Watkins says in his incisive *Hip Hop Matters,* "that the energy, loyalty, and passion that defined gang life could be guided toward more socially productive activities."[9] Bambaataa went on to found a performing group called The Organization, then later formed the Zulu Nation, a remarkable collective of New York artists that included Queen Latifah and LL Cool J.

Hip-hop emerged, Tricia Rose eloquently points out,

> from the deindustrialization meltdown where social alienation, prophetic imagination, and yearning intersect. Hip hop is a cultural form that attempts to negotiate the experiences of marginalization, brutally truncated opportunity, and oppression within the cultural imperatives of African-American and Caribbean history, identity, and community.[10]

Hip-hop would have many facets, but was essentially created as an oppositional form of identity, reflecting Bronx youth's collective struggle for self-recognition and meaning in bleak surroundings. "Alternative local identities were forged in fashion and language, street names, and most important, in establishing neighborhood crews or posses."[11]

In other words, rather than the identity of gang member, what took the South Bronx by storm was a racialized, oppositional identity based in culture. Watkins explains that Afrika Bambaataa professed, "Hip hop's real power and true significance resides in its capacity to empower young people to change their lives."[12] Cornel West sums up the essence of hip-hop culture:

> The basic aims of hip-hop music are threefold—to provide playful entertainment and serious art for the rituals of young people, to forge new ways of escaping social misery, and to explore novel responses for meaning and feeling in a market-driven world.[13]

To be sure, hip-hop did not spring like a rapping Minerva from the head of Afrika Bambaataa. While some want to define hip-hop as "authentic" black culture, in reality hip-hop is a marvelous hybrid, a merger of earlier blues, the West African griot, or call and response and emphasis on drumming, the Afro-Brazilian martial arts dance capoeira, and the Jamaican toasting tradition, as well as the African American celebration of male outlaws like "Stagger Lee."[14] Puerto Rican and other Latino influences were present in New York in the early years, and Mexican influences helped shape West Coast rap.[15] West African and Jamaican music, among others, make hip-hop essentially a "black Atlantic" culture, to extend an idea from Paul Gilroy's seminal work.[16]

Borrowing heavily from W. E. B. DuBois's concept of "double consciousness," Gilroy points out that "black culture"—like hip-hop—derives from many African, Caribbean, and European influences. The diversity of this culture is, in fact, its strength, speaking in many different voices and with many different messages. The postmodern deconstruction of "authentic," essentialist identities has a paradigmatic example in the amazing global pastiche of hip-hop. The struggle over these contradictory tendencies and various identities, I argue, is of central importance for the future of our youth.

THE TWO FACES OF GANGSTA RAP

Gangsta rap has always been a powerful voice as one kind of hardcore rap.[17] Gangsta rap has been popular, in essence, because it expresses the rage of the gang member in the ghetto and his defiance of the white man's system, particularly the police. This black rage has always found a cultural outlet, in music with the blues, and in the angry, passionate writings of Richard Wright, James Baldwin, Toni Morrison, and many others. For example, Eldridge Cleaver, the former convict and Black Panther, shocked many with *Soul on Ice* by writing that the rape of white women was "an insurrectionary act . . . defying and trampling on the white man's law."[18]

What is often missed in the numerous denunciations of Cleaver's quite real ideas of male supremacy is his self-reflection over this rage on the book's very next page. There Cleaver says that he could not "approve the act of rape," that his actions as a rapist cost him his "self-respect." The man, Cleaver, vowed to give his rage a cultural solution: "That is why I started to write. To save myself." This became Cleaver's way of reacting to nihilism. Similarly, the "rage" that comes from recognition of "the permanence of racism" sets both the emotional and creative conditions for the emergence of the cultural response of gangsta rap.

The popularity of gangsta rap comes from its ironic and defiant nature, its hardcore beats, and its very negativity in a world that appears unchangeable. At times, Ice Cube says, "there is no message, just reality." Ice-T adds: "This music isn't supposed to be positive. It's supposed to be negative, because the streets are negative." Ice Cube argues that gangsta rap is hated because it is telling the truth about the ghetto, not sugarcoating racism and poverty. "We tell kids the truth. . . . The world is an ugly place."[19]

Pious condemnations of "gangsta rap" by notables like Bob Dole or Bill Clinton ring hollow when these same politicians shamelessly accept millions in campaign contributions from the movie stars of Hollywood, America's first and foremost evil empire of sex and violence. Many denunciations of the influence of rap on young people are humorless, missing its irony and how rappers poke fun at white America. How else are we to understand Tupac Shakur's hilarious taunt that listening to him is like watching "OJ All-Day. Picture me 'Rollin!'"? Or enjoy any video from the aptly named "Ludacris."

Robin D. G. Kelley tries to counter the moral majority tide by pointing to rap's cultural nature: "Lest we get too sociological here, we must bear in mind that hip hop, irrespective of its particular flavor, is music."[20]

The power of gangsta rap to thrill black youth is why important, street-smart black religious figures like Louis Farrakhan have come to its defense and worked directly with rappers to organize gang truces and stop the violence. Gangsta rap is the power of negativity to keep on living in the awareness of ghetto conditions that are unlikely to be improved by government, business, or liberal whites. It is a "form of 'testimony' for the underclass" and its gangs.[21] Like the blues, its style and message can "stare painful truths in the face and persevere without cynicism or pessimism."[22]

But that said, gangsta rap is more than words of rebellion. In the early nineties, rap's east coast and west coast represented ganglike enemies and a feud that would cost hip-hop some its most talented stars, such as Tupac and the Notorious B.I.G. Those wars were real and lethal, but also a grim reflection of the music industry's amoral capacity to exploit even murder for profit.

Keith Clinkscales, in 1997 the CEO of *Vibe,* a prominent hip-hop magazine, said that the "marketing of evil" is a "double-edged sword." "Murder," Clinkscales argued, apparently without irony, "is not good for business." While Clinkscales personally cannot "condone some of the nihilism and misogynistic elements," hip-hop artists, he says, "should have the opportunity to have their work judged by the market."[23] The sound you hear is not "hip, hippity, hop" but "ka-ching."

CORPORATE HIP-HOP

It was the revolution in information technology that transformed the music business and led to the "discovery" of rap. *Billboard,* the music magazine, had traditionally provided ratings of the popularity of songs for the industry. These ratings were based on the sampling of opinions of music store owners. In 1991 the music industry switched over to a computerized count of sales, called SoundScan, and the results shocked insiders and outsiders alike. Rap music was incredibly popular, based on actual sales, and a giant market waiting to be devoured.[24] SoundScan reported that N.W.A.'s classic, *Niggaz 4 Life,* sold 900,000 copies in the first week it was out, and Dr. Dre's *Chronic* sold a previously unheard-of 3 million copies.[25] "Look at the top of the SoundScan," said Ice Cube in 1996. "All the top SoundScans are actually hardcore rap."[26]

A potential white clientele for black artists had been exploited before by music companies. Michael Jackson's 1983 "Thriller" music video had massive crossover appeal. "Yo! MTV Raps" was introduced in 1989, with impressive ratings among blacks and whites. Already by 1991 it was reported that suburban whites then made up the largest customer base for rap music.[27] When the SoundScan numbers went through the roof, you could almost see music industry moguls wiping the drool off their wide-eyed, money-hungry faces.[28]

What they bought and packaged was the hardcore beats of gangsta rap, to which they added the most stereotyped messages, aimed to appeal to white consumers who wanted to vicariously experience a fantasized, exotic ghetto life. The more violence and sex the better, following Hollywood's tried-and-true formula. Artists were pressured to add more "authentic" street violence to their lyrics and to look the part of the gangster, flanked in their videos with scantily clad sex objects. "Everywhere I go," Tupac deadpans, "I see the same 'ho.'"

Entrepreneurs like Death Row Records' Suge Knight saw the dollar signs in the crossover appeal of gangsta rap. Suge's real genius was in "shaping street culture for consumption by the youth of America."[29] In big music companies a devotion to sex and violence almost ruled out other forms of hip-hop. KRS-One reflects on his experience working at Time Warner: "They wanted artists who basically thugged it out and pimped it out and it was a disappointment."[30] The rap mogul Russell Simmons puts it bluntly: "I don't like the trend toward so many gangster records in rap, but I am an art dealer and that's what is selling now."[31] Gangsta rap today has become an almost wholly owned subsidiary of *corporate* hip-hop. "To white dominated mass media," bell hooks adds, "the controversy over gangsta rap makes great spectacle."[32] Mike Davis hits it on the head: "Hollywood is eager to mine Los Angeles' barrios and ghettoes for every last lurid image of self-destruction and community holocaust."[33]

Pushing gangsta rap on the air might help explain its popularity among fantasizing white teens, but the rhymes of violence indisputably resonate with, and derive from, the street. The SoundScan database came out in 1991 just as the crack wars were at their most intense. Tupac's "To Live and Die in LA" was a creative expression of street-level reality. Homicide rates in U.S. cities reached record highs as gangs competed for drug markets and for the chance to "get rich or die trying," striving to turn their daily nightmares into the American Dream. "By the summer of 1993," Kelley says, "gangsta rap had been reduced to 'nihilism for nihilism's sake.'"[34]

This harrowing experience of a life lived close to death shaped a street-based "gangsta" identity. "I never sleep," Nas raps, "cause sleep is the cousin of death." As Kelley writes:

> The criminalization, surveillance, incarceration, and poverty of black youth in the postindustrial city have been the central themes in gangsta rap and thus constitute the primary experiences from which cultural identities are constructed. . . . a new "ghettocentric" identity in which the specific class, race, and gendered experiences in late-capitalist urban centres coalesce to create a new identity—"Nigga."[35]

I was doing research in Milwaukee in 1991 with a staff of former gang members as community researchers to chart what happened to the gangs I had studied in the first edition of *People and Folks*.[36] The sounds of our office were racked with N.W.A. on the boom box, and we cruised the city listening brazenly with open windows to N.W.A.'s "Fuck tha Police." The guys laughed at the misogynist tales in cuts such as "Just Don't Bite It," claiming, and almost convincing themselves, that N.W.A.'s raps were what life in the crack house was *really* like. The all-time-high murder totals in Milwaukee were reflected in the violent gangsta rap music my staff loved to play. I watched my "gangster" staff emulating the "gangsta" or "nigga" identities performed by N.W.A.

On the one hand, gangsta rap's booming popularity, constant play, and erotic, money-worshiping music videos reinforce racist stereotypes among whites. On the other hand, these stereotypes also have had an influence on gang members themselves. This new, studio-produced gangsta or nigga identity now influences how actual gang members, and other youth, see themselves: life imitating art imitating life in a manner that would make Jean Baudrillard proud.[37] The internalization of the gangsta identity, defined crudely by the twisted imagination of white record company executives, is one of the most pernicious consequences of the rise of rap music worldwide.[38]

Hip-Hop's Challenge to the Gangsta

But while the record companies were exploiting the violence for their own profits, there were also intense reactions within the hip-hop community.

Hip-hop began as a life-affirming street culture, and the music industry was systematically turning it into an updated minstrel show, with no black-face needed. As Afrika Bambaataa disdainfully said, some gangsta rappers "need a check up from the neck up."[39]

The struggle against hip-hop's corporate, exoticizing tendencies was well known on the streets if not among criminologists. Hip-hop had civil rights–era predecessors in the Last Poets, a group of militant rappers founded after the murder of Dr. Martin Luther King Jr. The great Gil Scott-Heron struggled mightily against the depoliticization of the black community in the 1970s, calling for a renewed commitment to struggle in his famous rap "The Revolution Will Not Be Televised." Already in 1984, KRS-One, a major player in hip-hop history, had taken to the air with a passionate plea: "If you wanna get to the tip top, stop the violence in hip hop." Rap, for KRS-One, was "rebellious music not gangster music."[40]

In fact it was both, and the struggle against the glorification of the gangsta identity continued full force with such brilliant performers as Public Enemy, who scored with their "Burn Hollywood Burn," "Fight the Power," and other hot cuts. Tupac's career displays both sides of this dialectic, the "thug life" and the community activist, with Tupac's roots going back to his famous Black Panther mother, Afeni Shakur.[41] In the last few years, a reaction to the west coast/east coast gangsta beats has taken center stage, with a south-ern, more house party sound from artists such as Juvenile, Outkast, Arrested Development, and, of course, Missy Elliott.

What is crucial is the struggle to define an identity, one that is "oppo-sitional and liberatory" but does not go over the poetic cliff into nihilistic despair and self-destruction.[42] West comments, "One way of understand-ing the sub-genre of gangsta rap is as an extreme, exaggerated, metaphoric form of the struggle for recognition."[43]

What mainstream social science and the public alike lose sight of is that the culture of hip-hop has spawned multiple conflicting identities and divided loyalties, in a manner succinctly defined by hooks and, on a more general level, Craig Calhoun.[44] Some of these identities are merely dressed-up versions of an All-American, "keep your mind on your money and your money on your mind" culture. The seduction of gangsta rap by the big bucks of the music companies has stripped the authenticity of the streets from much of it, and if gangsta rap began as tragedy, it too often reigns as farce. Oppositional identities of thug, pimp, revolutionary, drug dealer, party girl, or playboy are put on stage as a bald and often ironic challenge to mainstream culture.

It is also a reality that rapping today is a way to "get paid," a way to find work and make money in the ghetto. The road to success of a rapper does not necessarily depend on education, rich investors, or connected friends. Rap has become a widely practiced form of the informal economy, a potential bridge to a hoped-for music contract. Being a rapper can be a career alternative to drug dealing. Rappers are today's Horatio Algers, "pulling themselves up by their own bootstraps" or, in this case, microphones. While the big music companies demand conformity as the price of success, a booming digital underground also exists where rappers perform and compete and develop their art.

What in fact has been going on in hip-hop culture since its creation is a vivid, no-holds-barred struggle between a host of different identities, some destructive, some liberatory, some playful, but nearly all defiant and much loved by the world's youth. This kind of struggle is inherent in any living culture and, I think, needs to be joined by those who wish to seriously combat the influence of the gangster lifestyle. I explore this further by looking first at gangsta rap's infamous misogyny and then at hip-hop around the world and its central importance for gangs.

WHO'S A TRAMP?

Salt-N-Pepa, an early female hip-hop trio, in a lively, fun-loving rap, turns the label of "tramp" on its head.

> So I dissed him, I said you's a sucker, get your dirty mind out the gutter. . . .
> Then I walked away, he called me a tease, you're on a mission, kid, yo *he's*
> a . . . tramp.[45]

The misogyny of gangsta rap has always been contested by many female rappers, as well as some men.[46] That protest is part of a centuries-long struggle by black women against patriarchal attitudes. As Nancy Guevara says,

> The undermining, deletion, or derogatory stereotyping of women's creative role in the development of minority cultures is a routine practice that serves to impede any progressive artistic or social development by women that might threaten male hegemony in the sphere of cultural production.[47]

While many male rappers dismiss the misogyny of their lyrics as "just words," these words, like the rhymes of violence, have a consequence for the identities of male and female alike.

The deindustrialization that has devastated poor minority communities has had a predictable effect on male notions of identity. Loss of even the capacity to play the role of breadwinner has reinforced historic feelings of powerlessness for black men and has led to exaggerated, defensive notions of masculinity. But the new urban conditions also have impacted young girls,[48] and both genders, in and out of gangs, have been heavily influenced by gangsta rap and consumer culture.

As hip-hop has matured, female performers have gotten more play and display nearly the same range of identities as males, both liberatory and self-destructive. Lil' Kim, for instance, as I write, has just been released from prison for lying in court in the trial of another rapper. Kim's sexualized raps and videos have her spitting out lines like these from "Get Yours":

> Sayin that you rich and all, tell me what'chu bitchin for
> Maybe cause I'm gettin mine—well is you gettin yours?

Just as female gang members take on different identities and roles, some more independent, others strongly dependent on males, female rappers span the range of identities of bitch, goddess, street fighter, killer, strong woman, and sex object. As Elliott told an interviewer,

> But I can say that um, women in the Hip Hop field is gettin' more respect now. We're able to say what the guys use to say or what they say now 'cause at first we couldn't do that, but now it's like we're more open and we are more respected now in the business then we were like 10–12 years ago when people like Latifah and Monie was out you know. So I think we starting to get a lot more respect. As females now and being able to just voice our opinion on how we feel about certain subjects.[49]

Female rappers, as well as males, turn to religious, ethnic, and racialized identities to resist urban conditions and mainstream culture. Quite naturally, females as well as males feel pride in their religion, race, or ethnic group. However, the sexism of men complicates female identity. Iris Rivera, a Puerto Rican graduate student doing her thesis on female identity and hip-hop, says of her own experience:

As an adolescent I listened to the "old school" style of hip hop, and during the early nineties I was immersed in the "new school" culture, often times buying and listening to misogynist music because of its ethnic beat and my identification with lyrics that denounced police brutality, systematic racism, and promoted the plight of the "ghetto blues."[50]

Rivera captures the contradiction between self-respect as a woman and the need to identify with her own, oppressed group. Joan Moore looks at Muslim gang girls in Europe who face a similar dilemma, of rebelling against traditional, patriarchal norms while strongly opposing the discrimination faced by Islam.[51] Mary Devitt and I tried to capture this internalized conflict with the notion of "fighting female": Milwaukee gang girls loved to fight but many rejected traditional female roles, asserting their independence from men who saw them only as "pillow queens."[52] The identities of gangsta rap both reflect and inform the identities on the street of female as well as male gang members.

For males, as a response to marginalization, gangsta rap is used to construct the "warrior" role, as for example Ice-T's in sending his "message to the soldiers, welcome to the struggle!" In this worldview women become either the protected or the seductive, but always an object, not a subject. This sexist notion has its roots in the history of the denial of legitimate work to black men and their corresponding feelings of loss of self-worth. "Every day black males face a culture that tells them that they can never really achieve enough money or power to set them free from racist white tyranny in the work world."[53]

The legacy of slavery and the burden of racism are magnified by American consumer culture that demoralizes men and women of every race who are not "masters of the universe." The glamorizing of gangsta rap—which includes the absurd, off-camera return to insurance agents of rented gold chains by rappers after shooting their music videos—has created an enormous industry of hip-hop consumption.

The well-dressed hip-hop consumer needs to understand the etiquettes and cues to proper dress and behavior, and spend the big bucks to acquire the name brands. This affects women as well as men, but the framing of fashion for women reinforces their role as sexual object. Old school rappers like Salt-N-Pepa, Lauryn Hill, and Queen Latifah spin out counternarratives, and Elliott and the new wave of female rap superstars cast an independent image that is both imposing and erotic.[54] But the MTV master image remains women as "bitches and ho's," high-heeled, scantily clad, big-breasted babes, shaking their "booties" in a "tip drill" for the guys.

Just as gangsta rap glamorizes ghetto violence, misogyny is also an all-too-real aspect of life on the streets. Lisa Maher explains, "Hierarchies within the drug economy serve to reproduce the gender, race, and class relations" of mainstream society, where women occupy menial and sexualized places.[55] While female gang members rebel and stand on their own, women in gangs, as in mainstream society, are dependent on males and are sexualized, objectified, and exploited. Women, including female gang members, are much less violent than media claims or their BET image.[56] However, music video female violence, reflecting the Hollywood success of tough-as-men but-still-sexy icons like Lara Croft or GI Jane, is basically a new, marketable twist to traditional male fantasies like 50 Cent's "Candy Shops."

Today the identity of the "pimp" has become a corporate hip-hop synonym for the stereotyped black male. The best example is 2006 Academy Award winner Three 6 Mafia's "It's Hard Out There for a Pimp."

> Man it seems like I'm duckin dodgin' bullets everyday. . . . But I gotta stay paid, gotta stay above water. . . . Couldn't keep up with my hoes, that's when shit got harder.

Pimp raps like these promote crude stereotypes of ghetto life and cover over a profoundly misogynist message in their catchy beats. Anyone, like me, who has had the unsettling experience of not being able to stop humming 50 Cent and Snoop's hypnotic but disgusting rap "P.I.M.P." can understand the problem.

Finally there is corporate hip-hop superstar Kanye West, who went platinum with his stereotype of the "gold digger." On the streets, gold diggers are a problem for unemployed males only in their wildest dreams, but millionaire West probably does speak from his own "diamonds-are-forever" experience. Corporate hip-hop, in its treatment of violence, money, and women, is in essence an unholy blend of ghetto fantasyland and suburban stereotype. It reinforces the worst caricatures of gang members among the white public and then glamorizes them to the ghettos and barrios.

One countertrend within hip-hop is exemplified by Muslim influence, with Public Enemy, Rakim, and others reflecting strong, conservative cultural sentiments. Maulana Rod Karenga, a powerful 1960s voice of cultural nation-alism, similarly expresses an anticonsumer, Afrocentric critique.

> Finally, we must *realize* and *resist* the continuing attempt of the corporate world to benefit from the tragedy and creativity of rap. Early it discovered that it could sell racist stereotypes for a profitable price, seduce infantile mil-lionaires into savaging themselves and their community under the concern for artistic and personal freedom and it will not miss the opportunity to in-crease its sales by turning communal and private pain into a profitable pub-lic spectacle. It will certainly convince young people and old that buying the records of one who has passed (Tupac) is the most appropriate and conve-nient way to honor the dead regardless of the problems posed for the living. After all, in a consumer society we are taught that buying is the way we can cure all ills from frustration and headache and other pain to ongoing oppres-sion. But again, the oppressor cannot be our teacher and ours is the future that we dare conceive and struggle to bring into being.[57]

While there is widespread resistance among male and female rappers, Muslims and other religious leaders, and much of the public to the gang-ster and "pimp and ho" images, this resistance has little chance of changing corporate hip-hop. As in the rest of Hollywood, sexualized images of women are the norm, and racist stereotypes of the "super fly" black male still abound. Indeed, I join with hooks in believing that substantial progress in the cre-ation of any "liberatory" identities is possible only if the fight against racist stereotypes is joined to the fight against misogyny in both rap music and mainstream U.S. culture.[58]

A WORLD OF HIP-HOP

Any serious investigation or even Google search into hip-hop's reach will quickly reveal that it is a worldwide cultural phenomenon. The 2005 World Hip-Hop Summit in Africa sponsored the "Messengers of Truth" project, which

> is about empowering disenfranchised girls and boys living in slums by giving them a chance to voice their views and opinions on decisions affecting their livelihoods and by facilitating their access to skills training, job opportunities, information and means of communication.[59]

In an interview with Michael Eric Dyson, Toni Morrison many years earlier argued

that what unifies hip-hop throughout the world is its emergence from "the others" within the empire: for instance the Turks in Germany and the Algerians and North Africans in France—who bring profound changes in the nation's discourse.[60]

Gangsta rap, though, is not the only musical style that emulates and idolizes defiant gang dealers. In Mexico, the *corrido,* or a style of folk songs, is one of the most popular forms of music. The "narcocorrido" is the Mexican form of gangsta rap, glorifying drug smugglers who risk all for money and fame and snub the Yanquis to boot. Chalino Sánchez and other singers appear on album covers replete with menacing guns and cowboy hats. Even Mayan gangs or *pandillas* in San Cristóbal happily rap out the latest cuts.[61]

In Sierra Leone, as in most African countries, American gangsta rap fills the airways, and youth gangs take the names of Crips, Bloods, X-Clan, and Niggas with Attitude (N.W.A.).[62] But in Sierra Leone, Ibrahim Abdullah writes, these Western influences are combined with an indigenous music called the *milo,* which originated in the 1940s among *rarri* boys. The *milo* was a form of music among the very poor, not a musical genre of the more educated. Like gangsta rap, "*milo* music did not carry any social message about their conditions in society. The lyrics dealt with the vulgar and the profane."[63]

Rap music rocks around Africa, Latin America, Asia, and Europe as well. In Brazil, a distinctive Brazilian rap is the most popular music in the favelas. The sound of machine guns and themes of shoot-outs with police reflect a violent reality. Members of the rap group Filosofia Gangsta say they perform gangsta rap

not because of the message per se but due to the form in which the messages are conveyed, the aggressive style. We use this label as a style of identification. We preach gangsterism against the horrible things that happen in the ghetto.[64]

When I was in Vigário Geral, the popular Grupo Cultural Afro Reggae ran a cultural program in a neighborhood center. A group of local youth performed a variety of art forms for us, such as drumming and dancing, and gave a musical lesson on AIDS education. In the tradition of Afrika Bambaataa, the Grupo saw culture as a way to pull kids away from the drug factions. As in the United States, street culture may express violent realities, but it is mainly constructing an oppositional identity, one that can refuse to give in to despair. In São Paulo, it is estimated there are at least thirty thousand rap groups that call themselves "gangstas" or "posses."[65]

South Africa is also a hotbed for rap music, which has long been intertwined with politics, as well as the musical dance form Kwaito.[66] One rapper, Devious, comments, in words that echo Ice Cube and Ice-T:

> I am a strong believer in the truth and therefore I don't beat around the bush when it comes to exposing it. I also believe in telling it like it is. "No sugar coated fairy tales." Strictly undiluted realness. When I say real, I mean real people, real situations and real emotions. I feel it's important to write about our reality. As it is important for you to acknowledge it.[67]

Zubz, MC of the Origins Band, explains his take on the universal appeal of hip-hop:

> I don't believe in local hip hop. I think the term needs to be re-visited. I believe in South African hip hop. Zimbabwean hip hop. African hip hop. I believe in the spirit of the music. It's soul. There's no such thing as a "local" soul. I hate the debate that rages on between "local" and "American." It's based on arguments based on little to do with the music, or art form, or culture, but on personal agendas aimed at propagating subjective opinion.[68]

African rappers understand the meaning of black Atlantic culture, since a major influence on American rap was the West African griot. Senegal's Daara J's hot release "Boomrang" expresses this history. The group's MC, Faada Freddy, says

> Hip-hop was born in Africa [and] went around the world to come back to Africa, like a boomerang that has been thrown from the motherland and is back home, . . . The first time we heard Grandmaster Flash rapping on a hip-hop track, everybody was like, "OK, we know this because this is tasso [the rhythmic oral history in Senegal]."[69]

France was the first European country where hip-hop made it big, mainly with youthful, dark-skinned immigrants from the Maghreb living in high-rises in *banlieues*. In 1984 the first TV show "Hip Hop" picked up the raps of the earlier "free radio" movement, and hip-hop's mesmerizing beats spread from there to the rest of Europe.[70]

In the barrios of New York and Miami as well as in San Juan, Reggaeton is a blend of Jamaican music with strains of reggae, dancehall, and hip-hop. Reggaeton, originated by the "philosopher," the Puerto Rican rapper Vico C, is another example of the power of black Atlantic culture, created as a true voice of Latino and Caribbean youth, not just a "Latino hip-hop." Native forms of hip-hop from New Zealand to Chile to the *banlieues* of Paris embrace rap for the same reasons as American youth, as a resistance identity.

A final example, Palestine, points out the potential of hip-hop as a culture of liberation. "Rap is our way of resisting occupation," Nadir Abu Ayash tells Al Jazeera. He raps:

Do you remember, or do you choose to forget
that your army, against us, aggressed
my voice will continue to echo, you'll never forget
You call me terrorist when I'm the one who's oppressed.[71]

Jackie Salloum, a filmmaker whose Web site, http://www.slingshot.com/, is filled with video and information on Palestinian rap, says youthful performers in Gaza and the West Bank "throw rhymes like others throw rockets." Similar sentiments can be found on http://www.arabrap.net, with the popular group DAM. There are also instances of Palestinian and Israeli rap groups performing together, though there is also a right-wing Israeli rapper, Subliminal, with his jeweled Star of David necklace, spinning nationalist, Zionist imagery.

The list could go on, from Maoris in New Zealand to youth in Greenland and Japan, but the main point is that hip-hop is a worldwide resistance identity, though not the same one for everyone. It can be destructive, narrowly nationalist, fun-loving, bigoted, misogynist, or revolutionary. Rather than locate meaning for gang members in a narrow "delinquent subculture," I have chosen to look at how a broader youth culture has been influenced by gang life and, in turn, shapes meaning in the lives of gang members on the street.

Gangsta Rap and Religious Fundamentalism

One way to better understand gangsta rap's worldwide appeal and potential is to compare it with fundamentalist religion. Both rap and fundamentalism provide a deep and rich cultural meaning to their adherents. That cultural meaning for both consists of the creation of an identity that is at odds with the secular, civic identities of mainstream modern society. The gangsta and fundamentalist identities are primary for many of the people involved and strongly related to their racial or ethnic origins. These identities are relied on, as Castells says, to "shrink an uncertain world into a manageable size" for true believers.[72] While in some ways the values embraced by the two cultures are different, both often celebrate violence and masculinity, and demonize and ridicule the mainstream.

Importantly, both gangsta rap and religious fundamentalism are part of broader systems of meaning—hip-hop and traditional religions. They both also have had political leanings. Thus many Christian fundamentalists function as a conservative pressure group to the U.S. Republican Party. Hindu and Islamic governments in India and the Middle East attempt to survive by placating fundamentalist critics, like al-Qaeda, that demand loyalty to the Koran and Islamic Umma, not the state.

Sean "P. Diddy" Combs's 2004 "Vote or Die" campaign was an attempt to tie the hip-hop nation to the U.S. Democratic Party. "Consciousness rappers" like Chuck D of Public Enemy joined Air America Radio and pushed for the participation of hip-hop-influenced youth in electoral politics. But many rappers refused to take the pledge of allegiance to the flag of the Democratic Party of cultural conservatives like Tipper Gore. KRS-One called the decision to vote for one of the two parties like having to choose between "mumps or measles."

The main point, though, is that the "political" identities of both fundamentalist religion and gangsta rap are only one identity among many, and in sharp conflict with other identities. It is the overall "power of identity," Castells argues, that is the main force opposing the globalized power of the market and accompanying demoralization of the socially excluded. Conscious, or "positive," rap is but one identity, and attempts to narrow hip-hop to conscious rap would kill it as a living culture. There are many ways to provide meaning to young people in the face of persisting ghettos and jobless barrios and favelas. Trying to re-create the civil rights movement through hip-hop is only one of them.

Afrika Bambaataa had it right from the beginning: hip-hop today is performed with a "post–civil rights voice."[73] It is much more than "We Shall Overcome" with a beat. Bambaataa preached that hip-hop could give young people the power to change their lives. It is this power, to use Castells's terms, that could produce a new "project identity" of social movements with clear goals that could transform social relations.

If those of us of the older generation want to lend a hand and not get in the way of youth, we need to first speak their language. One way to reach gang members is to enter the broader world of rap music and the real, existing struggle over the gangsta identity's worship of drugs and violence, and disdain for women. Such a cultural battle can be won only with weapons from within the culture.

Gangsta rap is what Castells called a "culture of urgency," filled with individualist values, destructive of the community and the self. But hip-hop, by its origins and conflicted nature, is multifaceted cultural responses to nihilism, a search for ways out of being paralyzed by the void. Gilroy comments:

> In the simplest possible terms, by posing the world as it is against the world as the racially subordinated would like it to be, this musical culture supplies a great deal of the courage required to go on living in the present.[74]

Tupac grasps the full meaning of Derrick Bell's face at the bottom of the well when he simply says, "even though you're fed up, ya got to keep your head up." While the defiance of hip-hop is often condemned by the older generation, it is precisely that defiance in the face of meaninglessness and desolation that needs to be captured and turned from self-destruction to self-affirmation.

Hip-hop makes meaning for young people within ghettos, barrios, favelas, and urban spaces worldwide. It expresses the principal cultural contradiction in their lives, the nature of their identity. To complete my mission to understand the world of gangs, I more closely examine the contested urban spaces where these identities are grown and displayed. There is a secret war going on: an offensive by the prosperous classes, who are trying to reclaim for themselves spaces near downtowns that they once neglected but now covet. Police raids, schemes for "development," surveillance cameras, and widespread incarceration are weapons used against the "defensible spaces" of the ghettos and their gangs.

chapter 9

Contested Cities:
Gentrification and the Ghetto

When white folk who have never met before, start to talk to each other, friendly like, it means some n——'s goin' to die.

—JEAN-PAUL SARTRE, *The Respectful Prostitute*

There is a common, if counterintuitive, factor that closely links gangs, the ghetto, violence, police, and the prison: gentrification. Investment bankers, high-priced professionals, and other "symbolic analysts" want to live near their colleagues and close to "where the action is" in refurbished, what they warmly call "charming," spaces near the city center. If the ghetto and its gangs get in their way, then something's got to give, and it probably will not be the "Starbucks Army." This chapter is about the secret war now being waged over space in globalizing cities.

In some cities, particularly in Europe, the poor and immigrants are concentrated in outlying suburbs, but in some third world and most U.S. cities the poor live in older, rundown housing near the central business district. The new gentry is expanding out from downtown, concentric zone by concentric zone, pushing out those who had made these lands their home. Space in many cities is tied inextricably to race, and the gentrification of cities typically means a confrontation with the dark ghetto and its gangs—a confrontation that has nearly always been won by the forces of "law and order." Rates of violence in many, but not all, U.S. cities have, as a result, come down as wars on gangs, drugs, and crime were waged to make the city safe and attractive, particularly for its returning whiter-skinned inhabitants.

Gangs have long operated their illicit businesses in the defensible spaces of housing projects or in dense, low-income neighborhoods. But when these older areas that have been black or brown for decades begin to whiten, an architecture of affluence and security transforms the landscape. The youth of these areas become targets of police harassment and end up behind bars or under constant threat of revocation of parole or probation. Gangs must adapt or leave.

Urban spaces reoccupied by the gentry, however, seldom benefit the existing residents, whose longtime homes and low-income public housing are razed or rehabbed to be reborn as pricey condos. What is more important is that these "revitalized" areas seldom signal an end to the ghetto. Rather, as I show in Chicago, the truly disadvantaged are forcibly and firmly transferred to the city's less desirable zones, where an undying ghetto tragically re-forms.

The main point of this chapter is that valued spaces of cities have become a battleground in a fierce, if little noticed, war. Gangs are socially constructed by a compliant mass media as the demonized and dangerous other and become a threatening "enemy" that must be removed by any means necessary. This one-sided "new war" differs by city, and how the war is carried out has much to do with variations in urban violence.[1] The important role played by gangs in urban violence is among the reasons we need to consider gangs as *social actors*.

THE IMPORTANCE OF URBAN SPACE

Cosmopolitan professionals moving into "run-down" areas would be mortified to think of gentrification as their version of "ethnic cleansing." That term is reserved for "Neanderthals" like the late Slobodan Milošević, or "primitives" like the Hutu and Tutsi. But consider this comment by a community policing officer in Chicago's Humboldt Park, a Puerto Rican neighborhood undergoing gentrification.

> We've got a lot of yuppies who move here, buy houses at a bargain price, and then they rehab it. But it's not the same neighborhood. . . . it's noisy, congested, more diverse, and there's more crime. There are the same kids who've always played on the street—Latinos, blacks, Filipinos, Arabs. . . . Now all of a sudden these "pioneers" want us to "round up the Indians" and clean up the neighborhood for them. Basically they want everyone who's not like them to move somewhere else.[2]

Another Chicago police officer put it even more bluntly. In ordering Pete Haywood, a black male off a corner near where the Chicago Housing Authority's (CHA) Stateway Gardens were being torn down, the blue-clad defender of law and order brusquely said, "This ain't CHA no more. It's the white man's land now. You can't stand there."[3] Loïc Wacquant underscores this racialized discourse of "safety":

> The result is that everywhere the dominant strategy for ensuring physical safety in urban space is to avoid younger African Americans. In the dualizing metropolis, the appraisive slogan "black is beautiful" has been effectively supplanted by the vituperative adage, "black is dangerous."[4]

The broader context for gentrification today is the paramount importance of the spaces of cities in a globalized world, particularly in those "world cities" that John Friedmann and Goetz Wolff famously called the "control centers of the global economy."[5] The notion that the Internet and fluidity of capital would mean the decreased importance of cities has been laid to rest by Saskia Sassen, among others.[6] Sassen argues that the global city needs actual, physical spaces for the professional class to interact, to do business, to be entertained, and to consume their wealth. These spaces are best found near their workplaces, just as in the nineteenth century the industrial proletariat's housing quarters were constructed around major factories. Areas adjacent to downtowns—the slums of the second concentric circle of Chicago school fame—need to be "reclaimed" in the information era.

The 1960s are a turning point in my overall narrative in many ways. This decade marked the closing of the industrial era, the beginning of the information era, and the rise and fall of social movements. But it also meant the emergence of cities as crucial nodes in the globalization of finances and trade. Elites had to make a choice whether to abandon cities or "revitalize" them. Debates in the 1970s were filled with laments about the "Ungovernable" or "Unheavenly City."[7] Popular movies like *The Warriors* and *Fort Apache, the Bronx* portrayed the city as filled with gangs and out of control,[8] and films like *Death Wish* and its many sequels called for violent responses by the state and vigilante justice.

While the future of the city once appeared to be at risk, the movie *Escape from New York,* which portrayed Manhattan as a walled-off prison-ghetto, was never even a faint possibility. In reality the new global economy compelled New York City to urgently retool, to remake itself into a more "civilized" workspace and playground for the bankers and other professionals who lived in Manhattan. Arriving on cue, as Neil Smith says, was the "revanchist city," a city of revenge against minorities, immigrants, and the dark other.[9]

At the dawn of the information era, some—but not all—cities clearly saw the need to reclaim run-down spaces for the professional class and provide housing and consumer markets. Indeed, as Sassen implicitly argues, an expanding agglomeration of information workers is a trusty sign that a city has joined the global elite: "The downtowns of cities and key nodes in metropolitan areas receive massive investments in real estate and telecommunications while low-income city areas and the older suburbs are starved for resources."[10] Those industrial cities that failed to recognize this transition early on, like Detroit, Buffalo, and my hometown of Milwaukee, continue even into this century to lose population and have high rates of crime. These "rustbelt" cities waited too long to find their niche in the global economy and have become the big losers in the globalization game.[11]

In globalizing cities like Chicago, however, more affluent whites who had earlier left for the suburbs are returning, boosting urban population after decades of decline. One of my Chicago students, a Puerto Rican male whose family had resided for years in now-gentrifying Humboldt Park, tragicomically described what was happening as *"white flight. . . .* White people are fleeing the suburbs and taking our homes." Spatial mobility, defined by the Chicago school as a one-way ticket to the suburbs, has instead turned into a round-trip affair. The yuppie chickens have come home to roost and, in the areas of the city they covet, are systematically evicting those who reside there.

In traditionally black Atlanta, the *New York Times* reports large numbers of affluent whites are returning and significantly increasing their share of the overall city population. New York City is losing black population for the first time since the years after the 1863 racist "draft riots."[12] Importantly, what is occurring across the United States is not only a class but a racial transformation. Cities that were becoming increasingly black and run by black mayors have become cities where whites are returning, often trying to build alliances with Latinos, to take back or retain power.

Thus we have witnessed the passing of powerful black mayors—Harold Washington, David Dinkins, and Tom Bradley—and their replacement by white mayors Rudy Giuliani, Richard M. Daley, and Richard Riordan. LA's election of Antonio Villaraigosa is testimony to the growing power of Latinos everywhere. Though Villaraigosa is said to be a friend of the black community, overall fears of a white and Latino antiblack electoral bloc are not to be dismissed.[13] The startling removal of blacks and creoles from New Orleans and their replacement by Mexican immigrant workers in the wake of Hurricane Katrina may be a glimpse in fast-forward of what might turn out to be a new American paradigm of "ethnic cleansing."

WORLDWIDE PATTERNS OF GENTRIFICATION

In the United States, reclaiming the city and making it safe were closely related to the war on drugs and the steady increase in the rate of incarceration of black youth.[14] But the pattern of building secure walled communities and fortified urban villages is international in scope. In Cape Town, urban development in the 1960s meant the making safe of central areas of the city called "White Group Areas" and the expulsion of native blacks from them. Don Pinnock points out, "The heart of the city was to be torn out as a sacrifice to order, cleanliness and progress." He goes on to explain the extremes taken by the apartheid state, in echoes of Ebenezer Howard and Baron Haussmann's reconstruction of Paris.[15] "Over proposals for garden cities and green belts, planners talked of 'machine-gun zones,' 'buffer strips,' 'military roads,' and 'policeability.'"[16] In Cape Town, electric fences originally built to protect white settlers against lions are now used as a barrier against blacks.[17]

Beirut followed a different pattern before the devastating 2006 war with Israel. Following the long civil war of 1975–90, the city center was destroyed and in the 1990s became revitalized as a pan-Arab entertainment capital. Private developers "with barely disguised commercial interests and political ambitions" rebuilt central Beirut by evicting the current poor residents, which began to "eliminate the social fabric" and make the city center safe for the better off.[18] "The rich and privileged who moved there took shelter in their own 'bubbles' of country clubs, park-townlet preserves which now punctuate our landscape."[19]

Similar to French working-class *banlieues,* the Lebanese poor have been confined to "dahlia," shantytowns in south suburban Beirut, segregated by religious sects and existing "beyond the law."[20] One commentator points out that "what is happening in Lebanon, at least in a majority of areas, is a sectarian ghettoization."[21] The rapidly increasing wealth of pre-Israeli-bombed central Beirut stands in stark contrast to growing marginalized populations with a strengthened communal identity.

A still different tack, and one with sinister implications, has been taken by Singapore. In an attempt to promote both security and homogeneity, ethnic "kampung" settlements were forcibly dismantled and their population scattered after the 1950s and 1960s race riots. Singapore sees itself as the model information city of the future, with its per capita income now exceeding that of the European Union.[22] The suppression of dissent and ethnic difference that characterize this totalitarian city-state has become a model for the iron-fist approach to pacifying the city, though Singapore's city-state status makes generalization questionable. The fight against crime, as Manuel Castells says, is "a battle repeatedly lost over the past decades everywhere—except in Singapore."[23] Another commentator says, "In Singapore the streets are safe. There is virtually no crime and no unemployment."[24]

Singapore's economic miracle and its success ensuring this "public safety" showcase the use of force to suppress crime and forcibly remake urban spaces into zones of safety. Cities look far and wide for "magic bullets" to give them at least the appearance of security. The apparent success of Giuliani's "zero tolerance policies" in New York City have brought multimillion-dollar contracts to his consulting firm from cities as diverse as Mexico City and London. Many of these cities are worried that high crime rates will discourage the profitable tourist industry and have turned to Giuliani and others to help them restore law and order. Dennis Judd calls an aspect of the cleansing of cities a "tourist bubble" where the lucrative tourist spots are kept sanitized and Tracy Chapman's "subcity" stays hidden or is silently eradicated.[25]

One of the most striking studies of the urban war over space is by Teresa Caldiera, whose *City of Walls* describes São Paulo, Brazil.[26] Caldiera begins with a discussion of the "talk of crime," the discourse used by the more wealthy residents who are seeking islands of security as they renovate older urban areas. In São Paulo, as in U.S. cities, the criminals are defined as "nonwhite," and such "racial crime-talk " elaborates prejudices and is made up of "stereotypes."

The construction of walled communities in São Paulo, as in gentrified areas of Chicago or settlements on Palestine's West Bank, means the "symbolic reordering of the world" to justify, among other things, a blatant land grab and persecution of the other. What goes on in the talk of crime, whether in community policing meetings, discussions of urban planners and developers, or in small group chatter at coffee shops, is the emphasis on "the difference between good and evil." For the new frontiersmen, "good" means security and "evil" means crime. As Caldiera says, the "central justification" for "fortified enclaves . . . is the fear of violent crime."[27]

Caldiera describes the city in the language of war, the seizing of desired spaces in São Paulo from gangs and criminals, and the securing of them with armed violence by police or vigilantes. This is a familiar discourse in the United States where perpetual wars on crime, drugs, gangs, and, of course, terror have been waged by the state over the past decades. São Paulo, like Peter Marcuse's New York City, is a city that is combination enclave, ghetto, and citadel, the urban archetype in the global era.[28] "In order to feel safe," Caldiera sadly concludes, the well-heeled "have to build walls."[29]

Caldiera compares São Paulo with Los Angeles, which Mike Davis describes as a "fortress" protecting the white gentry in a black and Latino city that needs to be pacified by force. Davis relays the story of LA's city attorney, and later mayor, James Hahn, who used civil injunctions to clear some spaces of gangs. Hahn wanted to criminalize gangs and believed LA was in a "war," so "no constitutional rights are absolute." In faint echoes of Singapore, Hahn said he was no longer interested in rehabilitating gang members but in jailing them for as long as possible.[30]

Davis goes on to discuss the "helter-skelter" proliferation of LA black street gangs "at a terrifying rate" in a somewhat apocalyptic prediction of coming chaos. Davis wrote *City of Quartz* as homicide rates were increasing, a few years before the sharp drops in violence in the mid-1990s in Los Angeles and other cities. Police have used declines in violence to trumpet the effectiveness of zero tolerance tactics. While this trend has made liberal academics uncomfortable, the "crime drop" is an unaccounted-for, "stubborn fact."[31] Indeed, variations in violence, the secret war over space, the unprecedented incarceration of black youth, and the transformation of the ghetto in the "dual city" are closely related.[32]

THE GHETTO, PRISON, VIOLENCE, AND GANGS

The ongoing war over urban space is very much like the second U.S. war on Iraq. Massive firepower results in a clear-cut victory in the short term but hardly an end to hostilities. The "new war" going on in U.S. cities is similar to guerrilla resistance to superior U.S. military intervention around the world: a battle to halt the elimination of a group and the erasure of its identity. As Mary Kaldor says, "The violence in the inner cities of Western Europe and North America can, in some senses, be described as new wars" that are as much about identity as space.[33]

The struggle over urban space is where racialized "resistance identities" often come into conflict with the gentry. While the elite are determined that the ghetto must go, a cosmopolitan identity requires a few of the more "respectable" minority residents to remain to add "color" and "diversity." A lifestyle of affluence appreciates the cashbox-culture of ethnic shops and native goods, in a reasonable proportion to global brand-name stores like Banana Republic, Starbucks, or Victoria's Secret.

Another onerous result of this confrontation is the spatial extension of the ghetto and its gangs into prison. As I showed in chapter 1, gang identities infiltrate the prison, and prison culture, in turn, diffuses to the ghetto. Wacquant calls the ghetto a "collective identity machine" for its stigmatization of the excluded and the acceptance of this stigmatization by black ghetto dwellers.[34] For Wacquant, the ghetto and the prison share a "single carcereal continuum," a "deep kinship" as "instruments of forced confinement" of the U.S. black population. Wacquant's critique is a stinging rejoinder to liberals who reduce racism "essentially" to poverty and believe the ghetto is little more than a quantitative extension of ethnic enclaves.

> The unchecked intensification of its exclusionary thrust suggests the ghetto might be profitably studied not by analogy with urban slums, lower-class neighborhoods, and immigrant enclaves, but alongside the reservation, the refugee camp, and the prison, as belonging to a broader class of institutions for the forced confinement of dispossessed and dishonored groups.[35]

Wacquant places the emergence of regimes of "neo-liberal penalty" within the globalizing world where some populations have become superfluous and mechanisms of social control must be extended. Wacquant in effect theorizes Caldiera's walls of segregation to the United States and then shows how punitive U.S. polices are being exported around the world.[36] As Friedmann and Wolff argue in their seminal article on world city formation:

> Confronted with violence, the nation-state responds in coin. Given the severity of its fiscal constraints in the face of rising costs, it resorts to the simplest, least imaginative alternative: the application of brute force. The response is

acceptable to the new ruling class who generally prefer administrative to political solutions. But police repression can at best contain class violence; it cannot eliminate or significantly reduce it. Violence is here to stay.[37]

The reality of ghetto life today, however, is not a static or uniformly violent one, as some globalization studies seem to imply. Most ghetto walls are not surrounded by barbed wire, nor are they socially isolated zones completely cut off from the rest of the city. Violence is neither invariably high nor unresponsive to a multitude of external factors, even excluding the outlier of Singapore. Ghettos move, and walls are often shifting and invisible to outsiders,[38] unlike the deliberately visible electronic fences of "privatopia" or the monstrosity of the Israeli wall criss-crossing the West Bank.[39]

In the late 1990s significant reductions in violence occurred in most, but not all, U.S. cities, while poverty stayed relatively constant or even increased. Every city differs in how it fashions space for its favored professionals. How a city wages its war over space and against gangs may be an important factor in a city's level of violence. One way to understand how gentrification, the ghetto, police repression, gangs, and violence are tied together is to take a close look at the city where I work, Chicago.[40]

Gangs, Public Housing, and the Ghetto

"The effort to recolonize the city involves systematic eviction."[41] Smith's words could not have better described the effect of gentrification . . . in Chicago. While some cities, like Smith's New York, have in fact invested heavily in affordable and low-cost housing and have stabilized low-income and working-class areas like the South Bronx,[42] others like Chicago have adopted a conscious policy of "systematic eviction" of public housing tenants and any residents who get in the way of "revitalizing" neighborhoods.

Two related processes are underway in Chicago. The first, nearly complete as I write, has been the destruction of Chicago's high-rise public housing projects. The second is a simultaneous expansion of the gentry into the ghettos on the city's north, west, and south sides. Chicago's institutionalized gangs have complicated both processes.

Chicago's Segregated Public Housing

In the 1950s the postwar black population explosion meant that affordable housing had to be increased, and the issue was where. White aldermen outdid one another in refusing to allow public housing to be built in their wards, and the solution was to tear down existing housing within the black belt and put up high-rises. The *Chicago Tribune* points out, "Of the nearly 21,000 low-income family apartments built by the CHA from 1955 through 1968, all but about 2,000 were in high rises."[43]

Adam Cohen and Elizabeth Taylor, in their remarkable biography of Richard J. Daley, describe the public housing extravaganza:

> Hilliard Center was the final installment in the State Street Corridor. When it was completed in 1966, this strip of land one-quarter mile wide and four miles long was home to almost 40,000 poor black tenants. The five massive projects lined State Street—700-unit Harold Ickes Homes, 800-unit Dearborn Homes, 1,784-unit Stateway Gardens, and 4,415-unit Robert Taylor Homes—and took up thirty-four consecutive blocks, except for a stretch between 30th and 35th Streets where the campus of the Illinois Institute of Technology is located.[44]

Altogether, thirty-eight thousand units of public housing were created, which at its height housed as many as one hundred thousand poor black tenants, including tens of thousands of "nonleaseholders" residing there without CHA knowledge or approval. Their concentration and later dispersal are two of the sorriest chapters in Chicago's shameful history of racism.

The 1950s CHA strategy for containment of Chicago's black population unintentionally created "defensible spaces" for gangs who used the projects' spaces to run their drug and other illegal businesses with impunity. As I argued earlier, the existence of all-black, low-income public housing high-rises was not the main factor in the institutionalization of Chicago's gangs, but it was a major contributor. Gangs controlled the drug business within the projects and warred with one another in the spaces outside. Here is another Black Gangster Disciple's description of the high-rise drug business:

> Because, like in the days, the projects were making a lot of money. That's when I started really making money in the projects, because they was giving me two hundred dollar dime bags, that was two stacks. I was sixteen, that's when I started making my own money, real money. My man gave me two hundred bags, tell me to bring him back fifteen, I keep five. Then, you're going to slip two hundred bags in a day, easy. In the morning, from 12–5,

you're going to make so much money because that's when they're out. That's why everybody was fighting. People thought it was over gangs because you ain't getting along. It was over money, it was over money.[45]

Another Black Gangster Disciple describes the intensity of the warfare in Robert Taylor Homes:

A. [In the next building] they had a sniper. And he was standing right there in front of the building, he was shooting right there . . . and he shot him in the head.

Q. Was this a Mickey Cobra [a rival gang] building?

A. Right. Yeah, 'cause I was in the back, 'cause, you know, in our building, there's a little hole where you do the shoot out. . . . So, that's where I was, then when I came out, that's when I heard the whole commotion, I heard what happened to Sonny.

Q. How did it make you feel?

A. That was the first time in my life I felt f——ed up about what I was doing. Like, damn, that could've been me. We could've been switched spots easy. That's the first time made me think. It didn't stop me, but it made me think. Damn. Made me finally believe what kind of game I was in.[46]

Female gang members also sometimes took part in violence. Two Sisters of the Struggle (the BGD-allied female gang) explain:

R1. We was into it with the Iggies [residents of the nearby Harold Ickes Homes]. . . . We just shot at them. We was like, I hit, you know the Hilton [Robert Taylor Homes] got a lot of floors, and we was like on the . . . fourth, . . . I just shoot at them.

R2. You could just shoot out the porch. It's like a big open thing. And . . . there's like a fence right here. It's, hey, you could just shoot. And, you know, they basically don't know where it's comin' from.[47]

The gang violence encouraged by the built environment of low-income high-rises was met with a variety of "sweep" tactics that consisted of CHA or Chicago police rampaging through buildings in a search for weapons, drugs, or wanted gang members. Like "search and destroy" missions in Vietnam, the sweeps almost always came up empty and cost the CHA $175,000 a pop to carry out.[48]

These tactics did nothing to lower Chicago's homicide rates that until the mid-1990s had been similar to New York City's, though considerably less than those of Detroit, Washington, D.C., or New Orleans. While murders dropped at mid-decade in most other cities, Chicago's homicide rate stayed stubbornly high. Every few years Chicago's police and mayors chanted the official mantra of yet another war against crime and gangs. But in the mid-1990s the slogans conveniently coincided with the plans of developers to grab the prime spaces of public housing that now were needed to house a quickly expanding professional class. Big money meant this time something would happen.

Destruction of Public Housing High-Rises, Displacement, and Violence

The five sets of housing projects that lined State Street just south of the Loop were originally built during the first Mayor Daley's term to contain the black community and create a barrier between African American Bronzeville and the legendary Irish Bridgeport. But the second Mayor Daley was positioning Chicago as a big-time player in the global economy, and the financial markets and high-tech economy were booming. The new rich needed places to live and play. Occupying vital space to the south were thirty-four blocks of high-rises; on the north were the towers of Cabrini-Green; out west were the four projects that made up what was called "ABLA." The talk for the public was about crime, but the backroom conversations were about money.

The money was to be made on "development" on top of the spaces of the CHA. The CHA's "Plan for Transformation" called for the destruction of all but one of its 168 high-rises and nearly twenty thousand housing units, replacing them with a variety of mixed-income residences.[49] The CHA's thirty-eight thousand units were to be replaced by twenty-five thousand new units, but half of those would go to senior citizens. The CHA waiting list for housing by 2006 was over sixty thousand.[50] While promises to existing residents of their "right of return" were made, most tenants knew relocation in public housing was more talk than action.

If Chicago were Bosnia, of course, the creation of internally displaced people would be recognized as ethnic cleansing. The areas being "cleansed" of black and brown people are among the city's most run-down areas. They include vast expanses of what Arnold Hirsch called the "Second Ghetto," the all-black spaces of the city that were rebuilt through segregated housing projects.[51]

In 2004 Miloon Kothari, the United Nation's highest-ranking expert on housing issues, visited Cabrini-Green, a Chicago housing project slated for demolition. He stated that "evictions of public housing residents in the United States clearly violate international human rights, including the International Convention on the Elimination of All Forms of Racial Discrimination and the International Covenant on Economic, Social and Cultural Rights." CHA tenants thus qualify as "Internally Displaced People" and are entitled to special protection under UN guidelines.[52]

But while some attention was given to the many tenants who resisted displacement,[53] what was almost completely overlooked were the consequences of displacing tenants and nonleaseholders who were gang members. In Chicago institutionalized gangs claim nearly all neighborhood spaces, and the movement of gang members and branches from the highrises to other high-rises or neighborhoods proved lethal.

In the mid-1990s homicide rates were falling in most U.S. cities, particularly New York, as aggressive policing combined with communities fed up with violence and repeated attempts by gangs to call truces. But in Chicago, this momentum was interrupted by the displacement of thousands of families and many gang members. Susan Popkin, who studied the "transformation" of the Harold Ickes Homes, comments,

> Without security, Ickes was particularly vulnerable to outside gangs. By 1996, the CHA was vacating and demolishing buildings in other developments along the State Street corridor (where Ickes and Robert Taylor Homes are located), displacing their gang members from their usual turf. The dominant Gangster Disciples had been weakened by the conviction of more than thirty of its top warlords on federal conspiracy charges related to drug sales; as a result Ickes did not even have an effective gang to fight off intruders. Without guards or gang members to protect the development from outsiders, Ickes quickly became a battleground.[54]

The plan to demolish high-rises to reduce violence, if it was ever a serious concern, was backfiring. This Vice Lord points out the obvious:

> As the projects come down, they gonna start movin' in, in like our neighborhoods, like our neighborhoods, probably some suburbs. . . . I'm talkin' about, man, a war, a war that you've never seen before, man. 'Cause niggers

from the projects gonna come try to take over niggers' lands and shit and, ain't nobody gonna let it, you know what I'm sayin'. . . . It's gonna be a lot of people dyin' and getting' shot and getting' hurt, robbed.[55]

That is indeed what happened. Here is how one Black Gangster Disciple explains what went on when he moved to far south side Roseland after his building was demolished.

> The building got torn down, and [we] moved out here, and the people got mad that we low end [former Robert Taylor Homes tenants] people that come down are trying to take over. . . . and we say "Like, they can't get mad now, because our building got torn down, they moved us, the government moved us out here. Now, they can't stop us, we're going to serve in their set, sell weed or anything."[56]

All hell broke loose in what several gang members called the "wild, wild, west" where gang members from the projects attempted to resettle in areas already claimed by other gangs. Chicago's homicide rate, which had paralleled New York City's for decades, reached as much as four times higher than New York's, before finally dropping after the turn of the century and stabilizing.[57] But while displacement of public housing tenants in the 1990s took place on a large scale—a process that was not occurring in New York— a wave of gentrification was engulfing other spaces of Chicago's ghetto, making good use of the iron fist of Smith's "revanchist city."

GENTRIFICATION AND CHICAGO'S GANGS

For the past decade, developers have been prospecting areas in Chicago's north, south, and west sides for development. A field note I wrote in the late 1990s, as several gang members gave me a tour of their neighborhood, describes one such gentrified "island" surrounded by run-down homes and vacant lots in Englewood on Chicago's south side.

> Then there was "Boy's Town," a legendary area with a lagoon where in the past bodies kept being found.[58] Young kids were always warned: if you keep it up you'll end up in the lagoon. But when we saw it, it looked like a Miami resort. Middle class people in shorts walking around in their own private space, clearly set off from the rest of the area. The lagoon was clear, clean,

with a touch of azure. . . . The guys said that the drug game around Boys
Town had stopped. Too much heat, maybe . . . other opportunities. What
I saw throughout the north side of Englewood was lots of these middle class
islands, mainly black, but some white people as well.

The introduction of middle-class homeowners into a ghetto area prompts
major changes in social control. This Vice Lord describes what happens.

Q. Do you do things differently, because the yuppies are there? Do they bring
cops with them, because they're there?

R. The cops come real quicker, you know what I'm sayin', and just say, at
first . . . before the yuppies start movin' in there, it used to take 'em a
minute. Now our neighborhood is condominiums, condominiums, condominiums, condominiums, condominiums. So if a cop get called . . .
they comin' like this (snaps fingers), and we gettin' locked up. Ain't no
talkin' no more. You get locked up, 'cause they might like say this person
called the police on us . . . might point to this person and say this person called the police so, man, you get locked up now. Ain't no more talk,
okay, man, f——— [you], man. . . . no more breaks, so you getting' locked
up, 'cause they tryin' to prove a point. They tell you at the station, know
what, we just can't let you all go 'cause . . . these people starin' out the
window right here. If we let you all go, then what? Our jobs would be
f———ed up. So you goin' in. They tryin' to stop you from hangin' on the
corners, all that now.[59]

Sometimes the yuppie newcomers are afraid of the scary-looking dark young
men hanging out on the corners.

You gotta . . . do your thing different, like, um, disguise it some times like,
let's just say, if you hangin' out and, um, you got to piss in the gang way, oh,
you gotta do this and mask up now, 'cause when they by the yuppies, they
will tell your face, you know what I'm sayin', but they don't be, they don't
be callin' the police and none of that, 'cause, really, they kind of scared any-
way, so what they do is, how you doin' sir, ooh, and man, man, they goin'
about they business, you know, so they scared.

They don't stay scared. Police flood gentrifying neighborhoods with patrols
to protect them. But more troops alone are not enough. Chicago's version

of "shock and awe" includes a high-tech component that is a sure sign of things to come.

THE ELECTRONIC PANOPTICON

In Chicago, in the late 1990s, surveillance cameras were installed in certain neighborhoods to keep watch on crime. These "blue light" cameras were concentrated in high-crime zones, but they were also placed in the gentrifying areas of the near west and south side. Police are especially aggressive in gentrifying areas, with sudden shakedowns and pressure on minority males, of any age, standing on corners.

The west side particularly, the traditional home of the Conservative Vice Lords, was targeted for maximum surveillance. One consequence of this policy for Lawndale was inconceivable levels of incarceration and criminalization of the population. In 2002, according to a study by the Center for Impact Research, up to 57 percent of *all* adults, male and female, who lived in Lawndale were either behind bars or on probation or parole.[60] Being on "paper" puts tremendous power in the hands of police to intimidate citizens who could be immediately sent to prison for an arrest for a minor violation. Like in Alice's Wonderland, revoking probation or parole means the sentence comes first and no judge or jury is even required.

Chicago police, particularly on the west and south sides, have a long history of corruption and brutality. The "systematic" use of torture by Chicago police, exemplified by the infamous Commander Jon Burge, was given international publicity by Human Rights Watch.[61] Rather than being reined in after this long history of brutality, police are now being "set loose" even more by the mayor, who wants the area "cleaned up." One of the original Vice Lords, a man nearing his sixties, explained what that meant:

> You know in the Lawndale area they rebuilding now. They are rebuilding. It is a new thing coming in there now. The police really got Lawndale under tap. . . . Man where we use to stand on the corner—you can't even stand on the corner now. Three people they are going to pull up—get to walking I mean where we use to hang out all night—drinking wine and singing wow, wow. . . . oh no that ain't happening now. . . . Me and Bobbie and Mack can't stand there on that corner no more than about fifteen minutes they are going to tell us to move. You have got to go. I don't care what you have done you have got to go.[62]

The gangs were forced to adapt. Youngsters who had sold drugs on corners openly were "laid off," since they were too conspicuous. Drug sales skyrocketed, with beepers replacing drive-by corners. Older members, particularly those who could relate to the newcomers, monopolized sales. Tension between youth and older members surfaced. Police harassment became routine.

Chicago's experience echoes Caldiera's description of São Paulo: "Thus for many people everyday life in the city is becoming a daily management of barriers and suspicion, marked by a succession of little rituals of identification and humiliation."[63] Traveling around Lawndale in 2006 with several older Vice Lords, I came upon a telltale scene. A brand new "El" commuter train station stood in a nearly vacant area of the neighborhood. Several blocks down stood a brand-new police district station house. In between was a sign: "Coming Soon: Condominiums." This public invitation to a yuppie invasion was even clearer as I turned my head east down Ogden Boulevard. On a straight line down the street were the skyscrapers of the Loop, easily accessible by both train and car.

Bobby Gore told me that even back in the 1960s he didn't need Paul Revere to warn him the "yuppies were coming": "We recognized Lawndale as being prime land. With Lawndale being seven and a half or ten minutes from the Loop, we knew they were going to come this way."

It just took them a few years.

Space, Race, and the Contested City

The battle for space in the American city is essentially the continuation of a centuries-long struggle against racial oppression and segregation. Housing policies in the 1950s and 1960s were aimed at clearing ghetto lands to build highways to speed up the white move to the suburbs. That earlier "white flight" now is reversing itself, as whites "flee" back to the city to take back "their" land. Not emphasized enough by the Marxist class analysis of scholars like Smith, the quiet war going on over space in the city is the most recent echo of the first white invaders of "native" American land. As the Chicago policeman said, "This is white man's land now." The white return to the city means the era of urban "black power" may be over before it even had a chance to get rolling.[64]

In some gentrifying black communities, Chicago's African American middle class is often the first to settle in traditionally black areas. Some claim this shows gentrification is mainly a class issue. In fact, such selective settlement reveals the deep racist fears of whites to move close to black ghetto areas until they have been "pacified" and shown to be safe. Whites appear to have no such fears of moving into Latino areas, like Chicago's Humboldt Park, and there are few if any middle-class African Americans who gentrify Latino areas.

Gentrification everywhere, as Caldiera reminds us, is accompanied by a discourse that socially constructs a dark other as enemy. Using both the conservative rhetoric of racism and its liberal "wink and nod" variant, this discourse calls on law enforcement to take the lead in securing the frontier. "What is being reproduced at the level of the built environment," Caldiera says, "is segregation and intolerance."[65] Along with this return to the city has been the vast expansion of the U.S. prison system and the war on drugs, a not even thinly disguised war on black and dark-skinned youth. The chilling reminder that *three-quarters* of all those sentenced to prison for drug offenses are black is enough of a statement in a country where the vast majority of drug users are white.[66]

Cities significantly differ, however, in the way the war for space is carried out and what policies are implemented toward the poor black and minority residents of coveted spaces. As the crack wars came to an end in most cities in the mid-1990s, zero tolerance and other law enforcement campaigns resulted in sharp crime drops. In Chicago the displacement of tens of thousands of black residents, including institutionalized gangs, delayed that city's "crime drop" for several years. Still, Chicago's homicide rate seems to have stabilized at a level that remains nearly three times higher than New York City's.

Clearly, one factor for Chicago's relatively high homicide rate is the Windy City's history of institutionalized gangs and how in the 1990s these black and Latino gangs interacted with policies of "systematic eviction." What the case study of Chicago tells us is that the nature of the war over space will differ city by city and is probably a major influence in variations of violence. It also tells us that gangs influence the level of violence in a city, though perhaps not directly. In other words, gangs are what Alain Touraine calls "social actors" and must be taken into account in fashioning urban policies, and even, as I have shown, housing policy. This recognition of gangs has important implications for how we understand them and what we will do about them.

A Rose in the Cracks of Concrete

But the chances for any major transformation in the ghetto's predicament are slim until the anguish of the ghetto is in some way shared not only by its victims but by the committed empathy of those who now consider themselves privileged and immune to the ghetto's flagrant pathologies.

—KENNETH B. CLARK, *Dark Ghetto*

This book has presented evidence that gangs, whether we like it or not, are a "normal" feature of cities worldwide. The reader of these pages may not want to admit it but may have to reluctantly recognize that this world of gangs will not go away soon, if at all. But what, then, should we do?

In 1988 in *People and Folks* I opposed any programs sponsored by the U.S. Department of Justice as merely stuffing more resources into an already bloated law enforcement machine. I have not changed my mind, and the machine is now more bloated than ever. Today the Department of Home-land Security is making things worse by labeling gangs "domestic terrorists" and expanding even wider its draconian net.

I do believe there are effective, if difficult, actions that can be taken by individuals and groups willing to reach out to angry youth. Analysis need not mean paralysis. I would like to use this concluding section to urge both action and rethinking. These final pages therefore set out to accomplish two modest tasks. First, I reiterate why gangs are important today and why our traditional ways of thinking are ill equipped to understand them. Second, I summarize some lessons I have learned about how to combine research and action.

A Misunderstood World of Gangs

The vast majority of gangs are adolescent peer groups that have been social-ized to the streets. In other words, gangs today are mainly made up of *kids,* like they always have been, who are displaying "normal deviance," in Joan Moore's terms.[1] In the wake of a vast increase in urbanization and social and economic marginalization, gangs are spontaneously created in cities all over the world. The old, familiar gang problem becomes more compli-cated when we understand that many of today's gangs may have begun spontaneously, but then are conditioned by different kinds of preexisting groups of armed young men. It is the shaping and channeling of so many youth gangs into various kinds of armed groups that represents one of the most significant developments of late modernity.

Some gangs have institutionalized over decades in defensible spaces of cities like Chicago, Cape Town, or Rio de Janeiro. Youth growing up in these cities have an ever-present role model in local gangs. The gang is one business that is almost always hiring and may be the only chance many youth have to get a job. But these gangs are not merely economic agents: they develop rituals and ceremonies, a distinctive outlook, and interests of their own. Young people are strongly attracted to and find an identity in these organizations that are deeply rooted in ghettos, barrios, and favelas. Such institutionalized gangs are nearly impossible to destroy, short of total-itarian repression.

But the problem is broader than a limited number of cities with institu-tionalized gangs. Civil wars, ethnic rivalries, and an immensely profitable underground economy have produced various sorts of armed young men who also exist as role models for youth and an organized outlet for their frustrations. The complex world we live in is not made up of neatly defined groups, some criminal, some political, some cultural. The world of gangs comprises flexible forms of armed groups, some changing from gang to militia to criminal syndicate to political party, or some existing as all types simultaneously.

Jobs alone will not solve the problem, though a few more jobs anywhere would not hurt. Community-based agencies and nongovernmental orga-nizations that provide recreation, education, and cultural programs are nec-essary, but not sufficient. I have argued that the anger of gang members fundamentally comes from their conscious or unconscious recognition that "progress" is an illusion. No leader, party, or form of government has "delivered the goods" for the underclass, nor do men and women on the streets realistically expect them to in the near future. The bright promise of modernity has dimmed on the ghetto's mean streets and for many has already burned out. This situation presents long-term dangers to them and to us.

To understand these young men and women, I have theoretically crossed over, in Edward Said's sense,[2] and taken Cornel West and Derrick Bell as my guides, rather than rely on a deracialized, moribund, industrial-era criminology. I have argued that the outlook of gangs is not so much economic rationality as nihilism. This approach allows us to better understand why gang members are seduced by an ethic of hustling, of trying to make it any way they can. As Nas says in "Life's a Bitch," "That's why we get high, because you never know when you're goin' to go." You have to recognize the world is ugly, says Ice Cube, and a dog-cat-dog life prowls on every corner.

The rage from the streets is especially intense because so many black and minority youth are drowning in rivers of racism. How can you minimize the importance of race in understanding how Irish gang members from the Hamburg Athletic Association could run Chicago and one even become mayor, while the 1960s black Conservative Vice Lords, with the same dreams and aspirations, were killed or sent to prison? The traditional study of gangs has always minimized race and, as a result, finds indecipherable the racialized, hostile identities of the street.

For the past decades, the study of gangs has been more structural than cultural, mechanically hypothesizing outdated notions of delinquent subcultures that when applied describe no gang at all. The culture of the streets begins with race and ends with survival. It is at once a culture of urgency, outrage, and resistance.

To begin to understand, all we need to do is listen to our iPods. Nothing better captures the alienation and rage of the streets than gangsta rap, which both proclaims an alternative lifestyle and mimics the lives of the rich and famous. It is mainly within the worldwide cultural arena of hip-hop that the struggle for the future of our youth is being waged. To understand how gang members make meaning in their lives, *talk to them*—but first listen to their music.

Their music is urban and worldwide, and most youth now live in cities, where a sharp contest for space is being waged. The classic studies of cities looked at deracialized, ecological processes in the industrial era, but these processes are out of date in the global city. Gentrification has reversed the one-way movement of better-off whites to the suburbs and has brought them back to the city and into conflict with the dark ghetto and its gangs. This war may be a secret to the public, but it is all too real to minority youth in gentrifying neighborhoods who are tracked by surveillance cameras and hounded by police. City officials and developers are using all means at their disposal to ethnically cleanse the special places they wish to reserve for those who will pay top dollar for conveniently placed condos. The contested city will be the norm for the twenty-first century.

A Requiem for Traditional Criminology

This brief synopsis of *A World of Gangs* explains why I have concluded that traditional criminology has worn out its usefulness in helping us understand gangs. My critique of criminology's dated theoretical framework has led me to look elsewhere for inspiration. To cite Alain Touraine once again, we need to go beyond a classical sociology that "is still beholden to the nineteenth-century idea that society is an organic or a mechanical system, with its own laws, and that the function of sociological analysis is to dispel the illusion of the actor."[3]

The reader of this book cannot help but see that the gang members I have described are neither puppets of economic forces nor hard-core criminals imprisoned by cold-blooded calculations of "rational action." My theoretical schema is more cultural than structural and looks to existential rebellion, not broken families or jobless landscapes, to understand gangs' social behavior. I am indebted more to Jean-Paul Sartre than James Short. My theoretical inspiration is from Manuel Castells and Touraine, not Robert Park or Frederic Thrasher. I prefer the poetry of Luis Rodriguez to the prose of Malcolm Klein. As far as traditional criminology goes, I can only say, "De mortuis nil nisi bonum."

I am also uncomfortable with much of the practice of criminologists. When academics attempt to "do something," they typically act as designers or evaluators of anticrime or "at-risk" youth programs. C. Wright Mills calls this being an "Advisor to the King," and it is a role that can, and has been, performed ethically—Irving Spergel comes to mind. More often, however, the only beneficiaries of this role are the advisers themselves, in the form of research grants or heightened status, with results being written up in what Mills calls the "pretentious triviality" of obscure journal articles.[4]

Many criminologists, like U.S. journalists in the Iraq war, have become embedded in the law enforcement bureaucracies that are waging war on gangs, drugs, and terror, practicing a kind of domestic orientalism.[5] While most criminologists profess a liberal ideology, they may have not assimilated Alvin Gouldner's main point in his critique of Howard Becker: it is to values, not factions, that we social scientists owe our allegiance.[6]

If gangs are indeed made up of alienated youth who are angry with an unresponsive government, undying racism, and a blank future, then roles other than those of adviser, consultant, or evaluator are more urgently needed. Working these last years with communities torn by violence and with gang members who need jobs and education more than prison, I have struggled with understanding what role I, as a social scientist, can play. To conclude, I would like to briefly sketch out how my theory informs my own actions and argue that we are not helpless even in the face of cold, unforgiving conditions.

SOCIAL MOVEMENTS AND SOCIAL ACTORS

First, let me repeat: *gangs are not going away no matter what we do.* Conditions are too dire, the task too difficult, the anger too deep. However, like Bell's *Faces at the Bottom of the Well* or Albert Camus's *Sisyphus*,[7] I do not think dim prospects of victory necessarily mean the destruction of one's soul. Resistance to what might appear to be all-powerful forces need not be futile and might contain traces of the elixir of freedom. Short of the breathtaking transformations of the economy and polity I have favored throughout my life, my research has helped me in several ways to make an impact today on young lives. These are not by any means the only positive actions one could take, but these are the ones I have chosen, informed by theory and my own experience. I hope that they contain lessons for others who also want to act as well as understand.

The Importance of History

First, we need to publicize gangs who have succeeded in making good. Both street youth and the broader public need to know that something good can come from the streets. Those on the bottom of the social structure are capable of profound, even noble, action.

The scholar in me has found a way to make use of some rusty academic tools, and I have become something of a historian. The story of the

Conservative Vice Lords, told in chapter 6, holds major lessons for today. The capacity of the CVL to transform itself into a prosocial organization is both powerful as well as largely forgotten. Many of my Chicago students, even those born in Lawndale, were unaware of the accomplishments of the 1960s CVL. Youth in Lawndale, and on streets everywhere, need to learn the main lesson of the CVL, that a future other than drugs, violence, and the streets is possible *and in their own hands.*

At the same time, the savage repression of the CVL, along with the other gangs and the Black Panther Party, reveals the deep-seated racial hostility that still persists in the halls of power. There can be no progress, Frederick Douglass famously said, without struggle. What I have learned is that anytime gangs have embarked on a real transformation, they were violently opposed by police and others in authority. Change will not come easily, and this means any accomplishments will be the result of struggle and sacrifice on the part of our youth and us.

Publicizing the lessons of the 1960s CVL has become a major task of my scholarship. My Web site, http://gangresearch.net, reaches hundreds of thousands of people around the world. Its pages, "Shattered Dreams," are the most effective way I know to publicize the CVL legacy to a broad audience. On the site I show in pictures, video, audio, and words of the Vice Lords themselves what was done and, implicitly, what is still possible from street youth and their organizations. I firmly believe social scientists should not just expose poor economic conditions but also point out that gang members have participated and still do participate in social movements and work for the good of their communities.

In other words, there *is* hope for the streets, and it lies in the proven capacity of gang members to act in their own and their community's interest. This means that social change does not fundamentally lie in the criminal justice system, or in uplifting social programs, but in social movements.

The Key Importance of Social Movements

For both Touraine and Castells, social movements are crucial in the information era, more significant than class struggle or modernizing economies. Touraine particularly focuses on the real nature of democracy:

> It is not democracy that is triumphant today, but the market economy. To some extent, the market economy is democracy's antithesis, as the market

attempts to prevent political institutions from intervening in its activity, whereas democratic politics attempts to promote intervention so as to protect the weak from the domination of the strong.[8]

What both Castells and Touraine urge, in different ways, is for scholars to use their talents to encourage social movements of all types. However, the potential of gangs to create, or even be part of social movements, cannot be taken for granted.

Luis Barrios and David Brotherton are sterling examples of how academics can shepherd and publicize gangs as social movements, as their work on New York City's Almighty Latin King and Queen Nation (ALKQN) shows.[9] Barrios and Brotherton have showcased the bright, all-too-brief, five-pointed star of the ALKQN in books, films, and articles. They have also highlighted the often forgotten role of women with the ALKQN for respect and dignity. Like the 1960s CVL reported on in these pages and in David Dawley's book, the ALKQN was attacked and soundly defeated by the police, who dismissed its social activism as a cover for drug dealing. Like the CVL, the ALKQN's brief prosocial phase is dead; all that lives on is the memory of its members' deeds, documented in a fine book.[10] To deny gangs' *capacity* as social actors is what so much positivist criminology has been busy doing for the past fifty years, a project that I have taken sharp issue with in this book.

But while *A World of Gangs* has explained how gangs have the capacity to change in many ways, there are regrettably few examples of successful, long-term gang transformations. That this may be due more to police repression than the unwillingness of gang members is not the point here. Gangs are not homogenous entities or protorevolutionary organizations. In all gangs, like the ALKQN in New York and the CVL in Chicago, there are contradictory tendencies and factions. Some members did see the political rhetoric as a convenient cover to sell drugs and continue with violence and a brutal culture of hypermasculinity. Others strongly argued for a more community-based direction that stresses equality and the struggle for justice. Given the hopelessness on the streets, the lack of jobs, and the reality that the 1960s CVL and 1990s ALKQN failed, it is not surprising that so few gangs are tempted by social activism.

What I have learned is that gang members and their gangs are most properly labeled what Touraine calls "social actors" who are fully capable of acting in their community's interest, but also may not. This is what Saskia Sassen means by gangs having a "presence" in cities.

> The space of the city . . . becomes a place where informal or nonformal political actors can be part of the political scene in a way that is much more difficult at the national level. . . . street-level politics make possible the formation of new types of political subjects that do not have to go through the formal political system."[11]

The recognition of gangs as social actors means they are capable of transforming, if not likely to transform, into social movements, and much less into what Castells calls a "project identity" that seeks to change the overall social structure. However, there are specific issues that vitally concern gang members as well as other people in their communities. Under certain conditions, gangs can actively work together with their neighbors and move away from self-destruction. It is to these issues, I believe, that we should give our most urgent attention.

Police Brutality

First among these issues is police brutality and corruption. Exposing police misconduct is not an everyday activity for criminologists, who often feed at the trough of law enforcement and do not want to put possible research or evaluation grants at risk. But police brutality and corruption is such an ever-present reality, particularly in black ghettos, that antipolice brutality campaigns or demands for civilian control of police occur spontaneously and regularly.

Even when such movements do not exist, debunking the lies and distortions by law enforcement in the prosecution of gang members can be an important role for academics and human rights advocates. I have worked as an expert witness and have done research to expose the long history of police brutality and corruption in Chicago on my Web site. What is important about this issue is that police misconduct not only affects gang members but is an infectious racial disease that nearly everyone in black and minority communities instantly recognizes.

Police brutality and corruption undermine the legitimacy of government and mock any expectations that gang members should respect the law. Many police also act as if there were a war going on and, following James Hahn's reckless talk in Los Angeles,[12] believe that no rules should apply. Politicians are slow to criticize police, since they fear being labeled "soft on crime" and losing the next election. Still, most people are aware that unconstitutional and inhuman police practices abound on the streets. To paraphrase Gil Scott-Heron, a police officer can easily justify any action he or she takes by saying the offender or crime was "gang-related." While the laws of U.S. society are increasingly repressive, we must insist that the "guardians of law and order" abide by them.

Nothing written here denies or dismisses the reality of gang violence and the harm it does to its victims and communities. Who among us can understand how someone "could just kill a man?" A mother's murdered child should prompt our empathy and sympathy, no matter who the victim is. An entire, well-funded, criminal justice system exists to take vengeance on offenders. But we also need to find the courage to stand up and expose and condemn police violence and lies.

I believe that the exposure of police misconduct is the more appropriate and more necessary role for social scientists today, particularly for those studying gangs.

Gentrification

Another issue that has great potential for drawing gangs into political action is the secret war over space in our cities. In earlier times, gangs were used by landlords as arsonists to burn down the very neighborhoods that made up their turf to make way for more profitable development. As cities transform, the older neighborhoods become more valuable, and conflict intensifies. The police harassment in areas like Lawndale is not confined to gangs but to all youth, and, as my sixty-year-old Vice Lord in chapter 6 found out, the not-so-young as well.

While gentrification can mean the introduction of wealth into a community for the betterment of all, that is not the way it usually works, at least not in Chicago. Saving one's community, though, is a cause that can unite everyone, male and female, young and old, gang members included. This includes fighting for construction jobs and better schools that benefit gang members along with everyone else.[13]

But many community groups and citizens are reluctant to work with or are even opposed to the participation of gangs or others from the street. What I have argued in this book is that gangs are not merely social dynamite or social junk, "lost forever" and not able to function within broad community mobilizations. The extreme flexibility of the form of the gang documented in these pages supports my belief in the ability of gangs and gang members to change.

What is important within community-based movements is for those of us who understand the deep alienation of youth to promote a policy of both inclusion and nonviolence. We need to oppose the demonization and exclusion of gang members from community organizations and social movement by "respectable citizens" and stand forthrightly for cooperative, nonviolent social action on the part of all, including gang members.[14]

While this may sound fanciful, the lessons of the 1960s social movements may give cause to think again. Gangs were powerfully influenced by the nationalist, revolutionary, and social movements of those years. Like the CVL, they shed many of their old clothes and worked against violence and for rebuilding their communities. However, those same broader social movements in the end failed to significantly benefit those on the bottom of society, like the gangs. Consequently, when the movements subsided, repression stepped up, and when the industrial economy collapsed, nihilism and a rash of violence took over. We, and particularly our youth, are still burdened with this devastating legacy.

THE WAR ON TERROR AND GANGS

We also cannot ignore the one-sided policies of repression both within the United States and internationally. For example, as I write, the U.S. Gang Deterrence and Community Protection Act of 2007 has gathered bipartisan support. Domestically, this act federalizes many common crimes, which are "gang-related," applying a "mandatory minimum" of five years to them and the federal death penalty for any "gang-related" homicide. This bill has gathered steam by the demonization of Mara Salvatrucha 13 and the fanciful allegations of those like Newt Gingrich that gangs are allying with al-Qaeda in an unholy alliance of terror.

As Elana Zilberg, Tom Hayden,[15] and others have written, Mara Salvatrucha is not invading the United States but is an American creation, formed in the LA barrios to be joined by the sons and daughters of Salvadoran and other Central American immigrants after they fled the U.S.-sponsored civil wars. Trapped in barrios with few jobs or opportunities and gangs everywhere, young Central American kids did what poor kids everywhere do—

they joined the local gang. As they got into trouble, the U.S. Immigration Service deported not only teenagers but an entire gang as well.

The fight against deportations, like that against gentrification, has the potential to unite gang members with the broader community. My own expert witness work has found that deportation often threatens the very lives of some gang members. Broad support can be built for the basic human right to have a life free of terror and resist deportation.

MS-13 is a "gang without borders" not because it is a cotraveler with Osama bin Laden or Colombian drug lords but because of the history of U.S. intervention in Central America and U.S. policies of deporting those we forced to move to our shores in the first place. The equation of gangs with terrorists is absurd, but that has not stopped the mass media and a motley crew of Republicans and Democrats from panicking the public to support their latest crusade against children.

Not all the news is bad. In 2006 the presidents-elect of both Honduras and Haiti called for talks with gangs and other armed groups. This is a stunning rebuke to the U.S. policy of "Mano Duro," the Spanish translation of "zero tolerance." To recognize gang members as people to be *talked to* is a belief in their innate humanity and a willingness to try to understand those who previously had been seen only as an impersonal "enemy."

The UN also has adopted some promising approaches. When developing policy toward "child soldiers," the UN established guidelines of "disarmament, demobilization, and reconciliation," or "DDR."[16] This two-sided policy is a good guide toward working with gangs as well, and not just in the third world. It means that gangs who become active in social movements, for their part, must actively work to "stop the violence" within their own gang and with rivals. Democracy cannot tolerate violence, which, by definition, dehumanizes the other. On the side of the government, the principles of DDR mean that reconciliation, not war, is the aim of policy. This is a far cry from where we are today.

My main point is this: I believe it is crucial for social movements to reach out and include in their mobilizations the millions who are still left out, including the very large number of young people who inhabit the world of gangs. What I must admit is that while gangs today are involved with some social movements in Chicago and elsewhere, on the whole their nihilism prevents activism and traps gang members in a self-centered, desperate struggle for survival. Dim prospects of success, however, are not a reason to stop trying.

Hip-Hop and Don't Stop

But political involvement is not the only answer, and may not even be the most immediately important one. My analysis argues that cultural identity is at the core of resistance to the unfettered power of markets. On the streets, cultural identity means hip-hop and gangsta rap. "Democracy," Touraine says, "is best defined as a will to reconcile rational thought, personal liberty, and cultural identity."[17]

This means that the construction of street identities based on hip-hop, even if they are oppositional and destructive, need to be recognized as a legitimate expression of the frustrations of youth. Wasn't that how many of our older generation had tried to understand James Dean in *Rebel without a Cause?* Most of all, as Afrika Bambaataa said, hip-hop means the power of youth to choose their own identities and change their lives. It means young people can face the void and still keep on rapping.

But it does not mean that we need to sing the praises of identities that deny the rights of others—particularly identities that glorify violence and drugs and flaunt contempt for women. I have tried to show that while these more destructive identities have ghetto roots, they are marketed worldwide because the big media corporations control "gangsta rappers." We need to point out that the violence and misogyny of gangsta rap is not mainly a message from the streets but a message from the suites, or *corporate* hip-hop. We need to expose and oppose this individualist, consumerist, and exploitative music for its willful, destructive misleading of our youth.

But hip-hop's power is important because it is the voice not just of gangs or the streets but of youthful rebellion. It is not just the voice of African Americans, but is a black Atlantic sound, mixing cultures in a display of how diversity can make meaning in all our lives. In other words, as a resistance identity hip-hop has the power to unite people and demand basic human rights for all. Hip-hop is not a social movement but contains the seeds of many such movements, impatient to emerge. Teachers, youth counselors, academics, and all of us trying to reach out to gang youth have to first learn that h-i-p-h-o-p spells "rebellion." We need to join it, not fight it.

I end with lines from "The Rose That Grew from Concrete," by rap's poet laureate, Tupac Shakur:

Did you hear about the rose that grew
from a crack in the concrete?
Proving nature's law is wrong it
learned to walk without having feet.
Funny it seems, but by keeping its dreams
it learned to breathe fresh air.
Long live the rose that grew from concrete
when no one else ever cared.

NOTES

INTRODUCTION

1. The reader will be relieved that I have ignored criminology's nit-picking definitional fixation on "what is a gang." For example, see Richard A. Ball and G. David Curry, "The Logic of Definition in Criminology: Purposes and Methods for Defining 'Gangs,'" *Criminology* 33 (1995): 225–46.

2. Manuel Castells, *The Rise of the Network Society,* vol. 1 of *The Information Age: Economy, Society, and Culture* (Malden, Mass.: Blackwell, 2000), 303. See also Castells, *End of Millennium,* 2nd ed., vol. 3 of *The Information Age: Economy, Society, and Culture* (Malden, Mass.: Blackwell, 2000); Castells, *The Power of Identity,* 2nd ed. vol. 2 of *The Information Age: Economy, Society, and Culture* (Malden, Mass.: Blackwell, 2004).

3. Malcolm Klein, Hans-Jurgen Kerner, Cheryl L. Maxson, and Elmar G. M. Weitekamp, eds., *The Eurogang Paradox: Street Gangs and Youth Groups in the U.S. and Europe* (Dordrecht, The Netherlands: Kluwer, 2001); Scott H. Decker and Frank M. Weerman, eds., *European Street Gangs and Troublesome Youth Groups* (Lanham, Md.: AltaMira, 2005).

4. Ted Robert Gurr, *Peoples versus States: Minorities at Risk in the New Century* (Washington, D.C.: United States Institute of Peace Press, 2000); Ted Robert Gurr and Barbara Harff, *Ethnic Conflict in World Politics* (Boulder, Colo.: Westview, 1994).

5. Manuel Castells, *The Power of Identity,* vol. 2 of *The Information Age: Economy, Society, and Culture* (Malden, Mass.: Blackwell, 1997), 66.

6. I sharply depart from my colleagues by arguing that race has often been more important than space in understanding gangs. See also John M. Hagedorn, "Race Not Space: A Revisionist History of Gangs in Chicago," *Journal of African American History* 91 (2006): 194–208.

7. West defines "nihilism" in part as "the lived experience of coping with a life of horrifying meaninglessness, hopelessness, and (most important) lovelessness" (*Race Matters*

[New York: Vintage, 1993], 22–23). In his later work, West expands nihilism to be a much broader malady. See Cornel West, *Democracy Matters: Winning the Fight against Imperialism* (New York: Penguin, 2004).

8. Gus Russo, *The Outfit: The Role of Chicago's Underworld in the Shaping of Modern America* (New York: Bloomsbury, 2001).

9. William Julius Wilson, *When Work Disappears: The World of the New Urban Poor* (New York: Knopf, 1996).

10. Alain Touraine, "Beyond Social Movements," in *Social Movements: Critiques, Concepts, Case-Studies,* ed. Stanford M. Lyman (New York: New York University Press, 1995), 184.

11. Philippe Bourgois, *In Search of Respect: Selling Crack in El Barrio* (Cambridge: Cambridge University Press, 1995), 326.

12. bell hooks, *We Real Cool: Black Men and Masculinity* (New York: Routledge, 2004), 151, 27.

13. John M. Hagedorn and Mary L. Devitt, "Fighting Female: The Social Construction of the Female Gang," in *Female Gangs in America: Essays on Girls, Gangs, and Gender,* ed. Meda Chesney-Lind and John M. Hagedorn (Chicago: Lakeview, 1999), 256–76.

14. Cornel West, preface to *Hip Hop and Philosophy: Rhyme 2 Reason,* ed. Derrick Darby and Tommie Shelby (Chicago: Open Court, 2005), xi–xii.

15. Ayazi-hashjin Sherry, *Rap and Hip Hop: Voices of a Generation* (New York: Rosen, 1999), 11.

16. Tricia Rose, *Black Noise: Rap Music and Black Culture in Contemporary America* (Hanover, N.H.: University Press of New England, 1994), 101.

17. Derrick Bell, *Faces at the Bottom of the Well: The Permanence of Racism* (New York: Basic Books, 1992).

18. Michael Eric Dyson, *Holler If You Hear Me* (New York: Basic Books, 2001), 64.

19. Bourgois, *In Search of Respect;* Elijah Anderson, *Code of the Street: Decency, Violence, and the Moral Life of the Inner City* (New York: Norton, 1999).

20. Saskia Sassen, *The Global City: New York, London, Tokyo* (Princeton, N.J.: Princeton University Press, 1991); Sassen, "The Global City: One Setting for New Types of Gang Work and Political Culture?" in *Gangs in the Global City: Alternatives to Traditional Criminology,* ed. John M. Hagedorn (Urbana: University of Illinois Press, 2006), 112–33.

21. UN-Habitat, *Slums of the World: The Face of Urban Poverty in the New Millennium?* (Nairobi, Kenya: United Nations Human Settlements Programme, 2003); Harvey Warren Zorbaugh, *The Gold Coast and the Slum: A Sociological Study of Chicago's Near North Side* (Chicago: University of Chicago Press, 1929); Mike Davis, *Planet of Slums* (London: Verso, 2006).

22. Loïc Wacquant, "The New 'Peculiar Institution': On the Prison as Surrogate Ghetto," *Theoretical Criminology* 4 (2000): 377–89.

23. "Turns out, even gangs have gone global" is the opening line of the FBI synopsis of its top criminal investigative executive, Chris Swecker.

24. CNN, news report, June 10, 2002. Jose Padilla, former member of Chicago's Maniac Latin Disciples, is arrested and charged with trying to build and explode a radioactive "dirty bomb." He is held as an "enemy combatant" without charge and little availability to counsel. For legal background, see http://www.humanrightsfirst.org/us_law/inthecourts/supreme_court_padilla.htm.

25. For example, the Gang Deterrence and Community Protection Act of 2005. Here is Robert Clifford, head of an FBI task force investigating gang terrorist links in Central America: "The FBI, in concert with the U.S. intelligence community and governments of several Central American republics, have determined that there is no basis in fact to support this allegation of al-Qaeda or even radical Islamic ties to MS-13 (Mara Salvatrucha)" (USA Today Online, February 23, 2005, updated February 24, 2005, http://www.usatoday.com/news/world/2005-02-23-gang-salvador_x.htm).

26. For example, Senator Dianne Feinstein: "The bottom line is that gangs represent a serious national threat, and the problem calls for a serious national response" (http://feinstein.senate.gov/05releases/r-ganghill-intro.htm); Max G. Manwaring, "Street Gangs: The New Urban Insurgency" (Carlisle, Penn.: Strategic Studies Institute, 2005). "If the struggle against political enemies is defined as a struggle against evil, it will turn into a holy war. And in holy war there can be no compromise. Evil cannot be converted; it must be eliminated" (Mahmood Mamdani, *Good Muslim, Bad Muslim: America, the Cold War, and the Roots of Terror* [New York: Pantheon Books, 2004]). We are still reliving Ronald Reagan's "evil empire."

27. C. Wright Mills, *The Sociological Imagination* (London: Oxford University Press, 1959), 177.

28. Diego Vigil, *A Rainbow of Gangs: Street Cultures in the Mega-City* (Austin: University of Texas Press, 2002), 7.

29. Aside from works by Joan Moore, Luis Barrios, David Brotherton, Diego Vigil, and Tom Hayden, see Jim Short's careful discussion of this issue in "Gangs, Politics, and the Social Order," in *Delinquency, Crime, and Society*, ed. James F. Short Jr. (Chicago: University of Chicago Press, 1976), 129–63.

30. For a clear-sighted discussion of the pitfalls of government-funded research, see Roland Chilton, "Viable Policy: The Impact of Federal Funding and the Need for Independent Research Agendas," *Criminology* 39 (2001): 1–8.

31. http://www.uic.edu/cuppa/gci/.

32. Hagedorn, "Race Not Space"; John M. Hagedorn, "Race, Space, and the Institutional Gang: The Chicago School Reconsidered," in *Gangs in the Global City: Alternatives to Traditional Criminology*, ed. Hagedorn.

33. Hagedorn, *Gangs in the Global City: Alternatives to Traditional Criminology.*

34. Klein et al., *Eurogang Paradox.*

35. Luke Dowdney, ed., *neither War nor Peace: International Comparisons of Children and Youth in Organized Armed Violence* (Rio de Janeiro: 7Letras, 2005).

36. J. M. Hagedorn and F. Gutiérrez, "Chicago and Medellín: A History of Organized Armed Violence." Unpublished paper.

37. John M. Hagedorn and Brigid Rauch, "Housing, Gangs, and Homicide: What We Can Learn from Chicago," *Urban Affairs Review* 42 (2007): 435–56.

1. GHETTO, FAVELA, AND TOWNSHIP

1. Mike Davis, "Planet of Slums," *New Left Review* 26 (March–April 2004), http://www.newleftreview.net/NLR26001.8html (accessed November 13, 2006).

2. Dowdney, *neither War nor Peace*.

3. Philip Selznick, *Leadership in Administration: A Sociological Interpretation* (Berkeley and Los Angeles: University of California Press, 1957); John M. Meyer and Brian Rowan, "Institutionalized Organizations: Formal Structure as Myth and Ceremony," *American Journal of Sociology* 83 [1997]: 340–62.

4. Malcolm Klein, "Resolving the Eurogang Paradox," in Klein et al., *Eurogang Paradox*, 7–21. For a more theoretical view, see Cheryl L. Maxson and Malcolm Klein, "'Play Groups' No Longer: Urban Street Gangs in the Los Angeles Region," in *From Chicago to L.A.: Making Sense of Urban Theory*, ed. Michael J. Dear (Thousand Oaks, Calif.: Sage, 2000), 239–66.

5. W. I. Thomas and Florian Znaniecki, *The Polish Peasant*, ed. E. Zaretsky, 5 vols. (1918–20; rpt. Urbana: University of Illinois Press, 1996), 45 note 1.

6. Frederic Thrasher, *The Gang* (Chicago: University of Chicago Press, 1927).

7. UN-Habitat, *Challenge of the Slums: Global Report on Human Settlements* (Nairobi, Kenya: United Nations Human Settlements Programme, 2003); see also UN-Habitat, *Slums of the World.* "The term slum includes the traditional meaning, that is, housing areas that were once respectable or even desirable, but which have since deteriorated, as the original dwellers have moved to new and better areas of cities. The condition of the old houses has then declined, and the units have been progressively subdivided and rented out to lower-income groups. A typical example is the inner city slums of many historical towns and cities in both the industrial and the developing countries. The term slum has, however, come to include also the vast informal settlements that are quickly becoming the most visual expression of urban poverty. The quality of dwellings in such settlements varies from the simplest shack to permanent structures, while access to water, electricity, sanitation and other basic services and infrastructure tends to be limited. Such settlements are referred to by a wide range of names and include a variety of tenurial arrangements" (UN-Habitat, *Challenge of the Slums,* 8).

8. The UN calculates that worldwide 1.3 billion people live on less than US$1 a day, its official measure of extreme poverty, and 2.8 billion live on less than $2 per day (United Nations, "Report on the World Social Situation" [New York: UN Department of Social and Economic Affairs, 2005]).

9. Davis, "Planet of Slums," 9.

10. Ibid., 6.

11. Mohammed Ibrahim, "An Empirical Survey of Children and Youth in Organised Armed Violence in Nigeria: Egbesu Boys, OPC, and Bakassi Boys as a Case Study," in Dowdney, *neither War nor Peace,* 4.

12. UN-Habitat, *Slums of the World.*

13. http://www.crin.org/docs/edu_youth_conflict.pdf (accessed August 11, 2006).

14. Charles Green, *Manufacturing Powerlessness in the Black Diaspora: Inner-City Youth and the New Global Frontier* (Walnut Creek, Calif.: AltaMira, 2001), 16.

15. See Herbert C. Covey, *Street Gangs throughout the World* (Springfield, Ill.: Thomas, 2003).

16. UN-Habitat, *Street Children and Gangs in African Cities: Guidelines for Local Authorities* (Nairobi, Kenya: United Nations Centre for Human Settlements, 2000). For example, according to the introduction, "Local authorities have a major role to play in improving the living conditions of street children and gangs. The main framework for improving the living conditions for children is set out in the UN Convention on the Rights of the Child, in four broad areas: survival, development, protection and participation" (v).

17. See especially Susan Strange, *The Retreat of the State: The Diffusion of Power in the World Economy* (New York: Cambridge University Press, 1996).

18. See, for example, the essays gathered in Robert Park, *Race and Culture* (Chicago: University of Chicago Press, 1940).

19. William Foote Whyte, *Street Corner Society: The Social Structure of an Italian Slum* (Chicago: University of Chicago Press, 1943); Loïc Wacquant, "Three Pernicious Premises in the Study of the American Ghetto," *International Journal of Urban and Regional Planning* 21 (1997): 341–53; William Reno, *Warlord Politics and African States* (Boulder, Colo.: Rienner, 1998).

20. "The Fourth World comprises large areas of the globe, such as much of Sub-Saharan Africa, and impoverished areas of Latin America and Asia. But it is also present in literally every country, and every city, in this new geography of social exclusion" (Castells, *End of Millennium*, 3:168). Castells follows William Julius Wilson's "underclass" argument that economic restructuring has resulted in "a truly disadvantaged" left out of or, to use Castells's term, "socially excluded" from mainstream society (William Julius Wilson, *The Declining Significance of Race* [Chicago: University of Chicago Press, 1978]; Wilson, *The Truly Disadvantaged* [Chicago: University of Chicago Press, 1987]).

21. Castells, *End of Millennium*, 3:200; United Nations, "Report on the World Social Situation," chap. 2; Davis reports that forty-six countries are poorer today than in 1990 (*Planet of Slums*, 163).

22. Zygmunt Bauman, *Globalization: The Human Consequences* (New York: Columbia University Press, 1998).

23. Strange points out that in the West, "'Reform,' these days, is apt to mean cutting back on the activities of government, shrinking the bureaucracy and imposing husbandry and economy on government offices. It used, within living memory, to mean the exact opposite: using the authority of government to impose more humane and regulated behavior on business and the private sector in general" (*Retreat of the State,* xii).

24. Davis, *Planet of Slums,* 164.

25. Manuel Castells, *End of Millennium* (Malden, Mass.: Blackwell, 1998), 185 note 39.

26. Joan Moore argued that Mexican gangs in East Los Angeles were "quasi-institutionalized," in a formulation that anticipated this work (*Homeboys: Gangs, Drugs, and Prison in the Barrios of Los Angeles* [Philadelphia: Temple University Press, 1978], 40). Much earlier, Everett Hughes used the term "bastard institutions" to describe Chicago's rackets, though not specifically referring to gangs, as "illegitimate distributors of legitimate goods and services; others satisfy wants not considered legitimate. . . . Some of these bastard institutions are directly against the law, or the declared moral values of society." While Hughes was writing in an era of more substantial mobility, his conclusions bear repeating: "These bastard institutions should be studied not merely as pathological departures from what is good and right, but as part of the total complex of human activities and enterprises" (Everett Hughes, "Bastard Institutions," in *The Sociological Eye: Selected Papers,* ed. Everett Hughes [Chicago: Aldine, 1971], 99).

27. Philip Selznick, *TVA and the Grass Roots: A Study of Politics and Organization* (Berkeley and Los Angeles: University of California Press, 1949).

28. Ibid., 17, 21. Even a casual reading of Selznick's classic *Leadership in Administration*'s description of the process of institutionalization can see its applicability to persisting gangs.

29. The student, familiar with sociological theory, went on: "My experience and introduction into the gang is extremely contradictory to Thrasher's theory. This was by no means a spontaneously formed group of individuals. Everything was painstakingly planned and symbolic. His phrase 'espirit de corps' did not capture the essence of this organization. These men standing before me were not little boys who grew up with one another. Most of the brothers came from different sets and communities. The rituals were not child's play but rather matters of life and death. We were not integrated through conflict but rather through necessity. We all were in need of something. Whether it was money, popularity, attention, a family, or support, the gang was willing to artificially fill a void."

30. Selznick, *Leadership in Administration,* 17–18.

31. For a brief overview of the various perspectives of institutional and neo-institutional theory, see W. Richard Scott, *Institutions and Organizations* (Thousand Oaks, Calif.: Sage, 1995).

32. John M. Meyer and Brian Rowan, in a classic essay, describe institutions as "dramatic enactments of the rationalized myths pervading modern society" ("Institutionalized Organizations: Formal Structure as Myth and Ceremony"). See also Selznick's discussion of "socially integrating myths." He concludes by summarizing that "myths are institution builders" (*Leadership in Administration,* 151–52).

33. Jack Katz and Curtis Jackson-Jacobs, "The Criminologists' Gang," in *The Blackwell Companion to Criminology,* ed. Colin Sumner (New York: Blackwell, 2003), 92. I would add, mythmaking is also a central activity for males in the academy.

34. Selznick, *Leadership in Administration.*

35. Marshall W. Meyer and Lynne G. Zucker, *Permanently Failing Organizations* (Newbury Park, Calif.: Sage, 1989).

36. Andrew V. Papachristos, *A.D., After the Disciples: The Neighborhood Impact of Federal Gang Prosecution* (Chicago: New Chicago Schools Press, 2001).

37. Chicago Black Gangster Disciple member, interview with author, Chicago, 2003.

38. For a more detailed discussion of the concept, see John M. Hagedorn, "Gangs, Institutions, Race, and Space: The Chicago School Reconsidered," in Hagedorn, *Gangs in the Global City: Alternatives to Traditional Criminology,* 26–64.

2. STREET INSTITUTIONS

1. Hagedorn, "Gangs, Institutions, Race, and Space."

2. Rod Emery, *The Blueprint: From Gangster Disciple to Growth and Development* (Elgin, Ill.: Morris, 1996). See also the Gaylords' official history, Michael Scott, *Lords of Lawndale: My Life in a Chicago White Street Gang* (Bloomington, Ind.: AuthorHouse, 2004).

3. Luke Dowdney, *Children of the Drug Trade: A Case Study of Children in Organised Armed Violence in Rio de Janeiro* (Rio de Janeiro: 7Letras, 2003).

4. Andre Standing, *The Threat of Gangs and Anti-Gangs Policy* (Cape Town: Institute for Security Studies, 2005).

5. Wacquant, "New 'Peculiar Institution.'"

6. Dowdney, *neither War nor Peace,* 34.

7. James Jacobs, *Stateville: The Penitentiary in Mass Society* (Chicago: University of Chicago Press, 1977), 146.

8. David Dawley, *A Nation of Lords: The Autobiography of the Vice Lords* (Prospect Heights, Ill.: Waveland, 1992).

9. John R. Fry, *Locked-Out Americans: A Memoir* (New York: Harper and Row, 1973), 24.

10. Irving A. Spergel, *The Youth Gang Problem: A Community Approach* (New York: Oxford University Press, 1995).

11. Irvin Kinnes, *From Urban Street Gangs to Criminal Empires: The Changing Face of Gangs in the Western Cape* (Cape Town: Institute for Security Studies, 2000); Dowdney, *Children of the Drug Trade,* 43. Chicago's prison-gang connection was first laid out in the classic work of James Jacobs, *Stateville.*

12. The academic left has typically failed to understand the significance and reality of the streets. For example: "Marginals have no privileged role to play in the fight against dictatorship and for socialism. They have no organization with which to develop the struggle." On the contrary, it was the revolutionary left that lost its organization during the dictatorship and the "marginals" who built organizations in the favelas (João Quartim, *Dictatorship and Armed Struggle in Brazil* [London: NLB, 1971], 153).

13. Dowdney, *neither War nor Peace,* 31.

14. Jorge Atilio Silva Iulianeli, Luiz Paulo Guanabara, Paulo Cesar Pontes Fraga, and Tom Blickman, *Drugs and Conflict* (Amsterdam: Transnational Institute, 2004), 27.

15. Ted Legget, "Terugskeit: Growing Up on the Street Corners of Mannenberg, South Africa," in Dowdney, *neither War nor Peace,* 292–311.

16. These three cities are not the only ones that produced institutionalized gangs in the 1960s. In Jamaica, the political battles of the People's National Party (PNP) and the Jamaica Labor Party (JLP) after independence in the 1960s led to the recruitment of area gangs to join gunplay with politics. In Medellín and Cali, Colombia, the revolutionary groups formed in the 1960s like Fuerzas Armadas Revolucionarias de Colombia (FARC) (and later the drug cartels) provided an organizational outlet for the hundreds of youth gangs that have flourished in those cities. See Laurie Gunst, *Born Fi' Dead: A Journey through the Jamaican Posse Underworld* (New York: Holt, 1995); Francisco Gutiérrez Sanin and Ana Maria Jaramillo, "Crime, [Counter]insurgency, and the Privatization of Security: The Case of Medellín, Colombia," *Environment and Urbanization* 16 (2004): 1–14; Ivan Dario Ramirez, "Medellín: The Invisible Children of the Social and Armed Conflict," in Dowdney, *neither War nor Peace*, 174–94; World Bank, *Cali, Colombia: Toward a City Development Strategy* (Washington, D.C.: International Bank for Reconstruction and Development, World Bank, 2002).

17. "After oil, the second largest international commodity traded in the world is drugs" (S. Cohen, "Crime and Politics: Spot the Difference," *British Journal of Sociology* 47 [1996]: 12).

18. Sudhir Alladi Venkatesh, *American Project: The Rise and Fall of a Modern Ghetto* (Cambridge, Mass.: Harvard University Press, 2000).

19. See Dowdney, *neither War nor Peace;* Kinnes, *From Urban Street Gangs to Criminal Empires;* and Andre Standing, "The Social Contradictions of Organised Crime on the Cape Flats" (Cape Town: Institute for Security Studies, 2003).

20. Michael Morgensen, "Corner and Area Gangs in Inner-City Jamaica," in Dowdney, *neither War nor Peace*, 229–45.

21. Iulianeli et al., "Drugs and Conflict."

22. Oscar Newman, *Defensible Space: Crime Prevention through Urban Design* (New York: Collier Books, 1972).

23. Lydia Richardson and Adale Kirsten, *Armed Violence and Poverty in Brazil: A Case Study of Rio de Janeiro and Assessment of Viva Rio for the Armed Violence and Poverty Initiative* (London: UK Department of International Development, 2005).

24. Dowdney, *neither War nor Peace*, 28.

25. See Lucia Macorro, "A Tale of Two Cities." Unpublished paper.

26. Dowdney, *neither War nor Peace*. In Vigário Geral in 1992, responding to the killing of two corrupt police officers, a full-scale invasion of the favela resulted. After firing randomly on residents and killing twenty-three, the police reboarded their helicopters and flew off. In another favela, Rocinha, in January 2004, 1,200 police occupied the favela to stop a gang war. They failed (Richardson and Kirsten, "Armed Violence and Poverty in Brazil," 27).

27. Dowdney, *neither War nor Peace*, 59.

28. Venkatesh, *American Project*, 85.

29. Chicago Gang History Project, interview with author, Chicago, 2003.

30. See Arnold R. Hirsch, *Making the Second Ghetto: Race and Housing in Chicago, 1940–1960*, 2nd ed. (Chicago: University of Chicago Press, 1998).

31. Susan J. Popkin, *The Hidden War: Crime and the Tragedy of Public Housing in Chicago* (New Brunswick, N.J.: Rutgers University Press, 2000), 67.

32. See Arnold R. Hirsch, *Making the Second Ghetto: Race and Housing in Chicago, 1940–1960* (Cambridge: Cambridge University Press, 1983); and Thomas Lee Philpott, *The Slum and the Ghetto: Neighborhood Deterioration and Middle-Class Reform: Chicago, 1880–1930* (New York: Oxford University Press, 1978).

33. For a history of the spatial segregation of Cape Town's gangs, see Don Pinnock, *The Brotherhoods: Street Gangs and State Control in Cape Town* (Cape Town: David Philip, 1984). For a more detailed comparison between Chicago and South African conditions, see John M. Hagedorn, "Gangs in Late Modernity," in Hagedorn, *Gangs in the Global City: Alternatives to Traditional Criminology.*

34. Legget, South Africa Country Report, in "Terugskeit."

35. Gangs in Kingston, Jamaica, were also based on neighborhoods aligned with political factions in the Manley-Seaga years. For Jamaica, see Morgensen, "Corner and Area Gangs in Inner-City Jamaica"; and Gunst, *Born Fi' Dead.* Segregation and voluntary separation also characterize the growth of armed groups in Belfast and Mumbai.

36. See the almost identical story of Los Angeles gangs in Alejandro A. Alonso, "Racialized Identities and the Formation of Black Gangs in Los Angeles," *Urban Geography* 25 (2004): 658–74. Cf. Hagedorn, "Race Not Space," a revisionist history of Chicago gangs.

37. Felix Padilla, *The Gang as an American Enterprise* (New Brunswick, N.J.: Rutgers University Press, 1992). Ethnic identity was also crucial for Latino gangs. The Latin Kings had its origins in the 1950s as a Puerto Rican street gang, but aggressively recruited youth in all Latino neighborhoods and grew powerful in the 1960s. During the same time the Young Lords, which also began as a street gang, turned political, but stayed all–Puerto Rican and did not recruit youth. Consequently, the Young Lords did not survive the repression of the late 1960s. The Latin Kings, on the other hand, thrived in prison and still have thousands of members in Chicago and branches around the world (Chicago Gang History Project, interview with author, Chicago, 2003).

38. Ric Curtis and Travis Wendel, "Lockin' Niggas Up Like It's Goin' Out of Style: The Differing Consequences of Police Interventions in Three Brooklyn New York Drug Markets." Unpublished manuscript, New York City, 2003.

39. See Macorro, "Tale of Two Cities."

40. Jailson Souza de Silva and Andre Urani, *Brazil: Children in Drug Trafficking: A Rapid Assessment* (Geneva: International Labor Organization, International Programme on the Elimination of Child Labour, 2002).

41. A 1967 law, passed under the military dictatorship, prohibited even the discussion of racism (Benedita da Silva, *Benedita da Silva: An Afro-Brazilian Women's Story of Politics and Love* [Chicago: Food First Books, 1997], 133).

42. Victor Ramos, "The 'Pedagogy of Drums': Music and Art as Mediators between

Youngsters from Favelas and Policemen in Brazil" (presented at Conference on Music and Cultural Rights—Trends and Prospects, Pittsburgh, 2005).

43. For example, the Vigário Geral–based rap group, Grupo Cultural Afro Reggae.

44. Another clear-cut example of institutionalization of gangs in South Africa is the Marashea gangs around the gold mines near Johannesburg. Gary Kynoch's book, though he never uses the term, is a perfect illustration of how gangs institutionalize. This is a representative conclusion: "The gangs negotiated the hazardous terrain of apartheid sometimes by challenging, but more often by adapting to, the urban conditions imposed by the South African state" (Gary Kynoch, *We Are Fighting the World: A History of the Marashea Gangs in South Africa, 1947–1999* [Athens: Ohio University Press, 2005], 90). An ethnic element is involved as well, as Marashea gangs are Basotho from Lesotho and warred continuously among themselves but also against the Xosha and Zulu.

45. See Pinnock, *Brotherhoods;* Kinnes, *From Urban Street Gangs to Criminal Empires.* Mandrax is a tablet that was used as a sleeping pill. It is smoked to give a greater rush and is thought to be highly addictive. The central ingredient is methaqualone and is now largely imported by the gangs from Pakistan and India. See http://www.drugaware .co.za/mandrax.html. *Dagga* is marijuana.

46. Kinnes, *From Urban Street Gangs to Criminal Empires.*

47. Clive Glaser, *Bo-Tsotsi: The Youth Gangs of Soweto, 1935–1976* (Portsmouth, N.H.: Heinemann, 2000).

48. Luis Rodriguez suggests that the favoring of criminals over militants may be a conscious policy of the state. While the evidence is weaker for this proposition in Chicago and Rio, in Cape Town there is ample evidence to support Rodriguez's view. See Luis Rodriguez, *Hearts and Hands: Creating Community in Violent Times* (New York: Seven Stories, 2001).

49. Bill Dixon and Lisa-Marie Johns, *Gangs, Pagad, and the State: Vigilantism and Revenge Violence in the Western Cape* (Cape Town: Center for the Study of Violence and Reconciliation, 2001).

50. Suren Pillay, "Problematizing the Making of Good and Evil: Gangs and Pagad," *Critical Arts: A Journal of South-North Cultural and Media Studies* 16 (2002): 61.

51. Standing, "Threat of Gangs and Anti-gangs Policy." He goes on, "The perception of political exclusion among the colored community plays a major role in motivational and causal factors that keep people involved in gang activity."

52. There are also conflicts between "coloured" and "Indian" or "Malaysian." Gangsters are often seen as Eur-African (Pillay, "Problematizing the Making of Good and Evil").

53. Dixon and Johns, *Gangs, Pagad, and the State.*

54. For a typical view, see Chicago Crime Commission, "Gangs: Public Enemy Number One" (1995) and "The New Faces of Organized Crime" (1997). A more recent attempt to redefine many street gangs as organized crime is Sean Grennan and Marjie T. Britz, *Organized Crime: A Worldwide Perspective* (Upper Saddle River, N.J.: Pearson/ Prentice Hall, 2006).

55. Dowdney, *neither War nor Peace.*

56. Ibid., 31; Alba Zaluar, *Violence in Rio de Janeiro: Styles of Leisure, Drug Use, and Trafficking* (New York: UNESCO, 2005), 31–39.

57. Dowdney, *neither War nor Peace.* The mythologizing of gang leaders and drug dealers is best exemplified by the Mexican narcocorrido, traditional folk songs often commissioned by traffickers (Elijah Wald, *Narcocorrido: A Journey into the Music of Drugs, Guns, and Guerrillas* [New York: Rayo/HarperCollins, 2001]; Luis Astorga, "The Social Construction of the Identity of the Trafficker" [New York: UNESCO, 2005], 39–46).

58. Standing, "Threat of Gangs and Anti-gangs Policy."

59. Karl E. Weick, "Educational Organizations as Loosely Coupled Systems," *Administrative Science Quarterly* 21 (1976): 1–19.

60. Paul R. Lawrence and Jay W. Lorsch, *Organization and Environment: Managing Differentiation and Integration* (Homewood, Ill.: Irwin, 1969); John M. Hagedorn, "Neighborhoods, Markets, and Gang Drug Organization," *Journal of Research in Crime and Delinquency* 32 (1994): 197–219.

61. For example, I was told the Conservative Vice Lords today consist of "the Albany Vice Lords, Cicero Insane Vice Lords, Conservative Vice Lords, Ebony Vice Lords, Four Corner Hustler Vice Lords, Imperial Insane Vice Lords, Mafia Insane Vice Lords, Traveling Vice Lords, Undertaker Vice Lords, Unknown Vice Lords, and the only Latino Vice Lords are the Spanish Vice Lords not to be misconceived with the Spanish Lords that are not part of the Vice Lords" (interview with author, Chicago, 2004). There are more Vice Lord chapters, though, than this list.

62. See sample constitutions in George Knox, *An Introduction to Gangs* (Chicago: Wyndham Hall, 1996).

63. Chicago Gang History Project, interview with author, Chicago, 2003. The Milwaukee Kings are not to be confused with the Latin Kings, a sworn enemy.

64. Moore, *Homeboys.*

65. Chicago Unknown Vice Lord member, interview with author, Chicago, 2003.

66. If gangs have a history, it means they will inevitably go through stages of youth, adulthood, and old age (Meyer and Zucker, *Permanently Failing Organizations*). This is a characteristic of the population ecology school of organizational theory.

67. Consider this scene, reminiscent of Al Capone, of Cape Town's Hard Livings leader, Rashied Staggie: "The act of throwing money from a moving car was quite a spectacle. Staggie would first drive his car up and down the street and tell the children that he would be throwing money out when he returned. As a consequence, hundreds of people, including adults, were drawn into the street. They would wait for the car to pass and everyone would scramble at the first sight of fluttering money. Adults, children, old and young would run around to get their hand on some money. In this way, the gang leader would sometimes throw R20,000 [US$3,500] out of his car window for the community." This allowed Staggie to win large sections of the community to his side when he was in trouble with the law (Kinnes, *From Urban Street Gangs to Criminal Empires*).

68. Maxson and Klein, "'Play Groups' No Longer." Dear's edited volume, *From Chicago to L.A.: Making Sense of Urban Theory,* contains the basic assumptions and claims of the Los Angeles school. See also the argument by Katz and Jackson-Jacobs in "The Criminologists' Gang."

69. Malcolm Klein, "The Value of Comparisons in Street Gang Research," *Journal of Contemporary Criminal Justice* 21 (2005): 125–52.

3. THE PROBLEM WITH DEFINITIONS

1. Conerly Casey, "Mediated Hostility: Media, 'Affective Citizenships,' and Genocide in Northern Nigeria," in *Genocide, Truth, and Representation: Anthropological Approaches,* ed. Alexander Hinton and Kevin O'Neill (Durham, N.C.: Duke University Press, 2008). The actual quote was taken from an earlier version of this chapter, reprinted by permission of the author.

2. Jack A. Goldstone, "States, Terrorists, and the Clash of Civilizations," in *Understanding September 11,* ed. Craig Calhoun, Paul Price, and Ashley Timmer (New York: New Press, 2002), 151.

3. Klein, "Resolving the Eurogang Paradox," 10.

4. Covey, *Street Gangs throughout the World,* 69.

5. Decker and Weerman, *European Street Gangs and Troublesome Youth Groups.* The "Eurogang" definition of a gang is "any durable, street-oriented youth group whose involvement in illegal activity is part of their group identity" (ibid., 288). The editors, and Klein in a preface, insist that "the most important" contribution of the Eurogang research is perhaps the "utility of the definition of a street gang" (ibid., 304).

6. Not all urbanists were optimists. Spengler's dismay over the results of urbanism was the most extreme case, and Weber's insight of the iron cage of modernity was similarly bleak. The Chicago school, however, perhaps reflecting American vigor, countered European pessimism with the notion that the city can create the conditions for freedom. See the introduction in Richard Sennett, ed., *Classic Essays on the Culture of Cities* (Englewood Cliffs, N.J.: Prentice-Hall, 1969). More on this in chapter 6.

7. Alain Touraine, *Can We Live Together? Equality and Difference* (Stanford, Calif.: Stanford University Press, 2000).

8. Richard Wright, *Native Son* (New York: Harper and Row, 1940), 392; Frantz Fanon, *The Wretched of the Earth* (New York: Grove, 1963).

9. Cypress Hill, "Here Is Something You Can't Understand," *Stone Raiders* (Columbia Records, 2001).

10. West, *Race Matters.*

11. Norman Elias, *The Civilizing Process: The History of Manners* (1939; rpt. Oxford: Blackwell, 1994); Robert A. Nisbet, *History of the Idea of Progress* (New York: Basic Books, 1980).

12. Strange, *Retreat of the State,* 4; "The new power system is characterized . . . by the plurality of sources of authority . . . the nation being just one of these" (Castells, *Power of Identity,* 303).

13. Arundhati Roy, "Public Power in an Age of Empire," Democracy Now, August 2004, http://www.democracynow.org/static/Arundhati_Trans.shtml (accessed December 22, 2005).

14. Castells, *Rise of the Network Society*, 141. Touraine argues that "it is not conducive to democracy when the weakening of the state subordinates the whole of society to the interests of those with the strongest market position" (*Can We Live Together?* 232). One typical example is Kenya, where a Structural Adjustment Plan (SAP) by the World Bank and IMF was implemented in the early 1990s. Resistance by the Kenyan state was met by stopping international loans, and the government was forced to freeze employment of teachers and civil service. An end to price supports sent commodity prices skyrocketing, and students were forced to drop out of college because of sharp rises in the price of education. Unemployment and poverty shot up as the economy ground to a halt. Edwin Gimode pointed out that "the result was a potentially large criminal army" ("An Anatomy of Violent Crime and Insecurity in Kenya: The Case of Nairobi, 1985–1999," *Africa Development* 26 [2001]: 295–335).

15. Green, *Manufacturing Powerlessness*.

16. Quoted in ibid., 388.

17. Quoted in ibid., 357.

18. Steve Reyna, "Imagining Monsters: A Structural History of Warfare in Chad (1968–1990)," in *Globalization, the State, and Violence*, ed. Jonathan Friedman (Walnut Creek, Calif.: AltaMira, 2003), 279–307.

19. Davis, *Planet of Slums*, 201–2.

20. Basil Davidson, *The Black Man's Burden: Africa and the Curse of the Nation-State* (New York: Times Books, 1992); Harvey W. Zorbaugh, "The Natural Areas of the City," in *Studies in Human Ecology*, ed. George A. Theodorson (1926; rpt. Evanston, Ill.: Row, Peterson, 1961), 45–49.

21. Steve Sampson, "Trouble Spots: Projects, Bandits, and State Fragmentation," in Friedman, *Globalization, the State, and Violence*, 337.

22. Jean-François Bayart, Stephen Ellis, and Béatrice Hibou, *The Criminalization of the State in Africa* (Oxford: International African Institute, 1999), 88; Reno, *Warlord Politics and African States*. Castells uses the term "Predator State" (*End of Millennium*).

23. This argument is developed in Kajsa Ekholm Friedman, "State Classes: The Logic of Rentier Power, and Social Disintegration," in Friedman, *Globalization, the State, and Violence*, 343–77.

24. Davidson, *Black Man's Burden*, 12.

25. Reno, *Warlord Politics and African States*, 207. Reno chillingly summarizes, "There is a strong possibility that sub-Saharan Africa is returning to the 'heart of darkness'" (114).

26. Gimode, "Anatomy of Violent Crime and Insecurity in Kenya," 329.

27. Lately, U.S. gang culture has penetrated Central America, as the children of refugees of civil war returned home, either by choice or by deportation, and implanted gangs like Mara Salvatrucha in Central America. See especially Elana Zilberg, "Banished from the Kingdom," *American Quarterly* 56 (2004): 759–79.

28. "The extraordinary growth in the drug traffic industry since the 1970s has transformed the economics and politics of Latin America" (Castells, *End of Millennium,* 195).

29. For example, Deborah Poole and Gerardo Rénique, *Peru: Time of Fear* (London: Latin American Bureau, 1992); and Elaine Shannon, *Desperados: Latin Drug Lords, U.S. Lawmen, and the War America Can't Win* (New York: Viking, 1988); Gutiérrez Sanin and Jaramillo, "Crime, [Counter]insurgency, and the Privatization of Security"; World Bank, "Cali, Colombia."

30. Louise Shelley, "Corruption and Organized Crime in Mexico in the Post-PRI Transition," *Journal of Contemporary Criminal Justice* 17 (2001): 213–28. See also Castells's discussion of the PRI in *End of Millennium,* 276–86.

31. Paul Chevigny, *The Edge of the Knife: Police Violence in the Americas* (New York: New Press, 1995), 143.

32. Castells, *Rise of the Network Society,* 256–306.

33. Triads in China institutionalized in the eighteenth century as opposition to the Qing Dynasty. Like Italy's Mafia, Triads began as an opponent of foreign (Manchu) rule and then adapted to changed conditions by providing "protection" and controlling illegal goods. And like the Sicilians, Triad influence is felt all over the world. In Japan, the Yakuza rose to prominence through corruption from the vast arsenal and storehouses of the U.S. military after World War II and the Korean War. See Martin Booth, *The Dragon Syndicates: The Global Phenomenon of the Triads* (New York: Carroll & Graf, 1999); Robert Whiting, *Tokyo Underworld: The Fast Times and Hard Life of an American Gangster in Japan* (New York: Vintage, 2000).

34. In India's teaming cities, gangs are a well-publicized problem, with a clear Hindu-Muslim divide. Mumbai's Shiv Sena and its strongman, Bal Thackeray, uses *mitra mandals,* or groups of tough youth, as "voting gangs" both to keep the Sena in power and as shock troops against Muslims. In turn, the Muslim community has lent conditional support to the gangster Dawood Ibrahim, who has skillfully combined religious politics with his lucrative underground empire. See also Julia M. Eckert, *The Charisma of Direct Action: Power, Politics, and the Shiv Sena* (New Delhi: Oxford University Press, 2003); Suketu Mehta, *Maximum City: Bombay Lost and Found* (New York: Knopf, 2004); S. Hussain Zaidi, *Black Friday: The True Story of the Bombay Bomb Blasts* (New Delhi: Penguin, 2002).

35. Alfred W. McCoy, *The Politics of Heroin in Southeast Asia* (New York: Harper and Row, 1972).

36. Castells, *Rise of the Network Society,* 152.

37. Gary LaFree, *Losing Legitimacy: Street Crime and the Decline of Social Institutions in America* (Boulder, Colo.: Westview, 1998).

38. Suzella Palmer and John Pitts, "Othering the Brothers: Black Youth, Racial Solidarity, and Gun Crime," unpublished manuscript (2005); John Pitts, *The New Politics of Youth Crime: Discipline or Solidarity?* (Basingstoke, UK: Palgrave, 2000).

39. Elijah Anderson, "The Ideologically Driven Critique," *American Journal of*

Sociology 107 (2002): 1546–47. This is Anderson's detailed rebuttal of Wacquant's criticism of Anderson's social disorganization approach.

40. Castells, *Rise of the Network Society*, 152.

41. Dixon and Johns describe South Africa in the mid-1990s as "a fragile transitional State (that) views street gangsters, organised crime syndicates, armed vigilantes and civil society anti-crime groups as, to varying degrees, a threat to its jealously guarded monopoly on the use of legitimate coercive force" (*Gangs, Pagad, and the State*, 42).

42. Henry A. Giroux, *Fugitive Cultures: Race, Violence, and Youth* (New York: Routledge, 1996).

43. Edward W. Said, *Culture and Imperialism* (New York: Knopf, 1993), 336.

44. Craig Calhoun, *Critical Social Theory* (Oxford: Blackwell, 1995), 45.

45. Finn-Aage Esbensen, L. Thomas Winfree Jr., and Terrance Taylor, "Gangs and Definitional Issues," *Crime and Delinquency* 47 (2001): 105–30.

46. James F. Short and Fred L. Strodtbeck, *Group Process and Gang Delinquency* (Chicago: University of Chicago Press, 1965); Joan W. Moore, *Going Down to the Barrio: Homeboys and Homegirls in Change* (Philadelphia: Temple University Press, 1991).

47. If any further categorization makes sense, it is between those gangs that institutionalize and those that do not, and to differentiate those from majority and minority ethnic groups (Hagedorn, "Gangs in Late Modernity").

4. FROM CHICAGO TO MUMBAI

1. Michel Wieviorka, "The New Paradigm of Violence," in Friedman, *Globalization, the State, and Violence*, 129.

2. John P. Sullivan, "Gangs, Hooligans, and Anarchists—The Vanguard of Netwar in the Streets," in *Networks and Netwars*, ed. John Arquilla and David Ronfeld (Santa Monica, Calif.: Rand National Defense Research Institute, 2001), 99–128. See also Manwaring, "Street Gangs."

3. Sampson, "Trouble Spots," 327.

4. Richard Cloward and Lloyd Ohlin, *Delinquency and Opportunity* (Glencoe, Ill.: Free Press, 1960).

5. Martin Sanchez Jankowski, *Islands in the Street: Gangs and American Urban Society* (Berkeley: University of California Press, 1991).

6. Klein, "Resolving the Eurogang Paradox," 7–19.

7. Ibrahim Abdullah, "Youth, Culture, and Rebellion: Understanding Sierra Leone's Wasted Decade," *Critical Arts: A Journal of South-North Cultural and Media Studies* 16 (2002): 19–37.

8. Susan Shepler points out in an unpublished paper that there also is a long-standing cultural context in Sierra Leone of violence by youth and a quite different definition of "youth" and "childhood" than in the West ("The Social and Cultural Context of Child Soldiering in Sierra Leone," paper presented at the PRIO workshop, "Techniques of Violence in Civil War," Oslo, August 21–24, 2004).

9. Gutiérrez Sanin and Jaramillo, "Crime, [Counter]insurgency, and the Privatization

of Security"; Watchlist on Children and Armed Conflict, "Colombia's War on Children" (New York: Watchlist on Children and Armed Conflict, 2004).

10. Human Rights Watch, *"You'll Learn Not to Cry": Child Combatants in Colombia"* (New York: Human Rights Watch, 2003), 54. One other group with large numbers of females and young girls participating as armed combatants is the Tamil Tigers, the Liberation Tigers of Tamel Eelam in Sri Lanka. See, for example, Cynthia Brown and Farhad Karim, "Playing the 'Communal Card': Communal Violence and Human Rights" (New York: Human Rights Watch, 1995).

11. Alonso Salazar, "Young Assassins of the Drug Trade" (New York: North America Congress on Latin America, 1994); Watchlist on Children and Armed Conflict, "Colombia's War on Children."

12. See also Ramirez, "Medellín."

13. COAV Bulletin, http://www.coav.org.br/frame.asp?url=/publique/cgi/cgilua.exe/sys/start.htm?UserActiveTemplate=%5Fen&infoid=1846&sid=114 (accessed April 2, 2006).

14. Rob White, "Youth Gang Research in Australia," in *Studying Youth Gangs,* ed. James F. Short and Lorine A. Hughes (Lanham, Md.: AltaMira, 2006), 161–80.

15. Cameron Hazelhurst, "Observing New Zealand 'Gangs,' 1950–2000: Learning from a Small Country," in Hagedorn, *Gangs in the Global City: Criminology Reconsidered.*

16. Joachim Kersten, "Youth Groupings, Identity, and the Political Context: On the Significance of Extremist Youth Groupings in Unified Germany," in Hagedorn, *Gangs in the Global City: Alternatives to Traditional Criminology,* 210.

17. Klein, "Value of Comparisons in Street Gang Research." For example, see Maureen Cain's statement that in Trinidad and Tobago, Western views of "aging out of crime" are not valid. It doesn't happen like that (*Crime and Criminology in the Caribbean: An Introduction* [Kingston], vii).

18. Gimode, "Anatomy of Violent Crime and Insecurity in Kenya," 332. The situation in Nairobi resembles Dar es Salaam, Tanzania, where youth gangs with names like the Posta Group, Ja la Ku, and Kariakoo Group function as unsupervised youth. Significantly, often not discussed in gang studies, both Nairobi and Dar es Salaam have a structured racial hierarchy left over from colonialism of whites, Asians, Arabs, and Africans on the bottom (Green, *Manufacturing Powerlessness in the Black Diaspora*).

19. David Anderson, *Histories of the Hanged: The Dirty War in Kenya and the End of Empire* (New York: Norton, 2005), 189, 196.

20. Covey, *Street Gangs throughout the World,* 191; see also his comments on the Middle East: "The presence of street gangs in the Middle East is difficult to ascertain given the political turmoil characteristic of the region. Differentiating law-violating groups, organized crime, politically motivated groups, or organizations is difficult" (196).

21. "Chinese youth gangs are not simply expressions of adolescent mischief or young adulthood. . . . They are consciously formed by adults (within Chinatown) or by former gangs members (outside of Chinatown) rather than by noncriminal adolescents"

(Ko-lin Chin, *Chinatown Gangs: Extortion, Enterprise, and Ethnicity* [New York: Oxford University Press, 1996], 19–20).

22. Patricia Bibes, "Transnational Organized Crime and Terrorism," *Journal of Contemporary Criminal Justice* 17, no. 2 (2001): 243–58.

23. Kynoch, *We Are Fighting the World,* 3.

24. Emery, *Blueprint,* 14.

25. Interview with author, Chicago, 2003.

26. Moore, *Homeboys,* 361, 129.

27. Dowdney, *Children of the Drug Trade,* 52.

28. Marlon Carranza, "Detention or Death: Where the 'Pandillero' Kids of El Salvador Are Heading," in Dowdney, *neither War nor Peace,* 209–28.

29. Zilberg, "Banished from the Kingdom," 763.

30. Donna Decesare, "From Civil War to Gang War: The Tragedy of Edgar Bolanos," in *Gangs and Society: Alternative Perspectives,* ed. Louis Kontos, David Brotherton, and Luis Barrios (New York: Columbia University Press, 2003), 283–313.

31. Children in Organised Armed Violence, "From Guerrillas to Gangs," Paraná Online, November 18, 2002, http://www.paranaonline.org.br.

32. For Ecuador, see Kleber Loor, "Ecuador's Pandillas and Naciones: A Dreadful Reality and a Challenging Task: From Victims to Victimizers," in Dowdney, *neither War nor Peace,* 195–208.

33. See, for example, Wieviorka, "New Paradigm of Violence," 107–39.

34. Donal B. Cruise O'Brien, "A Lost Generation? Youth Identity and Decay in West Africa," in *Postcolonial Identities in Africa,* ed. Richard Werbner and Terence Ranger (London: Zed Books, 1996), 55–74.

35. Friedman, "State Classes," 367, 369.

36. Asef Bayat, "Cairo's Poor: Dilemmas of Survival and Solidarity," *Middle East Report* 202 (Winter 1996): 6.

37. Castells, *End of Millennium.*

38. Alexander Salagaev, "Evolution of Delinquent Gangs in Russia," in Klein et al., *Eurogang Paradox,* 195–202.

39. Gloria La Cava and Rafaella Y. Nanetti, "Albania: Fight the Vulnerability Gap" (Washington, D.C.: World Bank, 2000), 16, 31.

40. John C. McCall, "Juju and Justice at the Movies: Vigilantes in Nigerian Popular Videos," *African Studies Review* (December 2004), http://www.umass.edu/anthro/asr/ (accessed November 4, 2005).

41. Julia M. Eckert, *The Charisma of Direct Action: Power, Politics, and the Shiv Sena* (New Delhi: Oxford University Press, 2003). The comparison of Richard J. Daley and Bal Thackeray is almost too exact to have escaped previous notice.

42. Suketu Mehta, *Maximum City: Bombay Lost and Found* (New York: Knopf, 2004).

43. Arjun Appadurai, "Spectral Housing and Urban Cleansing: Notes on Millennial Mumbai," *Public Culture* 12 (2000): 627–51.

44. Clive Glaser, *Bo-Tsotsi: The Youth Gangs of Soweto, 1935–1976* (Portsmouth, N.H.: Heinemann, 2000); James Curry, David Philip, and John M. Hagedorn, "Gangs in Late Modernity," in Hagedorn, *Gangs in the Global City: Alternatives to Traditional Criminology;* Nelson Mandela, *Long Walk to Freedom* (Boston: Little, Brown, 1994); John M. Hagedorn, "Gangs in Politics," in *Youth Activism: An International Encyclopedia,* ed. Lonnie R. Sherrod, Constance Flanagan, and Ron Kassimir (London: Blackwell, 2004).

45. Alonso, "Racialized Identities and the Formation of Black Gangs in Los Angeles," 666. See also the history of black and other LA gangs in Vigil, *Rainbow of Gangs.*

46. Ibid., 668.

47. Alexander Cockburn, "Blood Money," *New Statesman and Society* (1992), http://gangresearch.net/GangResearch/Policy/cripsbloodsplan.html (accessed November 1, 2005). Tom Hayden adds, "When the Panthers were demolished, nonpolitical fighting gangs symbolized by the Crips emerged in the vacuum" (*Street Wars: Gangs and the Future of Violence* [New York: New Press, 2004], 167).

48. David Brotherton and Luis Barrios, *Between Black and Gold: The Street Politics of the Almighty Latin King and Queen Nation* (New York: Columbia University Press, 2003); David C. Brotherton, "Toward the Gang as a Social Movement," in Hagedorn, *Gangs in the Global City: Alternatives to Traditional Criminology,* 450–69.

49. Interview with author, Chicago, 2003.

50. Morgensen, "Corner and Area Gangs of Inner-City Jamaica."

51. Gunst, *Born Fi' Dead,* 104.

52. "People just grow in da system. You live what you learn, generation after generation" (area gang member, quoted in Dowdney, *neither War nor Peace,* 239).

53. *Economist,* November 4, 2004. See also Covey, *Street Gangs throughout the World.*

54. See also Marie Smythe and Patricia Campbell, "Young People and Armed Violence in Northern Ireland," in Dowdney, *neither War nor Peace,* 260–69.

55. Caracas Journal, March 6, 2006, http://www.thedailyjournalonline.com/article.asp?ArticleId=228558&CategoryId=12393.

56. Poole and Rénique, *Peru.*

57. Luis Martinez, "Youth, the Street, and Violence in Algeria," in *Alienation or Integration of Arab Youth,* ed. Roel Meijer (Padistow, UK: Curzon, 2000), 83–105.

58. Robert Muggah, "Securing Haiti's Transition: Reviewing Human Insecurity and the Prospects for Disarmament, Demobilization, and Reintegration" (Geneva: Small Arms Survey, 2005), 31.

59. "'What is happening today in the suburbs is true anger—a "No" to permanent stigmatisation, to insults and daily acts of discrimination,' Mouloud Aounit, secretary-general of the Movement of Struggle against Racism, told the crowd" (BBC News, http://news.bbc.co.uk/2/hi/europe/4430540.stm [accessed November 12, 2005]). See also David Brooks, "Gangsta, in French," *New York Times,* November 10, 2005.

60. Oskar Verkaaik, *Migrants and Militants: Fun and Urban Violence in Pakistan* (Princeton, N.J.: Princeton University Press, 2004), 87.

61. Walter Miller, "Youth Gangs in the Urban Crisis Era," in Short, *Delinquency,*

Crime, and Society, 91–122. For a more balanced yet skeptical view of gangs and politics, see Short, "Gangs, Politics, and the Social Order," in Short, *Delinquency, Crime, and Society,* 129–63.

62. W. Durant, *The Renaissance: A History of Civilization in Italy from 1304–1576 A.D.* (New York: Simon and Schuster, 1953), 150. And the Christian gang tradition may go back even farther. In the fifth century, Cyril, Bishop of Alexandria, employed "shock troops," called *parabalani,* against the enemies of the faith. They "were viewed with such terror that the emperor himself had to ask that their numbers be limited to 500" (Charles Freeman, *The Closing of the Western Mind: The Rise of Faith and the Fall of Reason* [New York: Knopf, 2003], 268).

63. C. Brown and F. Karim, *Playing the "Communal Card": Communal Violence and Human Rights* (New York: Human Rights Watch, 1995), 20.

64. Here's how U.S. Ambassador Warren Zimmermann described the "Tigers": "The dregs of society—embezzlers, thugs, even professional killers—rose from the slime to become freedom fighters and national heroes" (*Origins of a Catastrophe* [New York: Times Books, 1999], 152). Mary Kaldor reports that the UN determined there were "eighty-three paramilitary groups on the territory of the former Yugoslavia" (*New and Old Wars: Organized Violence in a Global Era* [Stanford, Calif.: Stanford University Press, 1999], 47).

65. James Ron, "Territoriality and Plausible Deniability: Serbian Paramilitaries in the Bosnian War," in *Death Squads in Global Perspective: Murder with Deniability,* ed. Bruce A. Campbell and Arthur D. Brenner (New York: St. Martin's, 2000), 287–312. See also Kaldor, *New and Old Wars.*

66. I am indebted to Erin Conley, PhD student in criminal justice at the University of Illinois–Chicago, for discussions on her dissertation research on death squads.

67. Bruce Campbell, "Death Squads: Definition, Problems, and Historical Context," in Campbell and Brenner, *Death Squads in Global Perspective,* 2.

68. Ibrahim, "Empirical Survey of Children and Youth," 246–59.

69. Human Rights Watch, *The Bakassi Boys: The Legitimation of Murder and Torture* (New York: Human Rights Watch, 2002), http://www.hrw.org/reports/2002/nigeria2/ (accessed November 6, 2005).

70. Peter Ekeh, "Bakassi Boys," Urhobo Historical Society, http://www.waado.org/ NigerDelta/Documents/ConstitutionalMatters/PoliceVigilante/ReviewBakassiBoys -Ekeh.html (accessed November 6, 2005).

71. Ibid., 255.

72. Ibid., 257.

73. Ibid., 249.

74. Donald M. Nonini, "American Neoliberalism, 'Globalization,' and Violence," in Friedman, *Globalization, the State, and Violence,* 187.

75. Agnes Zenaida V. Camacho, "Children and Youth in Organised Armed Violence in the Philippines," in Dowdney, *neither War nor Peace,* 270–91.

76. Agnes Zenaida V. Camacho, *Children and Youth in Organised Armed Violence*

in the Philippines (Rio de Janeiro: University of the Philippines, Center for Integrative and Development Studies, Psychosocial Trauma and Human Rights program, 2005), 36. See also the chilling interview with a child hit man on page 33.

77. I am indebted to papers by my student Nixon Camillien for a deeper understanding of Haitian conditions.

78. Wozo Productions, video history of Haiti's rebellion, http://www.wozoproductions .org/pages/video_pages/video_six.htm (accessed November 7, 2005).

79. Human Rights Watch, "Haiti: Hundreds Killed Amid Rampant Impunity," April 14, 2005.

80. "The recruitment of street children by local gang chiefs in the commission of violent crimes is not uncommon, given the desperate poverty of the kids and the coercive intimidation of non-cooperatives by the gangs" (J. Christopher Kovats-Bernat, "Anti-Gang, Arimaj, and the War on Street Children," *Peace Review* 12 [2000]: 417). This was written about conditions during Aristide's reign.

5. NO WAY OUT

1. Wyn Craig Wade, *The Fiery Cross: The Ku Klux Klan in America* (New York: Simon and Schuster, 1987); Eckard V. Toy Jr., "Right-Wing Extremism from the Ku Klux Klan to the Order: 1915–1988," in *Violence in America: Protest, Rebellion, Reform,* ed. Ted Robert Gurr (Newbury Park, Calif.: Sage, 1989), 131–52; David Mark Chalmers, *Hooded Americanism: The History of the Ku Klux Klan* (New York: Watts, 1981).

2. Pete Simi, "Hate Groups or Street Gangs? The Emergence of Racist Skinheads," in *Studying Youth Gangs,* ed. James F. Short Jr. and Oorine A. Hughes (Lanham, Md.: AltaMira, 2006), 150.

3. Scott, *Lords of Lawndale,* 167.

4. Ibid., 169.

5. Ibid., 179.

6. Ibid., 95, 109.

7. Walter Miller, "White Gangs," in *Modern Criminals,* ed. James F. Short (New Brunswick, N.J.: Transaction, 1970), 45–84; Spergel, *Youth Gang Problem.*

8. Moore, *Going Down to the Barrio;* Vigil, *Rainbow of Gangs;* Carl Taylor, *Dangerous Society* (East Lansing: Michigan State University Press, 1989); Padilla, *Gang as an American Enterprise.*

9. Malcolm Klein, citing Short and Strodtbeck's work, argues that the similarities between gangs of different ethnic backgrounds far exceeds their differences, thus eliminating any need to examine the impact of structures of racism (Klein, *The American Street Gang: Its Nature, Prevalence, and Control* [New York: Oxford University Press, 1995], 70–71, 105–10; Short and Strodtbeck, *Group Process and Gang Delinquency*).

10. Spergel, *Youth Gang Problem,* 161–63.

11. This is the standard method of social science. See, for example, Robert J. Sampson, "Urban Black Violence: The Effect of Male Joblessness and Family Disruption," *American Journal of Sociology* 93 (1987): 348–82.

12. Wacquant, "Three Pernicious Premises in the Study of American Ghetto."

13. "The ethnic group-, class-, and nation-based perspectives all neglect the specificity of race as an autonomous field of social conflict, political organization, and cultural/ideological meaning" (Michael Omi and Howard Winant, *Racial Formation in the United States: From the 1960s to the 1990s* [New York: Routledge, 1994]).

14. Thrasher, *Gang*, 381–82.

15. Ibid., 392.

16. "It is probably the breaking down of local attachments and the weakening of the restraints and inhibitions of the primary group, under the influence of the urban environment, which are largely responsible for the increase of vice and crime in great cities" (Robert Park, "The City: Suggestions for the Investigation of Human Behavior in the Urban Environment," in *Classic Essays on the Culture of Cities*, ed. Richard Sennett [Englewood Cliffs, N.J.: Prentice-Hall, 1969], 112). See also, in the same volume, Georg Simmel, "The Metropolis and Mental Life," 47–60. This volume has an excellent overview of these issues.

17. Émile Durkheim, *The Division of Labor in Society* (New York: Free Press, 1933). See also Thomas and Znaniecki, *Polish Peasant*.

18. Eric Hobsbawm, *The Age of Extremes: A History of the World, 1914–1991* (New York: Vintage, 1997). See also Jock Young, *The Exclusive Society* (London: Sage, 1999).

19. Robert K. Merton, "Social Structure and Anomie," *American Sociological Review* 3 (1938): 672–82.

20. Cloward and Ohlin, *Delinquency and Opportunity;* Frances Fox Piven and Richard A. Cloward, *Regulating the Poor: The Functions of Public Welfare* (New York: Pantheon, 1971). Cloward was a key architect of the National Welfare Rights Organization.

21. Touraine, *Can We Live Together?* 125–27.

22. George Jackson, *Blood in My Eye* (New York: Random House, 1972).

23. hooks, *We Real Cool*, 15. Tom Hayden also argues that the mushrooming of gang violence was the result of the failure of the civil rights movement to take root in the north (*Street Wars*, 23).

24. See also Rodriguez, *Hearts and Hands*.

25. West, *Race Matters*.

26. Ibid., 24, 28. Compare this with W. E. B. DuBois, writing in 1902 about the end of Reconstruction: "Whatever of good may have come in these years of change, the shadow of a deep disappointment rests upon the Negro people" (*The Souls of Black Folk* [1902; rpt. New York: Penguin Books, 1989], 7).

27. "All told the civil rights movement succeeded in directing significant economic and social benefits of the middle-class social order to people of color. . . . the black middle class doubled in size between 1960 and 1980 to 36% of all blacks" (Andrew L. Barlow, *Between Fear and Hope: Globalization and Race in the United States* [Lanham, Md.: Rowman and Littlefield, 2003], 173).

28. Tupac, "I Wonder If Heaven Got a Ghetto," *R U Still Down? (Remember Me)* (Interscope, 1997).

29. Wilson, *Truly Disadvantaged;* John M. Hagedorn, *People and Folks: Gangs, Crime, and the Underclass in a Rustbelt City* (1988; rpt. Chicago: Lakeview, 1998).

30. David Harvey, *A Brief History of Neoliberalism* (New York: Oxford University Press, 2005), 171.

31. Sanyika Shakur, *Monster: The Autobiography of an L.A. Gang Member* (New York: Penguin Books, 1993), 220.

32. Robert B. Reich, *The Work of Nations* (New York: Vintage, 1991).

33. "I'm thinking here of President Lula of Brazil. Lula was the hero of the World Social Forum last year. This year he's busy implementing IMF guidelines, reducing pension benefits and purging radicals from the Workers' Party. I'm thinking also of the former president of South Africa, Nelson Mandela. Within two years of taking office in 1994, his government genuflected with hardly a caveat to the Market God. It instituted a massive program of privatization and structural adjustment that has left millions of people homeless, jobless and without water and electricity" (Arundhati Roy, *Nation,* February 9, 2004, http://www.thenation.com/doc/20040209/roy).

34. Alain Touraine, *Critique of Modernity* (Oxford: Blackwell, 1995), 2. This has also long been a theme of Latin American scholars. See Andre Gunder Frank, *Latin America: Underdevelopment or Revolution: Essays on the Development of Underdevelopment and the Immediate Enemy* (New York: Monthly Review Press, 1970).

35. Ralph Fevre, *The Demoralization of Western Culture: Social Theory and the Dilemmas of Modern Living* (London: Continuum, 2000), 1.

36. John Gray, *Enlightenment's Wake: Politics and Culture at the Close of the Modern Age* (London: Routledge, 1995), 15.

37. Zygmunt Bauman, *Community: Seeking Safety in an Insecure World* (Cambridge: Polity, 2001), 113.

38. Castells, *Power of Identity,* 9. For example, Maryse Esterle-Hedibel points out that Algerian Muslim youth form gangs "in reaction to and in defense against the outside world, with a sign reversal of the stigma, making it a part of its identity" ("Youth Gangs in France: A Socio-Ethnographic Approach," in Klein et al., *Eurogang Paradox,* 205).

39. Touraine, "Beyond Social Movements," 183.

40. Castells, *Power of Identity,* 64.

41. Ibid.

42. Shakur, *Monster,* 225–26.

43. Interview with author, Chicago, 2003.

44. DuBois left the United States for Ghana near the end of his life: "I just can't take anymore of this country's treatment. . . . Chin up, and fight on, but realize that American Negroes cannot win" (quoted in Henry Louis Gates and Cornel West, *The Future of the Race* [New York: Knopf, 1996]). On the increasing levels of racism in the United States, see Barlow, *Between Fear and Hope.*

45. Albert Memmi, *The Colonizer and the Colonized* (New York: Orion, 1965), xii.

46. Omi and Winant, *Racial Formation in the United States;* Kimberlé Crenshaw,

Critical Race Theory (New York: New Press, 1995); bell hooks, *Ain't I a Woman? Black Women and Feminism* (Boston: South End, 1981).

47. Robin D. G. Kelley, *Yo Mama's Disfunktional!: Fighting the Culture Wars in Urban America* (Boston: Beacon, 1997).

48. Bell, *Ain't I a Woman?* ix.

49. Ibid., 12. See also Touraine's comments that in these times the "Subject" is a "tragic figure" that is "fighting for survival" in a rapidly decaying world (*Can We Live Together?* 83).

50. Tupac, "Keep Ya Head Up," *Strictly 4 My N.I.G.G.A.Z.* (Interscope, 1993).

51. Howard Winant, *The World Is a Ghetto: Race and Democracy since World War II* (New York: Basic Books, 2001).

52. Gunnar Myrdal, Richard Mauritz, Edvard Sterner, and Arnold Rose, *An American Dilemma: The Negro Problem and Modern Democracy* (New York: Harper and Brothers, 1944).

53. Edward W. Said, *Orientalism* (1979; rpt. New York: Vintage, 1994).

54. Kersten, "Youth Groupings, Identity, and the Political Context."

55. Pitts, *New Politics of Youth Crime.*

56. Davidson, *Black Man's Burden.*

57. Arjun Appadurai, "Dead Certainty: Ethnic Violence in the Era of Globalization," in *Globalization and Identity: Dialectics of Flow and Closure,* ed. Birgit Meyer and Peter Geschiere (Oxford: Blackwell, 1999), 305–24; for an analytic treatment, see Castells, *End of Millennium.*

58. Nina Glick Schiller and Georges Fouron, "Killing Me Softly: Violence, Globalization, and the Apparent State," in Friedman, *Globalization, the State, and Violence,* 203–48.

59. Said, *Orientalism,* 45.

60. Ralph Ellison, *Invisible Man* (New York: Vintage, 1947).

61. Elijah Anderson, *Streetwise: Race, Class, and Change in an Urban Community* (Chicago: University of Chicago Press, 1990), 167.

62. Ibid., 182.

63. Cohen, "Crime and Politics," 16.

64. Richard Sennett, *Flesh and Stone: The Body and the City in Western Civilization* (New York: Norton, 1994).

65. Bell, *Faces at the Bottom of the Well,* 12.

66. DuBois, *Souls of Black Folk,* 173–74.

67. Touraine, *Critique of Modernity.*

68. Jennifer L. Hochschild, *Facing Up to the American Dream: Race, Class, and the Soul of the Nation* (Princeton, N.J.: Princeton University Press, 1995).

69. Wilson, *Declining Significance of Race;* Wilson, *Truly Disadvantaged.*

70. John M. Hagedorn, "Post-Industrial Gang Violence," in *Youth Violence,* ed. Michael Tonry and Mark H. Moore (1988; rpt. Chicago: University of Chicago Press, 1998), 457–511; Hagedorn, *People and Folks.*

6. A TALE OF TWO GANGS

1. The argument of this chapter builds on Hagedorn, "Race Not Space."

2. This is academically called "racial formation" (Omi and Winant, *Racial Formation in the United States*, 55ff.).

3. Herbert Asbury, *The Gangs of New York: An Informal History of the Underworld* (New York: Thunder's Mouth, 2001); Martin Scorsese, *Gangs of New York* (Miramax Films, 2002). See also John M. Hagedorn, "The Gangs of . . . ," *Chicago Tribune,* January 19, 2003, http://gangresearch.net/Archives/UIC/Courses/history/The%20Gangs %20of%20.%20.%20.html.

4. Eric H. Monkkonen, *Murder in New York City* (Berkeley: University of California Press, 2001), 120. In fact, Monkkonen calculated that the profits from graft and patronage at that time was at a scale to the profits made in the 1990s by gangs from the sale of cocaine (73).

5. Steven P. Erie, *Rainbow's End: From the Old to the New Urban Ethnic Politics* (Berkeley: University of California Press, 1988).

6. Thrasher, *Gang,* 74. On page 456, Thrasher states that "304" of the gangs were social athletic clubs. Numbers were not Thrasher's strong suit. It has been suggested that the number 1,313 that Thrasher claimed was the actual number of gangs in Chicago in fact was the address of a "red light" house of vice near Thrasher's outreach headquarters.

7. Carter H. Harrison [II], *Growing Up with Chicago: Sequel to "Stormy Years"* (1944), 229–30; "Political History of Bridgeport," http://www.uic.edu/orgs/LockZero/ V.html (accessed January 4, 2006).

8. Richard C. Lindberg, "The City That Never Was Legit," http://www.ipsn.org/ chiviol.html (accessed January 16, 2006).

9. Thrasher, *Gang,* 456.

10. Edwin H. Sutherland, *Criminology* (Philadelphia: Lippincott, 1924), 156.

11. Thrasher, *Gang,* 397.

12. Ibid., 470.

13. Asbury, *Gangs of New York.*

14. Adam Cohen and Elizabeth Taylor, *American Pharaoh: Mayor Richard J. Daley: His Battle for Chicago and the Nation* (Boston: Little Brown, 2000), 33.

15. "The Negro population increased from 44,103 in 1910 to 109,594 in 1920, an increase of 148 percent" ("The Negro in Chicago" [Chicago: Chicago Commission on Race Relations, 1922], 2). All facts, unless otherwise cited, come from this report.

16. Ibid. Twenty-three blacks and fifteen whites were killed in the riots, with 537 injured and over a thousand left homeless in the twelve days of rioting.

17. Ibid., 11–12.

18. Anthony M. Platt and University of California Berkeley, Center for the Study of Law and Society, *The Politics of Riot Commissions, 1917–1970: A Collection of Official Reports and Critical Essays* (New York: Macmillan, 1971).

19. Harry Haywood, *Black Bolshevik: Autobiography of an Afro-American Communist* (Chicago: Liberator, 1978), 81–83.

20. William M. Tuttle Jr., *Race Riot: Chicago in the Red Summer of 1919* (1970; rpt. Urbana: University of Illinois Press, 1996), 55. Tuttle corrects inaccuracies in the original Race Relations Commission Report.

21. "Negro in Chicago."

22. McDonough is still revered in the HAA. Former president Ray Murphy told of McDonough's love of eating and the belief among club members that McDonough ate himself to death in 1934 (Tamara Kerrill, "Where Friendship Is the Password," *Chicago Sun-Times,* March 17, 1996).

23. Thrasher, *Gang,* 199.

24. Ibid., 202.

25. Ibid., 216.

26. "Sociologists at the University of Chicago . . . viewed negroes as just another ethnic group whose segregation was largely voluntary and would prove to be only temporary. They subjected Chicago's social life to 'blinding scrutiny,' but they never saw the difference between the ethnic enclave and the black ghetto" (Philpott, *Slum and the Ghetto,* 139, 141).

27. Ibid., 199.

28. See, for example, Jesse Bernard, *The Sociology of Community* (Glenview, Ill.: Scott, Foresman, 1970).

29. Michael E. Funchion, "Irish Chicago: Church, Homeland, Politics, and Class— The Shaping of an Ethnic Group, 1870–1900," in *Ethnic Chicago: A Multicultural Portrait,* ed. Melvin G. Hollis and Peter d'A. Jones (Grand Rapids, Mich.: Eerdmans, 1984), 57–92.

30. DuBois, *Souls of Black Folk.*

31. Kerrill, "Where Friendship Is the Password."

32. Mike Royko, *Boss* (New York: Signet, 1971), 128.

33. Cohen and Taylor, *American Pharaoh,* 10. For a review of mainstream political science, see William J. Grimshaw, "Revisiting the Urban Classics: Political Order, Economic Development, and Social Justice," *Policy Studies Journal* 24 (1996): 230 44.

34. Nathan Thompson, *Kings: The True Story of Chicago's Policy Kings and Numbers Racketeers* (Chicago: Bronzeville, 2003). See also the talks of Timuel Black and Euseni Perkins to the Chicago Gang History Project at the Great Cities Institute, University of Illinois–Chicago.

35. David K. Fremon, *Chicago Politics Ward by Ward* (Bloomington: Indiana University Press, 1988), 159.

36. Cohen and Taylor, *American Pharaoh,* 271.

37. http://www.ipsn.org/chiviol.html.

38. Fremon, *Chicago Politics Ward by Ward,* 159.

39. Dawley, *Nation of Lords.*

40. Bennie Lee, http://gangresearch.net/ChicagoGangs/vicelords/Bennielee.html.

41. In the *Chicago Daily News* of July 18, 1968, President Alfonso Alford said, "We

are not a gang; we are a corporation, nonprofit and legally constituted in the State of Illinois" (http://gangresearch.net/cvl/cvlhistoryfinal/notagang.html).

42. Ibid.

43. "Kup's Column," *Chicago Sun-Times,* February 28, 1969.

44. Euseni Eugene Perkins, *Explosion of Chicago's Black Street Gangs* (Chicago: Third World, 1987).

45. http://gangresearch.net/ChicagoGangs/gangsandghetto/Perkins.htm. Lee adds, "Fred Hampton was assassinated because he became a political threat to the Illinois politicians. He helped to organize the LSD movement, pulling the minds of the Street Gang leaders to think in terms of the Civil rights movement" (ibid.).

46. Royko, *Boss,* 210.

47. Interview with author, Chicago, 2004.

48. http://gangresearch.net/ChicagoGangs/blackstonerangers/Fry/waralafry.html; Chicago Historical Association archives.

49. John Fry, counselor to the Blackstone Rangers, explains: "Crime is no longer what a judge determines criminals do, or what policemen report that criminals do; crime has become a state of the criminal's mind; crime is a propensity toward crime. Crime inheres in the gang member as his essence. Wherever he goes, crime goes with him. Whomever he meets is infected. He is a virus set loose to plague the city. By all means, action must be taken to prohibit contact between the virus-carriers and the uncontaminated. The police, with such a vision, cannot be faulted for striving to preserve the precious difference between the sick and the healthy by quarantining the plague area" (http://gangresearch.net/ChicagoGangs/blackstonerangers/Fry/waralafry.html).

50. Interview with author, Chicago, 2004.

51. Ibid.

52. Ibid.

53. Ibid.

54. Ibid.

55. Ibid.

56. Ibid.

57. Ibid.

58. Adolph Reed Jr., "Demobilization in the New Black Political Regime: Ideological Capitulation and Radical Failure in the Postsegregation Era," in *The Bubbling Cauldron: Race, Ethnicity, and the Urban Crisis,* ed. Michael Peter Smith and Joe R. Feagin (Minneapolis: University of Minnesota Press, 1995), 182–208.

59. Lise McKean and Jody Raphael, *Drugs, Crime, and Consequences: Arrests and Incarceration in North Lawndale* (Chicago: Center for Impact Research, 2002).

60. Wilson, *Truly Disadvantaged.*

61. Omi and Winant, *Racial Formation in the United States,* 55. The demonization of gangs can be seen as part of the "racial formation" of the Democratic machine in Chicago.

7. RECONSIDERING CULTURE

1. Kelley, *Yo' Mama's Disfunktional!*

2. Ruth Rosner Kornhauser, *Social Sources of Delinquency: An Appraisal of Analytic Models* (Chicago: University of Chicago Press, 1978). See the opening line of her influential book: "Culture in the modern world is everywhere at bay" (1).

3. Ronin Ro, *Gangsta: Merchandizing the Rhymes of Violence* (New York: St. Martin's, 1996).

4. Rose, *Black Noise*, 5.

5. West's views on hip-hop culture may have been responsible for his departure from Harvard. "After some time, Sealey interjected a question about the distinction between high culture and popular culture, citing West's 'leave-taking' of Harvard ("'Leave-taking!' I was pushed out!' West said, reenacting the boot he received) and the 'friction' it caused ('The clash!' West corrected him) as a collision between West's desire to blend all that there is to be blended with education with what perhaps Harvard wants to see itself as." West compared Harvard president Larry Summers's judgment of the album without having listened to it to what DuBois called "the a priori approach to the Negro." Summers "assumed it must be about G-strings, bling-bling, and so forth," West said, whereas the professor called it "danceable education"—an attempt to engage listeners with paideia and wake them up to the struggle for freedom and decency the music is rooted in. A new album is on its way, according to West. See http://www.hiphopconvention.org/issues/education/cornel.cfm (accessed February 3, 2006).

6. The Nazi holocaust would undermine this Enlightenment worship of technology and spark the beginnings of a postmodern critique (Max Horkheimer and Theodor W. Adorno, *Dialectic of Enlightenment* [1944; rpt. New York: Continuum, 1998]).

7. Ulf Hannerz, *Soulside: Inquiries into Ghetto Culture and Community* (New York: Columbia University Press, 1969), 183.

8. Wilson, *Truly Disadvantaged*, 61.

9. Robert J. Sampson and William Julius Wilson, "Toward a Theory of Race, Crime, and Urban Inequality," in *Crime and Inequality*, ed. John Hagan and Ruth D. Peterson (Stanford, Calif.: Stanford University Press, 1995), 38, 41, my emphasis.

10. This was also my argument in *People and Folks*.

11. Perhaps Wilson's views are not so far from mine. He advocates class-based "universal" solutions, since there is little hope the two political parties will act to solve a primarily racial problem. See Wilson, *Truly Disadvantaged*, 155.

12. Walter Miller, "Lower Class Culture as a Generating Milieu of Gang Delinquency," *Journal of Social Issues* 14 (1958): 5–19.

13. Hagedorn, *People and Folks*, 113.

14. For the centrality of race for white gang members, see the remarkable biography of the Gaylords by Michael Scott, *Lords of Lawndale*.

15. Anderson, *Streetwise*, 208.

16. Anderson, *Code of the Street*, 34.

17. These two types of families will be familiar to readers of Hannerz's *Soulside.*

18. Ibid., 36.

19. Ibid., 84.

20. Bourgois, *In Search of Respect,* 326; Lisa Maher and Kathleen Daly, "Women in the Street-Level Drug Economy: Continuity or Change?" *Criminology* 34 (1996): 465–92; Paul Willis, *Learning to Labor* (New York: Columbia University Press, 1981).

21. William Eric Perkins, *Droppin' Science: Critical Essays on Rap Music and Hip Hop Culture* (Philadelphia: Temple University Press, 1996).

22. Touraine, *Critique of Modernity,* 198. In his most recent book, Touraine refers to the dissociation of culture and social structure as "demodernization" (*Can We Live Together?* 25).

23. James D. Fearon and David D. Latain, "Violence and the Social Construction of Ethnic Identity," *International Organization* 54 (2000): 845–77; Stuart Hall, "Ethnicity: Identity and Difference," *Radical America* 23 (1989): 9–20.

24. Touraine, *Can We Live Together?*

25. Ibid., 320. For a clear exposition of the culture of the street and elite, see Jonathan Friedman, "Globalization, Dis-Integration, Re-organization: The Transformations of Violence," in Friedman, *Globalization, the State, and Violence,* 1–34.

26. Castells, *End of the Millennium,* 383.

27. Bourgois, *In Search of Respect,* 326.

28. Resistance identity, thus, in Castells's terms, becomes a "project identity" (*Power of Identity,* 8).

29. Arjun Appadurai, *Modernity at Large: Cultural Dimensions of Globalization* (Minneapolis: University of Minnesota Press, 1996), 13.

30. bell hooks, "Postmodern Blackness," *Postmodern Culture* 1 (1990): 15.

31. Alain Touraine, *Return of the Actor* (Minneapolis: University of Minnesota Press, 1988), 104.

32. Alain Touraine, *What Is Democracy?* (Boulder, Colo.: Westview, 1998), 110.

8. STREET WARS

1. This chapter is not intended to be a thoroughgoing academic critique of hip-hop, nor do I pretend to be a music critic. My intention is solely to understand how hip-hop lends meaning to the lives of gang members as a subset of youth as a resistance identity and how the public's understanding of gangs is shaped by music.

2. Bakiri Kitwana, *Hip Hop Generation: Young Blacks and the Crisis of American Culture* (New York: Basic Civitas, 2002).

3. Hip-hop, with all due respect to Chuck D, is *not* the "black CNN."

4. Many fine histories of hip-hop exist. See, for example, Rose, *Black Noise;* and Bakiri Kitwana, *Rap on Gangsta Rap: Who Run It? Gangsta Rap and Visions of Black Violence* (Chicago: Third World, 1994); Kitwana, *Hip Hop Generation.* I am also indebted to Katie Kaminski, whose research project was to put up the informative Gangs and Hip Hop site on gangresearch.net (http://www.uic.edu/orgs/kbc/hiphop/index.htm).

5. Perkins, *Droppin' Science.*

6. Giles Oakley, *The Devil's Music: A History of the Blues* (New York: Taplinger, 1977).

7. Imamu Amiri Baraka, *Blues People: Negro Music in White America* (New York: Morrow, 1999).

8. Rose, *Black Noise,* 31.

9. S. Craig Watkins, *Hip Hop Matters: Politics, Pop Culture, and the Struggle for the Soul of a Movement* (Boston: Beacon, 2005), 23.

10. Rose, *Black Noise,* 21.

11. Ibid., 34.

12. Watkins, *Hip Hop Matters,* 22.

13. Cornel West, preface to Darby and Shelby, *Hip Hop and Philosophy,* xi.

14. Oakley, *Devil's Music.*

15. For example, the mixed black and Mexican group, Cypress Hill.

16. Paul Gilroy, *The Black Atlantic: Modernity and Double Consciousness* (Cambridge, Mass.: Harvard University Press, 1993).

17. "Hardcore" takes its name from its community-centered, responsive lyrics, hard potent beats, and the use of the rapper's voice as a rhythmic instrument. Gangsta rap is typically, though not always, hardcore (Kitwana, *Rap on Gangsta Rap*).

18. Eldridge Cleaver, *Soul on Ice* (New York: Dell, 1968), 14.

19. Quotations from *Straight from the Streets,* Keith O'Derek and Robert Corsini (Los Angeles: Upfront Productions, 1999).

20. Robin D. G. Kelley, "Kickin' Reality, Kickin' Ballistics: Gangsta Rap and Postindustrial Los Angeles," in Perkins, *Droppin' Science,* 117.

21. hooks, "Postmodern Blackness."

22. West, *Democracy Matters,* 21.

23. Alison Stateman, "RAD RAP: Can the Hip-Hop Industry Turn the Beat Around?" 1997, http://www.prsa.org/juntop97.html (accessed December 2000).

24. Watkins gives a complete description of the introduction of Soundscan *(Hip Hop Matters).*

25. Kitwana, *Rap on Gangsta Rap,* 25.

26. Bruce Haring, *USA Today,* 1996, http://www.usatoday.com/life/enter/music/lem576.htm (accessed September 1997).

27. Kitwana, *Rap on Gangsta Rap.*

28. Hip-hop's promise of profits brings to mind Hunter S. Thompson's stinging line. "The music business is a cruel and shallow money trench, a long plastic hallway where thieves and pimps run free, and good men die like dogs. There's also a negative side" (http://urbanlegends.about.com/od/dubiousquotes/a/hunter-thompson.htm).

29. Watkins, *Hip Hop Matters,* 47.

30. KRS-One, interview, "Tenacity of the Cockroach: Conversations with Entertainment's Most Enduring Outsiders," *Onion,* April 2001.

31. Kelley, "Kickin' Reality, Kickin' Ballistics," 147.

32. bell hooks, "Misogyny, Gangsta Rap, and the Piano," *Z Magazine,* February 1994, http://race.eserver.org/misogyny.html (accessed February 2006).

33. Mike Davis, *City of Quartz* (New York: Vintage, 1990), 87.

34. Kelley, "Kickin' Reality, Kickin' Ballistics," 147.

35. Ibid., 136.

36. John M. Hagedorn, "The Emperor's New Clothes: Theory and Method in Gang Research," *Free Inquiry for Creative Sociology* 24 (1996): 111–22; Hagedorn, *People and Folks.*

37. Jean Baudrillard, *Simulations* (New York: Semiotext(e), 1983).

38. See Carl Husemoller Nightengale, *On the Edge: A History of Poor Black Children and Their American Dreams* (New York: Basic Books, 1993),

39. http://www.globaldarkness.com/articles/true_meaning_of_hip_hop_bambaata.htm.

40. http://www.urbanbassline.com/nightclub_guide/krs1.htm.

41. For the best biography of Tupac, see Michael Eric Dyson, *Holler If You Hear Me* (New York: Basic Books, 2001).

42. hooks, "Postmodern Blackness," 11.

43. West, *Race Matters,* 48.

44. Craig Calhoun, "Social Theory and the Politics of Identity," in Calhoun, *Critical Social Theory,* 9–36; hooks, "Postmodern Blackness."

45. Salt-N-Pepa, "Tramp," *Hot, Cool, and Vicious* (Next Plateau, 1986).

46. My student Iris Rivera has done important research for her forthcoming dissertation on the destructiveness of "gangsta rap" on female identity.

47. Nancy Guevara, "Women Writin', Rappin', Breakin'," in Perkins, *Droppin' Science,* 51.

48. See Joan W. Moore, "Female Gangs: Gender and Globalization," in Hagedorn, *Gangs in the Global City.*

49. http://www.daveyd.com/missyelliot.html.

50. Iris Rivera, "Gang Girls and Same Sex Misogyny: Hip Hop, Friend or Foe?" Unpublished manuscript, University of Illinois–Chicago, 2005.

51. Moore, "Female Gangs."

52. Hagedorn and Devitt, "Fighting Female."

53. hooks, *We Real Cool,* 26.

54. Missy Elliott, with her early unlikely music icon figure, is a good example of the power of the form of music video. The legendary director Hype turned rap music videos into an art form, mesmerizing audiences with creativity and the power of imagination that "could defy the rigid gender rules in pop culture." Hype's work with Missy, however, is dwarfed by what many call his misogynist videos showcasing women as sex objects. See Watkins, *Hip Hop Matters,* 214.

55. Lisa Maher, *Sexed Work: Gender, Race, and Resistance in a Brooklyn Drug Market* (Oxford: Clarendon, 1997), 19.

56. Meda Chesney-Lind, "Girls, Gangs, and Violence: Anatomy of a Backlash," *Humanity and Society* 17 (1993): 321–44.

57. Maulana Rod Karenga, http://www.us-organization.org/position/rap.html (accessed April 17, 2006).

58. See the brilliant historical treatment of this general theme in Gail Bederman, *Manliness and Civilization: A Cultural History of Gender and Race in the United States, 1880–1917* (Chicago: University of Chicago Press, 1995); or browse any of hooks's writings.

59. http://www.sustainabledevelopment.org/hiphop/hiphop.html (accessed May 2, 2006).

60. Dyson, *Holler If You Hear Me,* 116.

61. Jan Rus and Diego Vigil, "Rapid Urbanization and Migrant Indigenous Youth in San Cristobal, Chiapas, Mexico," in Hagedorn, *Gangs in the Global City,* 171, 173.

62. Lansana Fofana, "U.S. Influences Blamed for Delinquency in Sierra Leone," *Inter Press Service English News Wire,* May 6, 1997.

63. Abdullah, "Youth, Culture, and Rebellion," 27.

64. http://www.imageandnarrative.be/worldmusica/doveKpardue.htm.

65. Rosalyn Mburu, *Planet Hip Hop: A Brief Anthology in Search of Pride and Identity* (Barcelona: UN-Habitat, 2004).

66. Ibid.

67. http://www.africanhiphop.com/index.php?module=subjects&func=viewpage &pageid=77 (accessed February 23, 2006).

68. http://www.africanhiphop.com/index.php?module=subjects&func=viewpage &pageid=224 (accessed February 23, 2006).

69. http://www.npr.org/templates/story/story.php?storyId=4660446 (accessed February 23, 2006). You can listen to Daara J's hypnotic music on NPR's Web site, http:// www.npr.org/programs/asc/archives/asc75/#daara.

70. Mburu, "Planet Hip Hop."

71. Interview with Al Jazeera, March 13, 2000.

72. Castells, *Power of Identity,* 69.

73. Bill E. Lawson, "Microphone Commandoes: Rap Music and Political Philosophy," in Darby and Shelby, *Hip Hop and Philosophy,* 1/2.

74. Gilroy, *Black Atlantic,* 36.

9. CONTESTED CITIES

1. Kaldor, *New and Old Wars.*

2. Wesley Skogan, Aimee Fagan, Lynn Steiner, Jinha Kim, Jill Du Bois, Richard Block, and J. Erik Gudell, "Community Policing in Chicago, Year Seven: An Interim Report" (Chicago: Chicago Community Policing Evaluation Consortium, 2000), 118. I am indebted to Xavier Perez for bringing this quote to my attention. Perez is writing his dissertation on gentrification and violence in Humboldt Park.

3. http://viewfromtheground.com/archive/2003/03/state-street-coverage-initiative -its-white-mans-land-now.html%20 (accessed March 10, 2006).

4. Loïc Wacquant, "Race as Civic Felony," *International Social Science Journal* 181 (Spring 1995): 127–42. Also available in French, Spanish, Chinese, Arabic, and Russian.

5. John Friedmann and Goetz Wolff, "World City Formation: An Agenda for Research and Action," *International Journal of Urban and Regional Research* 6 (1984): 309–44.

6. Saskia Sassen, *The Global City: New York, London, Tokyo* (Princeton, N.J.: Princeton University Press, 1991).

7. Vincent Cannato, *The Ungovernable City: John Lindsay and His Struggle to Save New York* (New York: Basic Books, 2001); Edward C. Banfield, *The Unheavenly City* (New York: Free Press, 1970).

8. Neil Smith, *The New Urban Frontier: Gentrification and the Revanchist State* (London: Routledge, 1996).

9. Ibid., 44.

10. Saskia Sassen, "The Global City: One Setting for New Types of Gang Work and Political Culture?" in Hagedorn, *Gangs in the Global City*, 112–33.

11. John M. Hagedorn, "I Do Mind Dying," *Milwaukee Magazine,* December 1999; George Ritzer, ed., "Rustbelt," *The Blackwell Encyclopedia of Sociology* (Oxford: Blackwell, 2007), 3967–69.

12. Sam Roberts, "New York City Losing Blacks Census Shows," *New York Times,* April 3, 2006.

13. For an insightful view of black resentment of Latinos, see Earl Ofari Hutchinson, http://www.alternet.org/columnists/story/36197/ (accessed August 13, 2006).

14. See, for example, Marc Mauer, *Race to Incarcerate* (New York: New Press, 1999); Michael Tonry, *Malign Neglect: Race, Crime, and Punishment in America* (Oxford: Oxford University Press, 1995).

15. Peter Hall, *Cities of Tomorrow* (Oxford: Blackwell, 1988).

16. Pinnock, *Brotherhoods,* 31–32.

17. Davis, *Planet of Slums,* 117.

18. Assem Salam, "The Role of Government in Shaping the Built Environment," in *Projecting Beirut: Episodes in the Construction and Reconstruction of a Modern City,* ed. Peter G. Rowe and Hashim Sarkis (Munich: Prestel, 1998), 132.

19. H. E. Gassan Tueni, "From the Geography of Fear to a Geography of Hope," in Rowe and Sarkis, *Projecting Beirut,* 285.

20. Ibid., 298.

21. Samir Khalif, "Contested Spaces and the Forging of New Cultural Identities," in Rowe and Sarkis, *Projecting Beirut,* 151.

22. Castells, *End of Millennium.*

23. Castells, *Power of Identity,* 357.

24. David Turnbull, "Soc. Culture: Singapore," in *Architecture of Fear,* ed. Nan Ellin (New York: Princeton Architectural Press, 1997), 239.

25. Dennis R. Judd and Susan S. Fainstain, eds., *The Tourist City* (New Haven, Conn.: Yale University Press, 1999).

26. Teresa P. P. Caldiera, *City of Walls: Crime, Segregation, and Citizenship in São Paulo* (Berkeley: University of California Press, 2000).

27. Ibid., 213.

28. Peter Marcuse, "The Enclave, the Citadel, and the Ghetto: What Has Changed in the Post-Fordist U.S. City," *Urban Affairs Review* 33 (1997): 228–64.

29. Caldiera, *City of Walls,* 101.

30. Davis, *City of Quartz,* 277–84.

31. Alfred Blumstein and Joel Wallman, eds., *The Crime Drop in America* (Cambridge: University of Cambridge Press, 2000).

32. John Hull Mollenkopf and Manuel Castells, eds., *Dual City: Restructuring New York* (New York: Sage, 1991).

33. Kaldor, *New and Old Wars,* 11.

34. This is what Castells means by "the exclusion of the excluders by the excluded."

35. Wacquant, "New 'Peculiar Institution'"; Wacquant, "Ghetto," in *International Encyclopedia of the Social and Behavioral Sciences,* ed. Neil J. Smelser and Paul B. Baltes (London: Pergamon, 2004).

36. Loïc Wacquant, "The Penalisation of Poverty and the Rise of Neo-Liberalism," *European Journal on Criminal Policy and Research* 9 (2001): 401–12.

37. Friedmann and Wolff, "World City Formation," 323.

38. See the one-hundred-year history of Chicago's shifting ghetto in animation on http://gangresearch.net/ChicagoGangs/gangsandghetto/chighetto20.htm.

39. Evan Mckenzie, *Privatopia: Homeowner Associations and the Rise of Residential Private Government* (New Haven, Conn.: Yale University Press, 1994). Kenneth Clark first referred to the "invisible walls" of the dark ghetto (*Dark Ghetto: Dilemmas of Social Power* [New York: Harper and Row, 1965]). See Peter Marcuse's history of walls, "Walls of Fear and Walls of Support," in Ellin, *Architecture of Fear,* 101–14.

40. The following discussion is indebted to the Harry F. Guggenheim Foundation. See Hagedorn and Rauch, "Housing, Gangs, and Homicide."

41. Smith, *New Urban Frontier,* 27.

42. Paul S. Grogan and Tony Proscio, *Comeback Cities: A Blueprint for Urban Neighborhood Revival* (Boulder, Colo.: Westview, 2000).

43. *Chicago Tribune,* December 2, 1986, quoted in Venkatesh, *American Project,* 7.

44. Cohen and Taylor, *American Pharaoh,* 333.

45. Interview with author, Chicago, 2003.

46. Interview with author, Chicago, 2003.

47. Interview with author, Chicago, 2003.

48. Popkin, *Hidden War.*

49. http://www.encyclopedia.chicagohistory.org/pages/253.html (accessed March 22, 2006). For the actual CHA Plan for Transformation, see http://www.thecha.org/transformplan/plan_summary.html.

50. Yittayih Zelalem, Janet Smith, Martha Glas, and Nancy Hudspeth, *Affordable Housing Conditions and Outlook in Chicago: An Early Warning for Intervention* (Chicago: Nathalie P. Voorhees Center, 2006), 1–57.

51. Hirsch, *Making the Second Ghetto.*

52. Coalition to Protect Public Housing, "Cabrini Tenants to File Lawsuit to Stop Chicago Housing Authority from Illegally Evicting Hundreds of Tenants," press release, 2004.

53. See the tenants' Web site, View from the Ground, http://viewfromtheground.com/index.php.

54. Popkin, *Hidden War,* 169.

55. Interview with author, Chicago, 2003.

56. Interview with author, Chicago, 2003.

57. Chicago, with its institutionalized gangs, has not seen its murder rate, as of this writing, drop much below three times that of New York City's. As in Los Angeles, the homicide rate may go back up, not keep falling.

58. This "Boys Town" is not to be confused with the gay space of Chicago's Lakeview neighborhood.

59. Interview with author, Chicago, 2003.

60. McKean and Raphael, "Drugs, Crime, and Consequences."

61. http://www.hrw.org/reports98/police/uspo53.htm (accessed March 26, 2006).

62. Interview with author, Chicago, 2004.

63. Caldiera, *City of Walls,* 314.

64. In Chicago, the Puerto Rican community is also being pushed out of Humboldt Park, as they were ousted before from the near west side and then Lincoln Park. I am indebted to research in Humboldt Park by Xavier Perez, who is writing his dissertation on gentrification in his home community.

65. Caldiera, *City of Walls,* 334.

66. Stephen A. Donziger, ed., *The Real War on Crime: The Report of the National Criminal Justice Commission* (New York: HarperPerennial, 1996).

CONCLUSION

1. Moore, *Going Down to the Barrio.* Moore borrows this term from Gary Alan Fine, *With the Boys: Little League Baseball and Preadolescent Culture* (Chicago: University of Chicago Press, 1987).

2. Said, *Culture and Imperialism,* xx.

3. Touraine, *Return of the Actor,* 139.

4. Mills, *Sociological Imagination,* 184. See also Foucault's mocking of criminology as a "garrulous discourse" that "lacks a coherent framework" (Michel Foucault, *The Archaeology of Knowledge* [New York: Pantheon, 1972], 47).

5. I find myself applying Arundhati Roy's wry comments to criminologists: "I'm not seeing that many radical positions taken by writers or poets or artists, you know? It's all the seduction of the market that has shut them up like a good medieval beheading never could" (http://www.alternet.org/story/36643/ [accessed August 13, 2006]). See also Said, *Orientalism.* Not only are gangs an "other" in Said's sense, but the imposition of Western categories of gangs and social control measures has a parallel in the construction of the Orient and its colonial control.

6. Alvin Gouldner, "The Sociologist as Partisan: Sociology and the Welfare State," *American Sociologist* (May 1968): 103–16.

7. Albert Camus, *The Myth of Sisyphus, and Other Essays* (New York: Knopf, 1955). For Camus, Sisyphus was the "absurd hero" who was cursed by the gods to eternally roll a large rock up the hill, only to see it roll back down. Camus ends his essay, however, with the words "The struggle itself toward the heights is enough to fill a man's heart. One must imagine Sisyphus happy" (91).

8. Touraine, *What Is Democracy?* 189.

9. Joan Moore as well is a model for academics, as she worked tirelessly in an earlier time for a self-help movement among "Pintos" in Los Angeles. Tom Hayden has brought his political skills to the university with great success, and Diego Vigil's activism has enhanced his scholarship. The late Richard Cloward is in many ways the model of the activist-scholar. Too few academics emulate Cloward, Dwight Conquergood, Moore, Barrios, Brotherton, and Hayden.

10. Brotherton and Barrios, *Between Black and Gold;* Dawley, *Nation of Lords.*

11. Sassen, "Global City," 110.

12. http://www.streetgangs.com/topics/1999/033099north.html.

13. This is not meant to be a definitive list of inclusive issues. Elections have also attracted gangs, and in many cities Latinos are a rising political power. For example, in Chicago, since 80 percent of the increase in the region's population in the last decades has been Latinos, they—and their gangs—are becoming key partners in new electoral coalitions. What needs to be weighed are the implications of these coalitions for the decline of urban black political power and how that might affect our capacity to reach out to black gangs. Each city will have a different constellation of forces and unique history and circumstances. See Zelalem et al., "Affordable Housing Conditions." Also important are local movements and organizations working to make ex-offenders' re-entry into community life more successful.

14. Touraine calls movements that are not democratic and practice exclusion "anti-movements" (*Can We Live Together?* 116, 119).

15. Zilberg, "Banished from the Kingdom"; Hayden, *Street Wars.*

16. For the UN definition of DDR and other resources, see http://www.undp.org/bcpr/ddr/body.htm. For an application of DDR to gangs or youth in organized armed violence, see Dowdney, *neither War nor Peace.*

17. Touraine, *What Is Democracy?* 15.

INDEX

by Denise E. Carlson

John M. Hagedorn is associate professor of criminal justice and senior research fellow at the Great Cities Institute at the University of Illinois–Chicago. He has studied gangs and violence for more than twenty years. He is author of *People and Folks: Gangs, Crime, and the Underclass in a Rustbelt City;* coeditor of *Female Gangs in America: Essays on Girls, Gangs, and Gender;* and editor of *Gangs in the Global City: Alternatives to Traditional Criminology.*

Mike Davis is professor of history at the University of California, Irvine. He is the author of several books, including *Planet of Slums, City of Quartz,* and *Ecology of Fear.*

Globalization and Community

Dennis R. Judd, SERIES EDITOR